# THE
# JACKSONIAN
# PERSUASION

# THE
# JACKSONIAN
# PERSUASION

## Politics and Belief

MARVIN MEYERS

STANFORD UNIVERSITY PRESS · STANFORD, CALIFORNIA · 1957

STANFORD UNIVERSITY PRESS, STANFORD, CALIFORNIA

LONDON: OXFORD UNIVERSITY PRESS

© 1957 by the Board of Trustees of the Leland Stanford Junior University / All Rights Reserved / Printed in the United States of America / Parts of Chapter 4, "The Great Descent," reprinted with the permission of *The Pacific Spectator* / *Library of Congress Catalog Card Number: 57-12515*

Published with the assistance of the Ford Foundation

# PREFACE

The Jacksonian persuasion, as understood in these pages, is not a magic formula explaining everything Jacksonians said or did. There were Jacksonians of many sorts, whose thoughts and actions make a large and many-faceted historical record. The biographer, the narrator of events, the historian of ideas and institutions, will find—has found—much else to write about the era. Finally, however, all inquirers come to problems of general interpretation.

In speaking of Jacksonian Democracy, as of the New Freedom or the New Deal, historians indicate the presence of a central pattern, however flawed and indistinct, which dominates a variegated field. Above all, it seems to me, they suggest a certain unity of understanding among contemporaries, concerning their great problems and aspirations. Wars and revolutions strike the clearest patterns into memory, but these are not the only patterns, nor are they always the most significant. Historians, in short, dramatize politics because politics, especially in democratic communities, dramatizes life. I have searched for the major plot expressed in Jacksonian political appeals, with the hope that character and scene and episode will thereby gain further meaning and order. Other problems, other views contained within Jacksonian Democracy, will stand in a stronger light if we can find the center of political concern.

Although I have built this work with a severe and sometimes obstinate determination to achieve my own understanding of the Jacksonians, I have encountered more than my share of generous encouragement and illuminating criticism. Richard Hofstadter's discerning critique of the manuscript and David Riesman's inventive comments have given me essential help; it is no accident that I could learn so much from these two men, whose works have quickened and educated my interest in American politics broadly conceived.

A year of splendid leisure at the Center for Advanced Study in the Behavioral Sciences provided both an unaccustomed privacy for thought and writing and easy access to a bright and varied company whose conversation offered many hints for present and for future use.

Of those at the Center, Merle Curti in particular was a gracious and rewarding critic.

Others who have commented helpfully on parts or problems of the work at different stages include Martin Diamond, Reuel Denney, Dumas Malone, Philip Selznick, and Wallace Stegner; but there have been many more who will know themselves what they have given in kindness and counsel, often at the moment of necessity.

Portions of this book first appeared in articles, and are used here with the kind permission of the publishers: "The Jacksonian Persuasion," *American Quarterly*, V (Spring 1953); "The Basic Democrat: A Version of Tocqueville," *Political Science Quarterly*, LXXII (March 1957).

MARVIN MEYERS

Chicago, August 16, 1957

# CONTENTS

# 1

# THE OLD REPUBLIC
# AND THE NEW

## AN INTRODUCTION

❧

James Parton, that excellent popular biographer of his eminent countrymen, consulted a map in 1859 to discover which notables had given their names most frequently to American places. I doubt that one can find a better brief guide to relative popularity, and to relative political significance for the people, than Parton's simple finding:

Washington ............ 198 times
Jackson ................ 191
Franklin .............. 136
Jefferson ............. 110
Clay .................. 42

Washington the founder; Jackson the defender; Franklin the practical preceptor; Jefferson the republican sage; and far below, Clay the adjuster and promoter.[1]

To have routed British veterans at New Orleans and cleared a region for settlement in the Indian campaigns gave Andrew Jackson a strong initial claim to national attention; and the military style which made him Old Hickory, Old Hero, put the claim in its strongest terms. Yet there had to be more to account for the passionate involvement of men's loyalties with Jacksonian politics: there had been other generals, other battles, other colorful personalities. At first, the battlefield reputation was enough: the unfailingly acute Governor Ford of Illi-

---

[1] James Parton, *Life of Andrew Jackson*, I, 236. Publication data on editions cited in this footnote and all following footnotes may be found in the Bibliography, pp. 220–29.

nois, an uneasy late Jacksonian, observed how eager politicians had flocked to the banner of "a popular and fortunate leader" in the early days. But Ford saw too, in the perspective of 1850, that Jackson had been the master figure of American political life during his two administrations and the eight years of his retirement, and that he "has since continued to govern, even after his death."[2]

Jackson entered the presidency a national hero out of the West; he became the great partisan protagonist of his generation. No man of his time was at once so widely loved and so deeply hated. His blunt words and acts assumed the character of moral gestures which forced men to declare themselves, for or against. The movement we have come to call Jacksonian Democracy borrowed more than a powerful name; it projected into politics a fighting image of the man who would save the republic from its enemies. Exactly where and how Andrew Jackson and his party met is a question for biographers; but once joined, they excited and focused the concerns of a political generation. George Bancroft's memorial panegyric, for all its Transcendental claptrap, comes to a truth about Jackson's political significance:

Before the nation, before the world, before coming ages, he stands forth the representative, for his generation, of the American mind. And the secret of his greatness is this: by intuitive conception, he shared and possessed all the creative ideas of his country and his time; he expressed them with dauntless intrepidity; he enforced them with an immovable will; he executed them with an electric power that attracted and swayed the American people.[3]

From contemporary commentators to recent scholars there has been agreement upon initial facts: that politics substantially engaged the interest and feelings of American society; that Jacksonian Democracy was a large, divisive cause which shaped the themes of political controversy; that the second quarter of the nineteenth century is properly remembered as the age of Jackson. Here agreement ends. The limits of the subject are in dispute: Is Jacksonian Democracy to be considered primarily as an affair of party politics, or as a broad political, social, and intellectual movement? What message did Jacksonian Democracy carry to society, whom did it reach, what did it

[2] Thomas Ford, *A History of Illinois*, pp. 103–4, 271. For an interesting sketch of the petty local maneuvering which led to Jackson's original candidacy, see Charles Grier Sellers, Jr., "Jackson Men with Feet of Clay," *American Historical Review*, LXII (April 1957), 537–51.

[3] George Bancroft, *Literary and Historical Miscellanies*, p. 479.

signify in the setting of the times? These are yet unsettled questions, for all the wealth of industry and talent spent upon them.

In one view of the subject, urban masses rise against a business aristocracy; in another, simple farming folk strike out at capitalist trickery; in still another, fresh forest democracy seeks liberation from an effete East. Some recent works discover at the heart of the movement hungry men on the make invading the positions of chartered monopoly. Some stress the strengthening of the presidency, or the heightening of nationalist sentiment. An older emphasis upon King Andrew, master demagogue, exploiting the gullibility of the masses for the sake of his own power, reappears in altered form—the shrewd politicos behind a popular hero learning to manage a new mass electorate by perfecting the organization and tactics of machine politics. Woven into many accounts are elements of the official Jacksonian version: the friends of limited and frugal government, equal rights and equal laws, strict construction and dispersed power, taking up from Jefferson the defense of the republic.[4]

These are not all the theses; and each is, of course, far more formidable in its author's custody than I have made it out in quick review. My object is simply to suggest the variety of plausible interpretations, and to suggest further the gaps and conflicts that invite a new effort to order our knowledge of Jacksonian Democracy. Much remains to be learned from precise and limited studies of the movement and the

[4] The historical interpretations of Jacksonian democracy are not, of course, so flat and monolithic as I make them out here. I have abstracted what seem to me central lines of argument and deployed them for my own purposes. The variety of interpretations may be represented by such works as Arthur M. Schlesinger, Jr., *The Age of Jackson*; Joseph Dorfman, *The Economic Mind in American Civilization*, Vol. II; Alexis de Tocqueville, *Democracy in America*; Frederick Jackson Turner, *The United States, 1830–1850*; M. Ostrogorski, *Democracy and the Party System in the United States*; Thomas P. Abernethy, *From Frontier to Plantation in Tennessee*; Louis Hartz, *Economic Policy and Democratic Thought*; and the excellent chapter iii in Richard Hofstadter, *The American Political Tradition*, together with the bibliographical essay, *ibid.*, pp. 353–57.

Vernon Louis Parrington's brief discussion of Jackson as an "Agrarian Liberal" is perhaps closer to the truth than many later studies; see his *Main Currents in American Thought*, II, 145–52. Harold C. Syrett has made a useful selection of Jackson's writings and assessed his role in *Andrew Jackson*. Bray Hammond's revealing observations on Jacksonian economic aims, with special reference to banking, are discussed in Chapter 4, *infra*. A recent work by William N. Chambers, *Old Bullion Benton: Senator from the New West*, uses the opposing terms "enterprise" and "arcadia" as the key to Jacksonian party divisions; the similarity to my own conception will be apparent in the following pages. A penetrating critical essay by R. W. B. Lewis— *The American Adam*—suggests in its treatment of cultural spokesmen many parallels to my analysis of political spokesmen.

period; but now, I think, the need is to keep the focus wide: to ask the small questions with constant reference to the large.

Accepting the conclusions of Jacksonian scholarship as so many diverse hints to be considered when occasion gives them relevance, I have undertaken a new reading of some familiar sources. Somehow Jacksonian Democracy communicated a message which touched off powerful political emotions. What was this message, and what conditions gave it force? The questions are not easily answered.

When the Jacksonian movement formed in the late 1820's America was far out upon a democratic course: political democracy was the medium more than the achievement of the Jacksonian party. The Jacksonians proclaimed popular principles with but little more insistence than the Whig supporters of Harry of the West or Old Tip. For most of the country the Federalist conservatism of Hamilton or John Adams was stone dead: its ghost walked only in the speeches of Jacksonians trying to frighten honest citizens out of their opposition. Government by the people was largely a matter of consensus and of wont. Basic principles and institutions were firmly settled; only their legal elaboration—for example, in suffrage extension and the increase of elective offices—was recent and still in progress. There was some party conflict over details, none over the general democratic direction. The completion of a popular regime seemed to follow an unquestionable logic.

Indeed the most consequential political changes entered silently, without formal consideration or enactment: changes in the organization and conduct of parties. The winning of elections became to an unprecedented degree the business of professionals who managed powerful machines. On the surface such developments might suggest a bureaucratization of political life; in main effect, however, they brought a novel intimacy to the relation between the people and politics. The political machine reached into every neighborhood, inducted ordinary citizens of all sorts into active service. Parties tended to become lively two-way channels of influence. Public opinion was heard with a new sensitivity and addressed with anxious respect. The bureaucratic science of machine operation was effective only in association with the popular art of pleasing the many. As never before, the parties spoke directly, knowingly, to the interests and feelings of the public. The Jacksonians initiated much of the change in the instruments and methods of popular democracy; they adopted new party ways with a natural ease and competence which earned them some electoral advantage; the Whigs understandably resented their success, and quickly followed their example. Thus the new party democracy, like democracy in the abstract, was a common element of politics and raised no substantial public issues between Jacksonians and their rivals. At most, the less successful partisans carped at the more successful.

Under the new political conditions parties were alert to interests everywhere in society. One is tempted to think that Jacksonian Democracy found a major class constituency, identified its concrete needs, catered to them in its program, won the interested vote, and so became a great political force; and that the Whigs did much the same thing with opposite interests and policies. Unfortunately, the scheme breaks down at critical points. The chief Jacksonian policies—opposition to special corporate charters, hostility toward paper money, suspicion of public enterprise and public debt—do not patently contribute to the needs of a distinctive class following. The parties show some interesting marginal variations in their sources of support; nonetheless —given the relatively loose class structure, the heavy concentration in the middle social ranks as then identified (farmers, mechanics, shopkeepers), the flexibility of careers and the mixture of interests—it seems clear that both parties must have reached broadly similar class constituencies to gain, as they did, only a little more or less than half the popular vote. In sum: social differences were subtly shaded and unstable; party policies were ambiguous in their probable effects upon group interests; and so no general and simple class difference appears in party preferences.

The flaws in this class-interest approach have provoked a reaction toward the view that the Jacksonian movement had no great insurgent mission. In this view, the parties were fraternal twins, devoted to the advancement of slightly varying business interests in a free economy, their essential similarity disguised by a series of practical quarrels which windy party leaders dressed up in a conventional grand rhetoric; the essential meaning of Jacksonian politics is found in the objective import of legal and institutional changes. But why did political language go so far beyond practical objects? Why did men respond out of all proportion to their manifest interests? How were they convinced that party differences were profound, persistent—mattered greatly? Why did some kinds of rhetoric touch the quick, others not? Here, as elsewhere, the revisionist temper seems too impatient with the impalpable motives, feelings, perceptions, which lie between external act and external consequences.

I have spoken of the sensitive relationship which developed between parties and people: not only interests but attitudes and feelings reached the receptive eye of politicians. And politics took on what might be called an expressive role, along with its traditional task of conducting the business of the state. Here one enters a region of elusive psychological fact buried in a fragmentary record of words and acts. But here I think the vital transaction between Jacksonians and their generation must be found.

The appeals of the Democracy were carried by ideas and rhetoric, by policies and public gestures. Taken singly, these elements point this way and that, and no one of them conveys a full notion of the party message that worked such large effects. Taken together, I think, they converge to form an urgent political message with a central theme. It will be my purpose to identify that theme and the nature of its appeal. "Ideology" is a conventional term for one aspect of my subject, "ethos" for another, but I have chosen the less formal "persuasion" to fit my emphasis upon a matched set of attitudes, beliefs, projected actions: a half-formulated moral perspective involving emotional commitment. The community shares many values; at a given social moment some of these acquire a compelling importance. The political expression given to such values forms a persuasion.

In Jacksonian political appeals I have found—as might be expected—distinct traces of every theme used by historians to explain the nature and import of Jacksonian Democracy. Jacksonian spokesmen drew upon an exhaustive repertory of the moral plots which might engage the political attention of nineteenth-century Americans: equality against privilege, liberty against domination; honest work against idle exploit; natural dignity against factitious superiority; patriotic conservatism against alien innovation; progress against dead precedent. A first ungraded inventory shows only a troubled mind groping for names to fit its discontent.

The great specific mission of Jacksonian Democracy was the war against the Monster Bank. Here the party formed, or found, its character. Here was the issue which stood for all issues. Broad popular fear and hatred of the Second Bank, evoked by Jacksonian appeals, cannot be understood simply as a matter-of-fact reaction to material injuries. The economic operations of the institution conferred some manifest general benefits, directly crossed the interests of only a limited group: its hand was not found upon men's throats or in their pockets. The Bank was called a Monster by Jacksonians. A monster is an unnatural thing, its acts are out of reason, and its threat cannot be estimated in ordinary practical terms. The effort to destroy the Monster Bank and its vicious brood—privileged corporations, paper money—enlisted moral passions in a drama of social justice and self-justification.

Broadly speaking, the Jacksonians blamed the Bank for the transgressions committed by the people of their era against the political, social, and economic values of the Old Republic. The Bank carried the bad seed of Hamilton's first Monster, matured all the old evils, and created some new ones. To the Bank's influence Jacksonians traced constitutional impiety, consolidated national power, aristocratic privilege, and plutocratic corruption. Social inequality, impersonal and intangible business relations, economic instability, perpetual debt and taxes, all issued from the same source.

Jefferson had brought into temporary equilibrium the formal ideal of a dynamic liberal society and the concrete image of a stable, virtuous yeoman republic. "It is," he wrote, "the manners and spirit of a people which preserve a republic in vigor." And God had made the independent citizen farmer "His peculiar deposit for substantial and genuine virtue." Nothing is more revealing than Jefferson's later concession of the need for domestic manufacturing, under the pressures of war: "Our enemy has indeed the consolation of Satan on removing our first parents from Paradise: from a peaceful agricultural nation he makes us a military and manufacturing one."[5] Now Jacksonian society was caught between the elements—the liberal principle and the yeoman image—and tried again to harmonize them. Americans were boldly liberal in economic affairs, out of conviction and appetite combined, and moved their world in the direction of modern capitalism. But they were not inwardly prepared for the grinding uncertainties, the shocking changes, the complexity and indirection of the new economic ways. Their image of the good life had not altered: somehow, as men and as a society, they hoped to have their brave adventures, their provoca-

[5] "Notes on Virginia," in *The Works of Thomas Jefferson,* ed. Paul Leicester Ford, IV, 85–86; "Letter to William Short, Nov. 28, 1814," in *The Writings of Thomas Jefferson,* ed. H. A. Washington, VI, 400.

tive rewards, their open-ended progress, and remain essentially the same. The practical outcomes of the free pursuit of economic interest had never been legitimated, or even fully associated with the abstract liberal principle. Yet the ideological and material attachment to the liberal code was too deep to be severed, even in considerable distress.

Thus many found in the anti-Bank crusade, and in the Jacksonian appeal generally, a way to damn the unfamiliar, threatening, sometimes punishing elements in the changing order by fixing guilt upon a single protean agent. A laissez-faire society with this source of corruptions cut out would re-establish continuity with that golden age in which liberty and progress were joined inseparably with simple yeoman virtues. Under the Jacksonian persuasion men could follow their desires, protest their injuries, affirm their innocence. In this direction one can begin to meet the Jacksonian paradox: the fact that the movement which helped to clear the path for laissez-faire capitalism and its culture in America, and the public which in its daily life eagerly entered on that path, held nevertheless in their political conscience an ideal of a chaste republican order, resisting the seductions of risk and novelty, greed and extravagance, rapid motion and complex dealings.[6]

The Jacksonian movement was forged in the Bank War. Its new machine carried its influence throughout American society; its Old Hero, at once the voice and the exemplar of Jacksonian values, linked the machine to the essential cause. However far Jacksonians went in

---

[6] There is a fascinating English parallel, suggested to me first by reading William Cobbett's *Life of Andrew Jackson*. The history is poor stuff, cribbed from an American biography; but the remarks of the old Federalist "Porcupine" of the Philadelphia press wars, turned angry social reformer back at home, reveal a profound admiration for the American "Irishman": "The bravest and greatest man now living in this world, or that ever has lived in this world, as far as my knowledge extends" (*ibid.*, pp. iii–iv). Cobbett praised Jackson for mastering the British (his book is dedicated to the Irish working people), the savages, and the Bank—"a monster perfectly insatiable; hypocritical as the crocodile, delusive as the syren, and deadly as the rattlesnake itself." Cobbett sees a perfect parallel between the Bank of the United States and the Bank of England in nature and social effects (*ibid.*, pp. vi–vii, 162, 185–86). All this is the more interesting because Cobbett is not in the "liberal" reform camp, and has no patience with "corn-bill nonsense, or HEDDEKASHUN" as social panaceas (*ibid.*, p. 196). G. D. H. Cole calls him an "agrarian tribune" who "wanted his old world back again, his memory—idealised like most men's early memories—of the England which he had known and loved before the great wars and the great factories came." G. D. H. Cole, *Persons and Periods*, p. 157. Cf. J. L. and Barbara Hammond, *The Bleak Age*, p. 32. For further evidence of Cobbett's social views and of his impression of nineteenth-century America, see, for example, *Rural Rides, A Year's Residence in the United States of America*, and *The Emigrant's Guide*.

adapting policies to the practical requirements of local conditions, special interests, and effective party operation, the movement continually returned to its core appeal: death to the Monster; life and health to the old republican virtues. However carefully the knowledgeable voter looked to his immediate interests—when they could be linked plausibly to party policies—he would always see the moral choice proposed by Jacksonian Democracy.

If the Jacksonian persuasion gained relevance and force from common social experience, common tradition, how then did the Whigs develop a distinct voice and a subtantial following? Reducing a complex matter to the utmost simplicity: the Whig party spoke to the explicit hopes of Americans as Jacksonians addressed their diffuse fears and resentments. To say this is to reverse a common historical appraisal. The Federalists had been, at the end, a party of fear and resentment. There is some loose justice in deriving Whiggery from Federalism; but only if one recognizes that the language of mob terror and elite guidance had gone out of general use before Jacksonians and Whigs assumed political leadership. Some unregenerate Federalists who worried openly about the dangers of extreme democracy still survived; Whig party leaders tapped them for campaign funds and otherwise wished them out of sight.

What the Whigs deliberately maintained in the inheritance was the ambitious scheme for economic progress through banks, tariffs, and public promotion of internal improvements. Clay's American System, the nearest approach to a coherent Whig policy, was a popularization of Hamiltonian economic designs and John Marshall's flexible interpretation of national authority. Whigs, too, fully associated themselves with the Old Republican idyll—Webster wept in memory of his father's forest hut; zealous clerks helped to clutter city streets with Harrison log cabins—but they felt no serious tension between past and present. Their cabin was a nostalgic prop, a publicity gimmick without focused moral content. The fulfillment of liberal premises in capitalist progress was for them entirely natural and unproblematic.[7]

The Whigs distinctively affirmed the material promise of American life as it was going; and they promised to make it go faster. They

[7] See in this connection two recent discussions of Whig leaders: Clement Eaton, *Henry Clay and the Art of American Politics*; Richard N. Current, *Daniel Webster and the Rise of National Conservatism*.

were inclined to see the corporation not as a nameless monster but as an engine of progress; public debt not as a curse on honest labor but as a sound gamble on a richer future. Ironically, depression gave them their greatest popular success; yet they did not take depression as an omen of profound social maladjustment. They could see only that an imperious demagogue with primitive economic notions had thrown society into crisis by his spiteful war against the Bank. Indeed the Whigs were so markedly an anti-Jackson coalition that often their positive message was obscured in mere personal invective. To some degree, perhaps, the Whigs did succeed in spreading the conviction that Jacksonian dictatorship menaced the integrity of the republic. Principally, however, the party appealed to interested hopes, offering concrete advantages to groups and sections, and a quickening of economic progress for society as a whole.

Succeeding chapters will present a series of related commentaries on the appeal Jacksonian Democrats made to their generation, and on the changing social situation which lent relevance and force to that appeal. Perhaps they can convey the effort of Jacksonian Democracy to recall agrarian republican innocence to a society drawn fatally to the main chance and the long chance, to the revolutionizing ways of acquisition, emulative consumption, promotion, and speculation—the Jacksonian struggle to reconcile again the simple yeoman values with the free pursuit of economic interest, just as the two were splitting hopelessly apart.

# 2

# THE RESTORATION THEME

## ON JACKSON'S MESSAGE

❧

On his way toward the presidency Andrew Jackson had gained a splendid military reputation and a loose distinction as the plain man's candidate against the hierarchs of the republican statesmen's club. The broadening of the franchise, the shift to direct choice of presidential electors, the fading of old party lines: all prepared the way for a national hero, combining dramatic flair with the common touch, to break the chain of decorous successions and seize the first place in American political life. The time was ready for the popularity principle to supplant the rule of cabinet promotions in the choice of president; Jackson was precisely the man for the opportunity. His plurality in 1824 and then the decisive majority in 1828 must be regarded first as personal triumphs of the Old Hero, a man whose patriotic deeds, "hickory" character, and exemplary progress from obscurity to fame had wakened a new sort of political enthusiasm. National pride and nascent class ambition were drawn to a natural protagonist.[1]

As Jackson's initial victories were essentially personal, so his early opposition took the form of an ill-matched anti-Jackson junto. Slowly during the first administration the personal factions, the scattered policy quarrels, entered wider, firmer groupings. With the declaration of the Bank War the Jacksonian Democratic party crystallized: a vastly popular leader and an effective organization had touched the cause which would animate the political life of a generation.

[1] Theodore Roosevelt, before he emerged as a Square Dealer and a Progressive, applied to the Jacksonian age the contemptuous label, "millennium of the minnows." *Thomas Hart Benton*, p. 78. See the whole work for a fascinatingly ambivalent treatment of the "Western" influence in American politics.

Andrew Jackson did not simply deliver his personal following to the party and shrink into a figurehead. Without his influence the Bank question might have provoked no more than a limited policy argument on familiar grounds. Because he was a commanding figure, and a man of simple, thundering judgments who found things right or wrong and made disputants friends or enemies, the war against the Bank became a general struggle to preserve the values of the Old Republic. A general of the best Roman breed—as partisans saw him— sworn to his people, instinctively just, had come in righteous wrath to strangle a conspiracy with tentacles in every vital part of American society.

One cannot think of Jackson in this situation as the doctrinal counselor, or as the architect of policy. His affirmations and especially his fierce denials have the force of elemental acts: one feels Old Hickory throwing himself into the breach. In his own estimate, and the favorable public's, Jackson was the guardian of a threatened republican tradition which demanded not adjustment or revaluation but right action taken from a solid moral stance. His presidential messages are ragged political philosophy, tendentious accounting, crude policy. Political opponents mocked the contents, but ruefully acknowledged the impressive popular effect. Jackson offered a broad public a moral definition of their situation, a definition that seemed to strike home. Thus Jackson's messages to Congress and the nation, construing out of immediate events the great struggle between people and aristocracy for mastery of the republic, offer a first approach to the appeal of Jacksonian Democracy.[2]

### The Real People

Jackson's contemporary rivals damned him for appealing to class against class; some modern writers praise him for it. Beyond question, his public statements address a society divided into classes in-

---

[2] Good general discussions of the emergence of Jackson as a national leader are: John Spencer Bassett, *The Life of Andrew Jackson*, 2 vols.; James Parton, *Life of Andrew Jackson*, 3 vols.; Arthur M. Schlesinger, Jr., *The Age of Jackson*; William Graham Sumner, *Andrew Jackson*. Thomas Hart Benton's *Thirty Years' View* (2 vols., 1854–56) is the richest contemporary commentary. John Ward, *Andrew Jackson: Symbol for an Age,* is a rewarding discussion of reputation which unfortunately tends to divorce the man from his crucial political role. John Spencer Bassett and J. Franklin Jameson (eds.), *Correspondence of Andrew Jackson* (7 vols., 1926–35), provides a valuable record of Jackson's self-image, and full proof of the sincerity of Jackson's polemical appeal.

vidiously distinguished and profoundly antagonistic. But to understand the meaning of this cleavage and this clash, one must see them within a controlling context. There is for Jackson a whole body, the sovereign people, beset with aristocratic sores.

The relentless and apparently irresistible invocation of "the people" in Jacksonian rhetoric is reflected in the diary of a wealthy New York City Whig, Philip Hone, who regularly grinds the phrase through his teeth; or, with accumulated effect, in the growling humor of a Whig delegate to the New York constitutional convention of 1846: "The love of the people, the dear people was all that the gentlemen said influenced them. How very considerate. The love of the people—the dear people—was generally on men's tongues when they wanted to gain some particular end of their own."[3]

In the opposition view Jackson—and Jacksonians generally—were the worst sort of demagogues, men who could appropriate with galling effectiveness both the dignity of the sovereign people and the passion of embattled classes. That is just the point for Jackson: there are the whole people and the alien aristocracy, and the political advantages which result from the use of this distinction further confirm its validity. Jackson's notion of the people as a social class is grounded first in the political order, more precisely in the republican order. From this fixed base, and with this fixed idea of the double character of the people, Jackson's representation of the group composition of society may be analyzed first as an expression of political democracy; and then—by what seems to me a necessary extension—as a judgment of the values which attach to distinct social situations.

In the most inclusive and high-toned usage, the people would comprise "all classes of the community" and "all portions of the Union." From their midst arises a general "will of the American people," which is something considerably more than a fluctuating majority vote (though the vote for Jackson is acknowledged as a fair index). There are interests of a class and sectional character, legitimate and often illegitimate; but also a pervasive common interest (which corresponds neatly with the main items of the Democratic platform). The general will is originally pure ("Never for a moment believe that the great body of the citizens of any State or States can deliberately intend to

[3] Allan Nevins (ed.), *The Diary of Philip Hone, 1828–1851*; W. G. Bishop and W. H. Attree (reporters), *Report of the Debates and Proceedings of the Convention for the Revision of the Constitution of the State of New York: 1846*, p. 179.

do wrong"); liable to temporary error through weakness (corruptionists will sometimes succeed in "sinister appeals to selfish feelings" and to "personal ambition"); and, in the end, straight and true ("but in a community so enlightened and patriotic as the people of the United States argument will soon make them sensible of their errors").[4]

A brief, sharp application of this view occurs in Jackson's argument for direct election of the president. The extent of American territory—Madison's chief reliance for controlling the threat of majority faction — suggests to Jackson the dangerous prospect of sectional parties, which in turn will present sectional candidates and, in the zeal for party and selfish objects, "generate influences unmindful of the general good." Evil comes from the official apparatus, the mechanical contrivances of the complex electoral system. However, "the great body of the people," armed with a direct presidential vote which can express the general "will," must always defeat "antirepublican" tendencies and secure the common good.[5]

These "antirepublican" forces are identified as the "intriguers and politicians" and their tools, who thrive on political consolidation, chartered privilege, and speculative gain. Jackson sums up their purposes in relation to the Bank War:

The bank is, in fact, but one of the fruits of a system at war with the genius of all our institutions—a system founded upon a political creed the fundamental principle of which is a distrust of the popular will as a safe regulator of political power, and whose ultimate object and inevitable result, should it prevail, is the consolidation of all power in our system in one central government. Lavish public disbursements and corporations with exclusive privileges would be its substitutes for the original and as yet sound checks and balances of the Constitution—the means by whose silent and secret operation a control would be exercised by the few over the political conduct of the many by first acquiring that control over the labor and earnings of the great body of the people. Wherever this spirit has effected an alliance with political power, tyranny and despotism have been the fruit.[6]

From these rough outlines one can derive the gross political conception of the people and the classes which Jacksonians carried into party battle. But Jackson's categories do not remain abstract units

[4] James D. Richardson (ed.), *Messages and Papers of the Presidents, 1789–1897*, III, 5, 118–19, 296.

[5] *Ibid.*, pp. 147–48, 176–77.

[6] *Ibid.*, p. 165.

in a formal democratic scheme. In political terms the people are the great social residuum after alien elements have been removed. To gain a sense of their nurture and character, as portrayed in Jackson's messages, is to learn the qualities Jacksonians honored. The theme of people vs. aristocracy, when concrete references were added, began to speak of broad opposing social values.

When Jackson writes of the people—"the real people"—he specifies planters and farmers, mechanics and laborers, "the bone and sinew of the country." Thus a composite class of industrious folk is marked off within society. It appears to be a narrower group than "the sovereign people" of democratic doctrine, though it would surely encompass the mass of inhabitants of the Jacksonian era. Historians who identify the favored Jacksonian class simply as the common man tell too little. Others, who make the separation between wage earners and capitalists, or by rich/poor, town/country, East/West, or North/South, accept what seem to me variable secondary traits. Jackson's "real people" are essentially the four specific occupational groups he names, the men whose "success depends upon their own industry and economy," who know "that they must not expect to become suddenly rich by the fruits of their toil." The lines are fixed by the moral aspects of occupation.[7]

Morals, habits, character, are key terms in Jackson's discussion of the people—and almost every other subject. Major policies, for instance, are warranted by their capacity to "preserve the morals of the people," or "to revive and perpetuate those habits of economy and simplicity which are so congenial to the character of republicans." And so with the differentiation of classes according to worth: the American "laboring classes" are "so proudly distinguished" from their foreign counterparts by their "independent spirit, their love of liberty, their intelligence, and their high tone of moral character." At a still higher level within the bloc of favored classes, those who work the land—"the first and most important occupation of man"—contribute to society "that enduring wealth which is composed of flocks and herds and cultivated farms" and themselves constitute "a hardy race of free citizens."[8]

The positive definition of the "real people" significantly ignores pursuits which are primarily promotional, financial, or commercial.

[7] *Ibid.*, p. 305.
[8] *Ibid.*, pp. 19, 67–69, 166, 162.

This does not mean that Jackson raises a class war against mere or whole occupational categories. (He was himself lawyer, officeholder, land speculator, and merchant at various times.) The point seems to be that virtue naturally attaches to, and in fact takes much of its definition from, callings which involve some immediate, responsible function in the production of goods. Vice enters most readily through the excluded pursuits, though it may infect all classes and "withdraw their attention from the sober pursuits of honest industry." Defective morals, habits, and character are nurtured in the trades which seek wealth without labor, employing the stratagems of speculative maneuver, privilege-grabbing, and monetary manipulation.[9]

Like the Jeffersonians, Jackson regularly identifies the class enemy as the money power, the moneyed aristocracy, and so forth. There is in these words undoubtedly some direct appeal against the rich, yet I would maintain that this is a secondary meaning. First, Jackson's bone-and-sinew occupational classes clearly allow for a considerable income range: it would be fair to say that upper-upper and lower-lower would enter only as exceptions, while there would be a heavy concentration at some middling point of independence. Income as an index of differential economic or power interest does not become a ground for the judgment of classes. Instead, Jackson links income with good and evil ways. The "real people" cannot expect sudden riches from their honest, useful work; and surplus wealth would in any case prove a temptation to antirepublican habits of idleness and extravagance. Briefly, a stable income of middling proportions is generally associated with the occupations, and with the habits, morals, and character, of the "real people."[10]

More important, however, is the meaning given to phrases like "money power"—and note that Jackson typically uses this expression and not "the rich." The term occurs invariably in discussions of corporations, particularly banking corporations; it signifies the *paper* money power, the *corporate* money power—i.e., concentrations of wealth arising suddenly from financial manipulation and special privilege; ill-gotten gains. If the suggestion persists in Jackson's public statements that such is the common way to large wealth, and certainly the only quick way, then it is still the mode and tempo of acquisition,

9 *Ibid.*, p. 302.
10 *Ibid.*, p. 305.

and not the fact of possession, which is made to damn the rich before Jackson's public.

Further, the money power is damned precisely as a *power,* a user of ill-gotten gains to corrupt and dominate the plain republican order. Any concentration of wealth may be a potential source of evil; but the real danger arises when the concentration falls into hands which require grants of special privilege for economic success. A wealthy planter (and Jackson was this, too) should need no editorial or legislative hired hands; a wealthy banker of this era cannot do without them, where incorporation requires special charter grants.

Thus, Jackson's representation of the "real people" in the plain republican order supplies at least tentative ground for an interpretation of Jacksonian Democracy as, in vital respects, an appeal to an idealized ancestral way. Beneath the gross polemical image of people vs. aristocracy one finds the steady note of praise for simplicity and stability, self-reliance and independence, economy and useful toil, honesty and plain dealing. These ways are in themselves good, and take on the highest value when they breed a hardy race of free citizens, the plain republicans of America.

The familiar identification of Jacksonian Democracy and its favored folk with the West has its points, but not when it blends into the image of the raw West. Jackson shows little sympathy for the rural operator, or the rootless mover and claim-jumper. Nor does the moral restoration projected in his public papers bear any resemblance to American primitivism in the Davy Crockett mode. Neither the forest shadows, nor the half-man, half-alligator tone, nor a wild-woods democracy lies at the heart of the Jacksonian persuasion. Rather, one sees a countryside of flocks and herds and cultivated farms, worked in seasonal rhythm and linked in republican community.

### Hard Coin and the Web of Credit

As a national political phenomenon, Jacksonian Democracy drew heavily upon the Bank War for its strength and its distinctive character. The basic position Andrew Jackson established for the Democratic party in relation to money and banking continued to operate as a source of political strength through the 1840's. So powerful, in fact, was the Jacksonian appeal that large sections of the rival Whig party finally capitulated on this issue explicitly for the purpose of saving the party's life. First shrewd Whig party managers like Weed of New York, and later most Whig spokesmen, were forced to sacrifice their policy convictions to escape identification as the "Bank Party."

Jackson's standard case against banking and currency abuses has already been sketched above. Within the matrix of his Bank War, the crucial class split is discovered and the general principles of Jacksonian Democracy take shape. However, the Bank War, viewed as a struggle for possession of men's minds and loyalties, does not simply offer a self-evident display of its own meaning. Out of the polemical language there emerges a basic moral posture much like the one which enters Jackson's representation of the republican order.

Jackson's appeal for economic reform suggests at bottom a dismantling operation: an effort to pull down the menacing constructions of federal and corporate power, and restore the wholesome rule of "public opinion and the interests of trade." This has the sound of laissez faire, but with peculiar overtones which give the argument a new effect. Poor Richard and the man on the make may share a common enemy with Jackson's plain republican; indeed the forest democrat, the poor man, and the workingman—social types variously proposed as natural supporters of Jacksonian Democracy—might see their several adversaries overthrown in Jackson's rhetoric. Yet, if Jackson gives promise of catching every man's particular enemy in a broad aristocracy trap, does he not promise still more powerfully a reformation and a restoration: a return to pure and simple ways?

Tocqueville, though he reaches an opposite conclusion, suggests very effectively this dismantling spirit:

The bank is a great establishment, which has an independent existence; and the people, accustomed to make and unmake whatsoever they please, are startled to meet with this obstacle to their authority. In the midst of the perpetual fluctuation of society, the community is irritated by so permanent an institution and is led to attack it, in order to see whether it can be shaken, like everything else.[11]

But what is it about the great establishment which provokes hostility and a passion for dismantling? How can the permanence of the Bank, set over against the perpetual fluctuation of society, explain the ceaseless Jacksonian complaint against the tendency of the Bank precisely

[11] Tocqueville, *Democracy in America,* I, 178–79.

to introduce perpetual fluctuation in the economic affairs of society? There is, I think, another and better explanation of the symbolic import of the Bank War.

The Bank of the United States, veritable incarnation of evil in Jackson's argument, assumes the shape of "the Monster," the unnatural creature of lust for wealth and power. Its managers, supporters, and beneficiaries form the first rank of the aristocracy: the artificial product of legislative prestidigitation. The Monster thrives in a medium of paper money, the mere specter of palpable value. The bank system suspends the real world of solid goods, honestly exchanged, upon a mysterious, swaying web of speculative credit. The natural distributive mechanism, which proportions rewards to "industry, economy, and virtue," is fixed to pay off the insider and the gambler.

To knock down this institution, then, and with it a false, rotten, insubstantial world, becomes the compelling object. Jackson removed the public deposits, so he said, "to preserve the morals of the people, the freedom of the press, and the purity of the elective franchise." Final victory over the Bank and its paper spawn "will form an era in the history of our country which will be dwelt upon with delight by every true friend of its liberty and independence," not least because the dismantling operation will "do more to revive and perpetuate those habits of economy and simplicity which are so congenial to the character of republicans than all the legislation which has yet been attempted."[12]

The Jacksonian appeal for a dismantling operation and the restoration of Old Republican ways flows easily into the hard coin argument. Hard coin, I have already suggested, stands for palpable value as against the spectral issue of the printing press. In plainer terms, Jackson argues before the Congress: "The great desideratum in modern times is an efficient check upon the power of banks, preventing that excessive issue of paper whence arise those fluctuations in the standard of value which render uncertain the rewards of labor." Addressing a later Congress, Jackson pursues the point: Bank paper lacks the stability provided by hard coin; thus circulation varies with the tide of bank issue; thus the value of property and the whole price level are at the mercy of these banking institutions; thus the laboring

[12] Richardson, *Messages and Papers*, III, 19, 166.

classes especially, and the "real people" generally, are victimized, while the few conniving speculators add to their riches.[13]

A related appeal to the attractions of stability, of sure rewards and steady values and hard coins, can be found in Jackson's belated warnings against the accumulation and distribution of the revenue surplus: an overflowing federal treasury, spilling into the states, would produce ruinous expansions and contractions of credit, arbitrary fluctuations in the price of property, "rash speculation, idleness, extravagance, and a deterioration of morals." But above all it is the banks and their paper system which "engender a spirit of speculation injurious to the habits and character of the people," which inspire "this eager desire to amass wealth without labor," which turn even good men from "the sober pursuits of honest industry." To restore hard coin is to restore the ways of the plain republican order. Dismantling of the unnatural and unjust bank and paper system is the necessary first step.[14]

### The Sum of Good Government

The one indispensable credential of public or private worth, whether of individual, or class, or trade, is conveyed by Jackson by the term "republican"; that which is antirepublican is the heart of evil. With all valuations referred to the republican standard, and that standard apparently a category of politics, one might expect some final revelation of the Jacksonian persuasion in Jackson's representation of the good state. The truth is, on my reading, somewhat different. The good republic he portrays—and remembers from the Revolutionary days of 1776 and 1800—is on the political side the ornament, the glory, and the final security of the worthy community, not its creator.

Jackson's sketch of a political system congenial to Old Republican ways uses nothing beyond the memorable summation in Jefferson's First Inaugural Address: "a wise and frugal government, which shall restrain men from injuring one another, shall leave them otherwise

13 *Ibid.*, pp. 164, 247–48. Parton, discussing Jackson's business career, observes this basic quality in the man: "Andrew Jackson was a man singularly adverse to anything complicated and of all complications the one under which he was most restive was Debt. He *hated* Debt." *Life of Andrew Jackson*, I, 243. Supporting evidence is thickly scattered through his correspondence. See, for example, Bassett and Jameson (eds.), *Correspondence*, VI, 40, 45–46, 52, 127, 135, 368–69.

14 Richardson, *Messages and Papers*, III, 246, 302.

free to regulate their own pursuits of industry and improvement, and shall not take from the mouth of labor the bread it has earned. This is the sum of good government, and this is necessary to close the circle of our felicities." The literal Jacksonian translation prescribes: the Constitution strictly construed; strict observance of the "fundamental and sacred" rules of simplicity and economy; separation of political authority from the conduct of economic affairs.[15]

Jackson's political remarks both parallel and support the general themes discussed in previous sections. His ideal is no government of projects and ambitions. It does its simple, largely negative business in a simple, self-denying way. Republican government must be strong, and yet avoid the elaboration of state machinery which would create an autonomous center of power. The hardy race of independent republicans, engaged in plain and useful toil, need no more than a stable government of equal laws to secure their equal rights. In Jacksonian discourse, government becomes a fighting issue only when it grows too fat and meddlesome. Again, the republic is defined and judged positively by its republicans and only negatively by its government.

The Bank War once more provides the crucial case. Jackson mobilized the powers of government for what was essentially a dismantling operation. His cure rejects any transference of the powers of the Bank to another central agency: to give the president the currency controls and the power over individuals now held by the bank "would be as objectionable and as dangerous as to leave it as it is." Control of banks and currency, apart from the strictly constitutional functions of coinage and regulation of value, should be "entirely separated from the political power of the country." Any device is wicked and dangerous which would "concentrate the whole moneyed power of the Republic in any form whatsoever." We must, above all, ignore petty, expedient considerations, and "look to the honor and preservation of the republican system."[16]

## A Summary Appraisal

In reopening the most obvious political source I have not intended to rehearse established facts about Jackson's policies and principles. Quite simply, I have examined the presidential messages again within a special framework: assessed them as a political appeal which brought

15 *Ibid.,* pp. 18, 108, 161–62.
16 *Ibid.,* pp. 7, 18, 111.

passing events under judgment, in the language of prevalent attitudes and beliefs.

At the level of explicit doctrine, Jackson's message seems to attack manifest violations of formal republican rules. Immediately, however, his rhetoric creates the great, essential opposition of the people and the aristocracy. The people, as a formal political category, becomes the "real people," with characteristic social virtues : the defining traits of the ideal yeoman-republican. The aristocracy, first specified as a definite privilege-holding clique, grows into a diffuse class with pervasive social vices : the mixed attributes of aristocratic arrogance, financial jobbery, and irresponsibly adventurous enterprise.

When the inexorable Old General pits himself against the Bank, he gives political urgency to the encounter of broad social principles. Through his messages and actions the Bank becomes the enemy at the gate, threatening destruction to the city of republican virtue : the commonwealth of plain, honest freemen; of simple, stable, visible economic relationships; of limited and frugal democratic government. Political supporters of the Bank merge with the class which lives on privilege, deceit, and speculation. The party of the president absorbs "the bone and sinew of the country" : the farmers and mechanics conditioned by their concrete situation to sustain the values of the Old Republic. Thus Jackson gives to the party contest the aura of a class struggle, distinguishing the classes not by their economic position as such, but primarily by their moral orientation.

One can deflate this rhetoric of moral crisis and incipient social war by insisting that the heart of Jackson's message was in its literal doctrinal formulas and in its limited action-clauses. Briefly: Jackson employed a conventional liberal argument against legal privilege and public economic meddling and latitudinarian construction of constitutional powers; he directed public policy against the Bank monopoly, against federal participation in local improvement projects, against excessive tariffs, public debt, and the use of public lands to furnish revenues for public spending. So Jackson reasoned, so he chose to act : the fact remains that his appeal swept over such confinements.

Andrew Jackson took his liberal political dicta from the previous generation, and with them took an image of the good republican life. Laissez-faire notions were embedded in a half-remembered, half-imagined way of life. When government governed least, society— made of the right republican materials—would realize its own natural moral discipline. In America, Jacksonians announced, the people were the true conservatives. The liberalism of Jackson's message did not communicate a liberating purpose: there was no vision of a fresh creation at the Western edge of civilization, certainly no dream of enterprise unbound. The rule of equal liberty served to condemn the aristocracy of privilege for sapping republican political institutions, and so to fix an enemy who could bear responsibility for the general erosion of republican social values.

In an age of violent growth and change, Jackson's appeal felt for the uncertainties and suspicions, the actual grievances, perhaps the latent guilts, of his people. He provided a dramatic definition of their discontents. The world of independent producers, secure in their modest competence, proud in their natural dignity, confirmed in their yeoman character, responsible masters of their fate—the order of the Old Republic—was betrayed. From the great visible centers of private wealth and power, a web of economic and political influence reached into every community, threatened every household in the land. Banks and corporations, with their paper mysteries, their secret hold on public men, their mask of anonymity, their legal untouchability, held invisible powers over the life of the community, greater even than their manifest controls.

Between its minimum and maximum terms the Jacksonian appeal could promise much for little: it would destroy the Monster Bank, and it would restore a precious social enterprise to its original purity. With one courageous local amputation, society could save its character—and safely seek the goods it hungered for.

# 3

# VENTUROUS CONSERVATIVE

## ON TOCQUEVILLE'S IMAGE OF
## THE DEMOCRAT

❦

Alexis de Tocqueville's classic commentary on American democracy[1] has been consulted by historians for every purpose but the simplest: as a key to the immediate subject of the work, Jacksonian America. In the sober view of history Tocqueville has figured as a philosopher, a prophet, a personage, and a source of brilliant phrases. Why not restore to him the office of observer, interpreting the scene he visited between the spring of 1831 and the late winter of 1832? Plainly, it would be absurd to treat Tocqueville as one more garrulous nineteenth-century tourist; but that is not the only way open. His work offers just what is most needed by the student of Jacksonian times: an integrative view of society and culture, grounded in experience.

The venturous conservative is my construction of the man beneath the skin of Americans met everywhere in Tocqueville's pages. This image—compounded of consistent human qualities perceived by Tocqueville in the institutions, laws, ideas, customs, manners, and feelings of the American democracy—reflects Jacksonian experience within the basic form of the democratic social situation. The central

[1] *Democracy in America,* originally published in French in two volumes, 1835 and 1840. I am much indebted to Professor George Pierson for his full, meticulous account of *Tocqueville and Beaumont in America* (1938), although I have not always followed his interpretations; so rich is the book in documentary quotation that it becomes as much a source book as a history. It should be clear that I am proposing an *additional* use of Tocqueville, one especially suited to the purpose of this study and consistent with Tocqueville's intention. Certainly his importance as a political and social analyst is not restricted to the particular subject of Jacksonian Democracy. See Appendix A, pp. 213–16, for further comment on *Democracy in America* as a historical source.

character of the *Democracy* is, at once and congruously, a recognizable Jacksonian contemporary; a representative American; inherently, the universal democratic man.

Among these interpenetrating aspects of social character, and their corresponding environments, Tocqueville plainly gives least weight to the immediate and particular. The Jacksonian era, in his perspective, has no unique structure. Observed traits of society and character and culture simply illustrate the consequences of a great seven-century democratic revolution in its American—penultimate—expression. This stress on continuity makes for sound general history: in the long view, comprehending Europe and America, there is compelling force in Tocqueville's bold comment that he saw "the destiny of America embodied in the first Puritan who landed on those shores." And so he can interpret the Jacksonian world as a democratic microcosm, refer the actions of its citizens to the generic social responses of the democrat as American.[2]

I would propose further that the particular experiences of the Jacksonian generation formed a pattern of their own, which reinforced the general effects ascribed by Tocqueville to a persistent social situation; and that the venturous conservative was, in a brief incarnation, exactly the Jacksonian who helped to work a social transformation as he invoked the virtues of the Old Republic. The value of this notion for the understanding of Jacksonian Democracy and its persuasion cannot be established in a short argument. Its merits can be judged only in the whole design of my study, which attempts an extended development of Tocqueville's lead.

The following discussion offers an interpretation of *Democracy in America*, intended first to recover a searching portrait of the new-world democrat as a historical social type. Implicitly, I shall be sketching out an analytic scheme to guide further inquiry into the contemporary meaning of the Jacksonian appeal. Tocqueville's sometimes doubtful incidental judgments on Jacksonian public affairs have been rebuked more than enough. One does not ask a visitor to grasp esoteric family references; and especially not when one can get instead the testimony of a mind with a rare gift for using the contrast between object and observer to reveal essential and determinative qualities. If Tocqueville missed political details, he found a most rewarding general approach to democratic politics. With the appraisal

2 *Democracy in America*, I, 290.

of social character and its conditions—of the venturous conservative in his American democratic situation—Tocqueville starts us toward a fresh understanding of the Jacksonians. In their community, as the *Democracy* suggests persuasively, politics becomes a medium for the expression of influences compounded at the heart of democratic society, a mirror more than a creator of the common life. "What is understood by a republican government in the United States," Tocqueville comments, "is the slow and quiet action of society upon itself."[3]

## The Democratic Situation

America is an illuminating case and not a realized blueprint of democratic development: a case uniquely valuable as the fully recorded experience of a people born to equality and tranquilly unfolding their endowment almost to its natural limits. The great democratic revolution in the Western world, extending over seven centuries, has thrown America into its vanguard to explore, within a special history and place, varieties upon a providential theme: equality. Tocqueville's general analysis of democracy represents an effort to define the common social situation created by equality, through which accident and choice must operate.

Every page of Tocqueville, beginning with the first sentence of the introduction, is an argument that equality of condition "is the fundamental fact from which all others seem to be derived"—at once the principle and the substance of the great social revolution.[4] Condition is, in this usage, the total social situation:

Gradually the distinctions of rank are done away with; the barriers that once severed mankind are falling; property is divided, power is shared by many, the light of intelligence spreads, and the capacities of all classes tend towards equality. Society becomes democratic, and the empire of democracy is slowly and peaceably introduced to institutions and customs.[5]

The primary theoretical task for Tocqueville is to discover how equality, the primal active element, can constitute a social system, democracy.

In searching out the social design of democracy, Tocqueville confronts the possibility that equality does not create a community at all,

3 *Ibid.*, I, 416.
4 *Ibid.*, I, 3.
5 *Ibid.*, I, 9.

but the negation of community. Radical equality is a solvent of bonds; of tradition, hierarchy, authority, and every joint articulating contemporaries and generations. Viewed strictly, from the elevation of an ideal aristocracy, democracy would seem a state of bedlam, a vast aberration, with system only in the mode of its departure from the norms of human association. Approaching democracy from above and behind, Tocqueville in America, one feels, could never quite subdue a sense of shock at what he saw : not a black void but a viable human condition with remarkable powers of expansion and persistence. It is as if a man removed the main supports of a massive structure and felt its terrible weight in his own hands; then withdrew and saw it still standing. Here I think Tocqueville's aristocratic values served him wonderfully, at first to find the essential contrast of the old and new condition; and then to force him to construct in theory a coherent order out of chaos.

In a dazzling passage Tocqueville sketches the primary response to leveled condition :

Among democratic nations new families are constantly springing up, others are constantly falling away, and all that remain change their condition ; the woof of time is every instant broken and the track of generations effaced. Those who went before are soon forgotten ; of those who will come after, no one has any idea : the interest of man is confined to those in close propinquity to himself. As each class gradually approaches others and mingles with them, its members become undifferentiated and lose their class identity for each other. Aristocracy had made a chain of all the members of the community, from the peasant to the king ; democracy breaks that chain and severs every link of it. . . .

Thus not only does democracy make every man forget his ancestors, but it hides his descendants and separates his contemporaries from him; it throws him back forever upon himself alone and threatens in the end to confine him entirely within the solitude of his own heart.[6]

This is the original democratic chaos—"individualism"—from which Tocqueville derives the essential pattern of the new order. Men set apart upon a social plain confront their strength and then their weakness. To think and act alone breeds boundless independence. To doubt or fail in independence out of common human insufficiency compels submission to the only eminence equality permits, the equal brotherhood. The masterless of democratic times invent the only authority tolerable, even conceivable, in their condition : themselves

[6] *Ibid.*, II, 99.

*en masse.*[7] In the absence of countervailing influence extraneous to the social structure, Tocqueville expects always to find democracy somewhere in the passage from an insupportable liberty-in-isolation toward an abject dependence on the majority. This logic of development cannot be reversed; at most its consequences can be modified, and then only by understanding the process, accepting its limits, and employing the peculiar means which it presents.[8] Thus the urgent call: "A new science of politics is needed for a new world."[9]

I do not wish to impose more rigor and completeness upon Tocqueville's ideal conception of the democratic situation than the author himself intended. The *Democracy* never pulls together a formal structure with all elements nicely integrated and all tendencies precisely specified. Perhaps it is misleading to apply the term "ideal type" to a broad characterization of a historical trend, used as a kind of wire master key for opening strange new things to view. At any rate my purpose here has been not to systematize Tocqueville's system, a major theoretical task in its own right, but to locate its central theme, as an aid to recognition of the democrat as American.

## American Variations

The *Democracy* is so full of paradox that the casual reader is moved to suspect the author either of a muddled head or of a willful eccentricity. Man in his pride, portrayed in bold primaries, gives way to man reduced to a gray mass; then reappears; then disappears again. There is no simple formula in Tocqueville for composing the antagonistic figures; yet there are guides which bring the difference within the range of comprehension. The fundamental source of paradox lies in the double potentiality of the democratic situation: toward radical independence; toward submergence in the brotherhood. The most powerful and enduring tendency in "pure" democracy is the passage from the former toward the latter: toward a soft totalitarianism peopled by shapeless men. If all the counterforces of accident and statecraft should converge, there could not be a second coming of the aristocratic virtues. Uniformity, conformity, mediocrity, and the rule of the felicific calculus are fixed returns of the equalitarian society.[10]

---

[7] *Ibid.*, I, 254–70; II, 8–12, 258–63, 316–21.
[8] *Ibid.*, I, 418; II, 287–96, 316–21.
[9] *Ibid.*, I, 7.    [10] *Ibid.*, I, 252–53; II, 332–34.

And yet, within the democratic range, variety remains significant: the independence unloosed by killing off the gods of traditional society persists in varying degrees, in different spheres of social action, according to the reinforcements brought by history, place, and the creative use of political means available to democratic leaders. Thus the American of the *Democracy* is the compound product of the universal democratic situation and a unique national experience. If the fundamental fact of American history has been the quiet unfolding of an equalitarian society[11]—the basic democratic situation—yet there are lesser facts which, in aggregate, weigh heavily upon the outcome. A historical beginning in the modern era, under conditions of substantial equality and middle-class homogeneity, has meant in Tocqueville's view not only the quick and thorough elaboration of a democratic society, but a unique deliverance from social revolution and its special consequences—notably, class hatred and a strengthened state. The English-Puritan heritage transplanted to America carried the most advanced democratic elements of the Old World, to shape the New exclusively along democratic lines; but further, the heritage brought special gifts which significantly altered the course of democratic development: especially, the values of individual liberty, local freedom, and morality grounded in religious belief.[12]

Historical influences count in giving American democracy a distinctive turn only as they are grounded in customs and institutions. Tocqueville credits America with several political inventions of critical importance for preserving its historical gifts; the most brilliant innovation, perhaps, is the design of the dual federal system, with a wide distribution of administrative functions. The constitutional separation of church and state, the guarantee of private rights, the assignment of important functions to the judiciary are further instances of a prudent statecraft, effecting the translation from historical possibility, through legal and institutional forms, into "habits of the heart" and mind which alter the consequences of the basic democratic situation.[13] And yet the greatest achievement of the American democracy in recasting its fate Tocqueville sees as an unintended process, a fortunate result of choices made with other ends in view.

---

11 *Ibid.*, I, 46–54.
12 *Ibid.*, I, 26–29, 30–35, 43–44, 62–67, 290–91; II, 6–7, 101, 243–44, 256.
13 *Ibid.*, I, 244–47, 271–72, 280, 299, 300–314, 324–25.

Returning to the fundamental analysis of the leveled society, contrasted with a model aristocracy, Tocqueville recalls the essential feature of nonarticulation, of shapelessness—"individualism" when expressed in terms of members' responses. As a result of local freedom, the broad extension of political rights, and a bold commitment to almost unlimited civil liberty, the Americans have stumbled upon the chief expedient in democratic times for avoiding the new despotism: voluntary association. The leading virtue of political democracy in America turns out to be the capacity to penetrate the citizen's isolation, join his self-interest to a wider group, and educate him in the wonderworking skills of organization; thus to fill the void between the weak individual and the overbearing mass with a buzzing congeries of voluntary ("civil") associations. Ironically, the achievement of American politics has been to convert political into private affairs, to train men for private action.[14]

So history and art intervene to give variety to providence, and the look of paradox to Tocqueville's pages. The accidents of geography have less autonomous influence: Tocqueville anticipates some recent critics of Turner by asking why comparable conditions in South America, Canada, and the United States have yielded such unlike national careers; and finds the answers in decisive differences of law and above all custom, introduced by varying historical beginnings.[15] The gift of space, rich resources, and unmenaced borders has meant a free field for the fulfillment of the democratic revolution: specifically, a full provision for material equality; a wide margin for error; elbowroom for liberty.[16] In Tocqueville's phrase, "Nature herself favors the cause of the people."[17] The sheer abundance of natural endowment—"a field for human effort far more extensive than any sum of labor that can be applied to work it"[18]—sustains the recessive tendency in democracy, the tendency toward independence. In a sense, the American environment perpetuates the democratic state of nature, the world of liberated equal isolates, by promising fabulous rewards to brave spirits. Brave *economic* spirits, one should add, excited by the material rewards which loom so large in the city of equality; not independent minds and characters.

14 *Ibid.*, I, 191–98, 241–44, 248–52; II, 102–20.
15 *Ibid.*, I, 319–23; see also pp. 316–17.
16 *Ibid.*, I, 288–98.      17 *Ibid.*, I, 291.      18 *Ibid.*, I, 297.

## Venturous Conservative

Unique American conditions work selectively upon the basic democratic situation to give a mixed, even a paradoxical, aspect to American society, in Tocqueville's wide perspective. One might conclude simply that the double potentiality in democracy—toward independence, toward dependence—made possible a certain interesting and in some respects hopeful variety in American life, which Tocqueville rendered in alternating images of equalitarian freedom and servitude. This easy resolution would, however, cost us some of the most powerful historical insights in the *Democracy*. Primarily, we would miss Tocqueville's most ambitious and, I think, most productive contribution toward a concrete synthesis of American character; i.e., his recurrent attempt to identify a patterned response to the American situation, in both its typical democratic and its unique American features. The phrase "venturous conservative" is mine, and the assembled argument for using it as a central expression for the antithetic elements in American character is mine again, derived from scattered interpretations in the text suggestive of a common theme.

"They love change," Tocqueville's provocative formula for American democrats goes, "but they dread revolutions."[19]  Thus:

Two things are surprising in the United States: the mutability of the greater part of human actions, and the singular stability of certain principles. Men are in constant motion; the mind of man appears almost unmoved. . . . In the United States general principles in religion, philosophy, morality, and even politics do not vary, or at least are only modified by a hidden and often an imperceptible process; even the grossest prejudices are obliterated with incredible slowness amid the continual friction of men and things.[20]

In elucidating the distinction between change and revolution, in exploring the interplay of mutable actions and frozen principles, Tocqueville provides a brilliant lead for the understanding of Jacksonian Americans.

Speaking from his full elevation—the French aristocrat looking down upon a dull provincial show—Tocqueville sometimes, rarely, dismisses his own problem with a noble yawn. What does all the shuffling of possessions, laws, and notions amount to in the scale of dramatic high policy, philosophic heresy, great revolution?

[19] *Ibid.*, II, 255.    [20] *Ibid.*, II, 257.

It is true that they [democracies] are subject to great and frequent vicissitudes, but as the same events of good or adverse fortune are continually recurring, only the name of the actors is changed, the piece is always the same. The aspect of American society is animated because men and things are always changing, but it is monotonous because all these changes are alike.[21]

But sympathy and curiosity force Tocqueville beyond mere boredom: the spectacle suggests man's fate, all of reality which can reasonably be expected to appear; and therefore a thing to be understood internally. Indeed, I would argue that Tocqueville often, in unguarded moments, forgot that he was conceding the world reluctantly to the providential dictum of the lesser good for the greatest number; and that he gaped and marveled at the American miracle—the continuous social explosion which contained itself, and prospered mightily.

The ultimate sources of American character are found in that radical equality of condition which makes men masterless and separate. Everything seems possible, nothing certain, and life short: the American "clutches everything, he holds nothing fast, but soon loosens his grasp to pursue fresh gratifications."[22] As traders the Americans overwhelm their rivals with the audacity of French Revolutionary generals;[23] as workers they are never "more attached to one line of operation than to another" and have "no rooted habits."[24] Commerce is "like a vast lottery."[25] Turner's famous sketches of a westering people are almost watery beside the restless image in the *Democracy,* of a "continuous removal of the human race" without parallel since "those irruptions which caused the fall of the Roman Empire."[26] Thus,

It would be difficult to describe the avidity with which the American rushes forward to secure this immense booty that fortune offers. . . . Before him lies a boundless continent, and he urges onward as if time pressed and he was afraid of finding no room for his exertions. . . . They early broke the ties that bound them to their natal earth, and they have contracted no fresh ones on their way. Emigration was at first necessary to them; and it soon becomes a sort of game of chance, which they pursue for the emotions it excites as much as for the gain it procures.[27]

All this rootless, anxious, driving quality Tocqueville invests in a panoramic view of American careers:

[21] *Ibid.,* II, 228–29.     [22] *Ibid.,* II, 236.     [23] *Ibid.,* I, 422–25.
[24] *Ibid.,* I, 425.     [25] *Ibid.,* II, 236.     [26] *Ibid.,* I, 293.     [27] *Ibid.,* I, 294–95.

In the United States a man builds a house in which to spend his old age, and he sells it before the roof is on; he plants a garden and lets it just as the trees are coming into bearing; he brings a field into tillage and leaves other men to gather the crops; he embraces a profession and gives it up; he settles in a place, which he soon afterwards leaves to carry his changeable longings elsewhere. If his private affairs leave him any leisure, he instantly plunges into the vortex of politics; and if at the end of a year of unremitting labor he finds he has a few days' vacation, his eager curiosity whirls him over the vast extent of the United States, and he will travel fifteen hundred miles in a few days to shake off his happiness. Death at length overtakes him, but it is before he is weary of his bootless chase of that complete felicity which forever escapes him.[28]

So far the social basis of American character, equality of condition, has been treated in a generalized way, as the unstructured social environment playing into a rich and spacious physical environment, giving to American life the qualities of "a game of chance, a revolutionary crisis, or a battle," and shaping the American as "a man of singular warmth in his desires, enterprising, fond of adventure and, above all, of novelty."[29] It is equally clear that restlessness, anxiety, insatiability are permanently embedded in an enterprising nature: Tocqueville's venturous American is no more the heroic Renaissance individual than he is a flexible Poor Richard, deriving his actions from his balance sheet.

A grinding tension is inherent in that bold pursuit of a success which

perpetually retires from before them, yet without hiding itself from their sight, and in retiring draws them on. At every moment they think they are about to grasp it; it escapes at every moment from their hold. They are near enough to see its charms, but too far off to enjoy them; and before they have fully tasted its delights, they die. . . .

In democratic times enjoyments are more intense than in the ages of aristocracy, and the number of those who partake in them is vastly larger; but, on the other hand, it must be admitted that man's hopes and desires are oftener blasted, the soul is more stricken and perturbed, and care itself more keen.[30]

In America Tocqueville saw "the freest and most enlightened men placed in the happiest circumstances that the world affords; it seemed to me as if a cloud habitually hung upon their brow, and I thought

[28] *Ibid.*, II, 136–37.     [29] *Ibid.*, I, 426.     [30] *Ibid.*, II, 138–39.

them serious and almost sad, even in their pleasures."[31] Indeed, so central was this worried quality in American experience that Tocqueville suspected life "would have no relish for them if they were delivered from the anxieties which harass them."[32]

Perhaps it is already evident how Tocqueville will discover tameness in the marrow of the tiger's bones. But the case will be clearer if first we trace the argument from condition to character along a more concrete line. All the previous references involve the pursuit of material success, the handling of material things. This is not, of course, accidental to Tocqueville's thesis. Most democratic energies, heightened by the extraordinary flux and freedom of American life, are channeled into one outlet. The direct pursuit of rank, privilege, honor, power, intellectual distinction has an aristocratic taint; money and goods alone are legitimate counters for the social competition of dissociated equals. The existence of competition is a given democratic fact: human energies must go somewhere in a society which does not prescribe fixed places and goals, which makes everything possible. But its intensity and direction are best understood from the conception of a social order in which men see first themselves and then a mass of almost-equals.[33]

In Tocqueville's penetrating analysis:

Whatever efforts a people may make, they will never succeed in reducing all the conditions of society to a perfect level. . . . However democratic, then, the social state and the political constitution of a people may be, it is certain that every member of the community will always find out several points about him which overlook his own position; and we may foresee that his looks will be doggedly fixed in that direction. When inequality of conditions is the common law of society, the most marked inequalities do not strike the eye; when everything is nearly on the same level, the slightest are marked enough to hurt it. Hence the desire of equality always becomes more insatiable in proportion as equality is more complete.[34]

Thus the intensity of democratic American striving. The direction, already partially explained, can now be given fuller definition. A major component of social equality in America is the narrowed spread of property differences, with a heavy concentration in the middle

---

[31] *Ibid.*, II, 136.      [32] *Ibid.*, II, 222.
[33] *Ibid.*, II, 128–30, 136–39, 154–57, 228–29, 244–47.
[34] *Ibid.*, II, 138.

range: the typical figures are "eager and apprehensive men of small property."

As they are still almost within the reach of poverty, they see its privations near at hand and dread them; between poverty and themselves there is nothing but a scanty fortune, upon which they immediately fix their apprehensions and their hopes.[35]

The case is very similar for the democratic rich and poor: "When . . . the distinctions of ranks are obliterated and privileges are destroyed, when hereditary property is subdivided and education and freedom are widely diffused, the desire of acquiring the comforts of the world haunts the imagination of the poor, and the dread of losing them that of the rich."[36] In total effect, then: "The love of well-being has now become the predominant taste of the nation; the great current of human passions runs in that channel and sweeps everything along in its course."[37]

With the urgent, worried striving for indefinite material success Tocqueville finds a marked propensity toward industrial and commercial callings; i.e., toward the most flexible pursuits which afford the quickest openings to large returns.[38] The seeming contradiction, in the heavy predominance of agricultural employment among Americans, Tocqueville resolves first by pointing to the rapid rate of growth in nonagricultural lines and then, more effectively, by attaching a special meaning to American farming.

Almost all the farmers of the United States combine some trade with agriculture; most of them make agriculture itself a trade. It seldom happens that an American farmer settles for good upon the land which he occupies; especially in the districts of the Far [i.e., Middle] West, he brings land into tillage in order to sell it again, and not to farm it: he builds a farmhouse on the speculation that, as the state of the country will soon be changed by the increase of population, a good price may be obtained for it. . . . Thus the Americans carry their businesslike qualities into agriculture, and their trading passions are displayed in that as in their other pursuits.[39]

Tocqueville does not hesitate to accept one of the sweeping consequences of his argument: that America is essentially a one-dimensional society, with a single basic life style, a single character type.

35 *Ibid.*, II, 253.    36 *Ibid.*, II, 129.
37 *Ibid.*, II, 130.    38 *Ibid.*, II, 154–57.    39 *Ibid.*, II, 157.

Equality of condition, American-style, defines a common social situation and enforces a common pattern of response (along the lines sketched above). Examining the possibility of sectional variation, Tocqueville concludes that the American South alone has preserved a unique social universe, founded upon the glaring anomaly, within a democratic order, of Negro slavery, and even this difference must collapse eventually. The West is partially distinct in nature and effects, yet basically within the unitary pattern.[40] In a fascinating set of wilderness notes[41] (which some future editor of the *Democracy* should append to the text), Tocqueville wrote that he had indeed expected geography to count for more in America, and abandoned this among other "traveller's illusions" only in the face of strong evidence.

In America, even more than in Europe, there is only one society. It may be either rich or poor, humble or brilliant, trading or agricultural; but it is composed everywhere of the same elements. The plane of a uniform civilization has passed over it. The man you left in New York you find again in almost impenetrable solitudes: same clothes, same attitude, same language, same habits, same pleasures. Nothing rustic, nothing naive, nothing which smells of the wilderness, nothing even resembling our [French] villages. . . . Those who inhabit these isolated places have arrived there since yesterday; they have come with the customs, the ideas, the needs of civilization. They only yield to savagery that which the imperious necessity of things exacts from them. . . .[42]

The most remarkable quality of the West, in short, is not its somewhat looser, rougher ways, but its capacity to reproduce almost from the moment of settlement the typical society and character of American democracy.[43]

At the center of this turbulence Tocqueville exposes—what he scarcely expected his French readers to credit—the soul of an archconservative: the steady citizen, the meek thinker, the pillar of property and propriety. To deal convincingly with such a strange compound he calls upon all his resources in history, politics, sociology, and psychology. His point is not to distinguish differences and place them separately upon plausible grounds, but to reconstruct a dynamic whole, a venturous conservative.

[40] *Ibid.*, I, 356–81, 392–95, 405.
[41] "Quinze jours au Désert," quoted in Pierson, *Tocqueville and Beaumont*, pp. 231–84.
[42] *Ibid.*, pp. 236–37.
[43] Tocqueville, *Democracy*, I, 290–92, 297, 316–17.

The men of the middle, preponderant in democratic times and overwhelmingly so in America, are unquiet souls, whipped into motion by acquisitive hunger and then arrested by possessive fears.[44] When Tocqueville portrays such men as the "natural enemies of violent commotions,"[45] he has in mind no inert lump of a dozing bourgeois but a nervous striver whose apprehensions mount with his success. The democratic competitor, shifting his efforts fluidly toward the quick opening to relative economic success (as the key to all felicity), finds himself in the midst of a universal competition of equals. With all the parts of his universe, himself included, in erratic motion, with no fixed terminus and no secure resting place, the democrat develops an acute awareness of loss and failure. He is never the contented success; rarely the jealous miser; and typically the unrelenting acquisitor, casting a nervous backward glance at what he has already gained.[46] The economic radical, in style of work, becomes the property-minded conservative: "between poverty and themselves there is nothing but a scanty fortune, upon which they immediately fix their apprehensions and their hopes."[47]

In the basic democratic situation, the strenuous pursuit of private welfare means the draining of vital concern from alternative commitments, notably to ideas and politics. There is simply very little attention available for revolutionary agitation.[48] This analysis has only a limited application to America, however, where free, democratic political institutions infuse the habits of freedom into almost the entire population:[49] "but if an American were condemned to confine his activity to his own affairs, he would be robbed of one-half of his existence; he would feel an immense void in the life which he is accustomed to lead, and his wretchedness would be unbearable."[50] It is not, then, political apathy which tames the American; instead he shapes the

[44] Ibid., II, 252–53, 128–30.
[45] Ibid., II, 252.
[46] Ibid., II, 154–57, 244–48, 228–29, 136–39.
[47] Ibid., II, 253. Even failure is not a clean-cut, ultimate catastrophe leading to emotional rejection of the economic system. The bankrupt has fallen in an equal competition, has a standing offer of new chances in new places, and so responds normally by renewing the struggle, abnormally by escaping into insanity, almost never by overt rebelliousness. (Tocqueville reports, as a common opinion, that American insanity rates are unusually high.) Ibid., II, 139, 236.
[48] Ibid., II, 253–55, 260.
[49] Ibid., I, 249–52.
[50] Ibid., I, 250.

quality of his political participation to correspond to and conserve his private-welfare interests.

An American attends to his private concerns as if he were alone in the world, and the next minute he gives himself up to the common welfare as if he had forgotten them. At one time he seems animated by the most selfish cupidity; at another, by the most lively patriotism. The human heart cannot be thus divided. The inhabitants of the United States alternately display so strong and so similar a passion for their own welfare and for their freedom that it may be supposed that these passions are united and mingled in some part of their character. And indeed the Americans believe their freedom to be the best instrument and surest safeguard of their welfare; they are attached to the one by the other. They by no means think that they are not called upon to take a part in public affairs; they believe, on the contrary, that their chief business is to secure for themselves a government which will allow them to acquire the things they covet and which will not debar them from the peaceful enjoyment of those possessions which they have already acquired.[51]

With such passionate devotion to the gains he has and seeks, the venturous American creates within himself a counterforce to his furious energies: "They love change but they dread revolutions."[52] Under a regime of almost unlimited political and civil liberty, the American democrat is perhaps the safest citizen in the world. Yet this is not the full measure of American conservatism: "amid the continual friction of men and things," Tocqueville observes, "the mind of man appears almost unmoved."[53] Here his classic analysis of equalitarian conformity, scarcely modified by anything unique to the American situation, records the suicide of individuality unbounded. If elsewhere Tocqueville emphasizes the "wide verge" of the "fatal circle" defined by a democratic social condition, it now becomes clear that accident and choice are critically significant only in one direction: the avoidance of political despotism (the total domination of "an immense and tutelary power"), mainly by releasing and focusing vast stores of private energy for the nonpolitical accomplishment of social tasks. Against the natural tendency of democracy to press minds into a dead uniformity Tocqueville's "new science of politics" uncovers no deep-rooted, durable restraints.[54]

The leveling of society, especially when accomplished by violent revolutionary means, initially unhinges all authority relations. But

[51] Ibid., II, 142.    [52] Ibid., II, 255.
[53] Ibid., II, 257.    [54] Ibid., II, 318, 332–33.

the shock of leveled liberty puts an insupportable strain upon the democrat:[55] "A principle of authority must then always occur, under all circumstances, in some part or other of the moral and intellectual world."[56] The location is determined by the basic democratic situation:

When the inhabitant of a democratic country compares himself individually with all those about him, he feels with pride that he is the equal of any one of them; but when he comes to survey the totality of his fellows and to place himself in contrast with so huge a body, he is instantly overwhelmed by the sense of his own insignificance and weakness. The same equality that renders him independent of each of his fellow citizens, taken severally, exposes him alone and unprotected to the influence of the greater number. The public, therefore, among a democratic people, has a singular power, which aristocratic nations cannot conceive; for it does not persuade others to its beliefs, but it imposes them and makes them permeate the thinking of everyone by a sort of enormous pressure of the mind of all upon the individual intelligence.[57]

Thus democrats—and Americans—turn toward public opinion as their source of moral and intellectual authority.[58] That a pervasive public opinion should exist in democratic society to assume the functions of authority, is understood by Tocqueville as a simple consequence of equality:

Men who are equal in rights, in education, in fortune, or, to comprise all in one word, in their social condition, have necessarily wants, habits, and tastes that are hardly dissimilar. As they look at objects under the same aspect, their minds naturally tend to similar conclusions; and though each of them may deviate from his contemporaries and form opinions of his own, they will involuntarily and unconsciously concur in a certain number of received opinions. . . . The leading opinions of men become similar in proportion as their conditions assimilate: such appears to me to be the general and permanent law; the rest is casual and transient.[59]

The democratic heretic who seeks a public hearing must speak at once to all: he has a legal permit, but no social platform—no claim to the attention of a busily preoccupied crowd, no initial concession of confidence in private intellectual authority to build upon.[60] "He strains

55 *Ibid.*, II, 3–12.    56 *Ibid.*, II, 9.
57 *Ibid.*, II, 10.    58 *Ibid.*, I, 263–65.
59 *Ibid.*, II, 258. See also *ibid.*, I, 303–7; II, 6, 10–11, 26–28, on the conservative reinforcement provided by religion, adapted to democratic circumstance and accepted "as a commonly received opinion."
60 *Ibid.*, II, 258–63.

himself to rouse the indifferent and distracted multitude and finds at last that he is reduced to impotence, not because he is conquered, but because he is alone."[61]

## Summary

The image of the democrat as American which I have assembled from Tocqueville's pages represents a most ambitious attempt to derive from the basic social situation of democracy (with local variations) a characteristic pattern of psychological response manifested broadly in the culture and life style of Jacksonian Americans. Certainly the boldest and possibly the most revealing feature of the portrait is the joining in dynamic tension of two major tendencies—toward independence, toward dependence. Tocqueville discovers the antithetic trends in the basic democratic situation, finds them in varying relations through every aspect of American life, and sees them exposed again in that duality of character which I have summed up in the phrase "venturous conservative." Condensing drastically, I would suggest that Tocqueville sees the process shaping the venturous conservative in two related ways. A comprehensive social equality is the common point of departure. Along one line: a world of almost-equals creates an anxious, urgent, flexible seeker of the next, most precious, most elusive increment of wealth and status; a seeker who, out of fear for his possessions and hope for his opportunities, becomes a firm conservative on property matters; and one who, from the depth of his material preoccupations, has little concern for radical revaluations of his moral universe. Along the second line: the masterless man, free to invent a fresh world, finds all the important value answers (and many petty ones) given in familiar, comfortable form by his own self-image magnified to authoritative dimensions—by the majority. In this direction little adventure survives; only a sort of surface confusion masking a congealed mass of values.

Tocqueville's venturous conservative is a historical type, perceived in wide focus. The portrait is built out of Jacksonian materials, but composed primarily to elucidate the enduring family traits of the democrat, with special reference to the American branch. As Tocqueville abstracted the democratic type from his Jacksonian observations, so I think one can profitably reverse the process, reviewing Jacksonian

[61] *Ibid.*, II, 255.

times in the light of Tocqueville's synthesis. His image of the venturous conservative pervades much of my discussion of the Jacksonian
persuasion. Tocqueville does not himself make the connection between
social situation, typical response, and the specific content of the Jacksonian political appeal; yet it seems to me a highly plausible association. The American who was involved in the continuous re-creation
of his social world, the continuous relocation of his place within it,
became the anxious witness of his own audacity. The consequence,
Tocqueville suggests, was the renewal of frenetic activity and, at the
same time, a powerful attachment to property and order. A further
response is evidenced, I would propose, in the effectiveness of the
Jacksonian political appeal: to hard money, personal enterprise and
credit, rural simplicity, and, broadly, to the pristine values of the Old
Republic.

# 4

# THE GREAT DESCENT

## ON COOPER AND THE AGE OF
## DODGE AND BRAGG

❧

For a generation or more the Leatherstocking has been ignored by the juvenile public. Meanwhile a body of solemn criticism has pretty convincingly translated Fenimore Cooper from adventure writer into moral commentator. By no rigorous standard can Cooper be made into a major thinker or a literary master. The sponsors of the revival have shown good sense in their restraint. Fenimore Cooper, reconsidered as a social critic, does not emerge with unsuspected qualities of originality, profundity, or subtlety. He offers rather the findings of a crusty, literal intelligence addressed to the fate of democratic values in America.[1]

In this revised approach to Cooper's work there is, I think, a useful opening for historians of Jacksonian society: a means of access to the ethos of a people undergoing drastic changes in their condition, and so a way of touching the contemporary meaning of such changes. The ample, often excellent literature of biography and criticism will support, and indeed invites, a further effort to draw from Cooper a direct commentary on Jacksonian manners and morals.

The evidence is strong that Cooper maintained a close attachment

[1] Valuable discussions of the "new" Cooper include: D. H. Lawrence, *Studies in Classic American Literature*, chaps. 4–5; Parrington, *Main Currents in American Thought*, II, 222–37; Robert E. Spiller, *Fenimore Cooper*; Dorothy Waples, *The Whig Myth of James Fenimore Cooper*; Henry Nash Smith, Introduction to James Fenimore Cooper, *The Prairie*, pp. v–xx; James Grossman, *James Fenimore Cooper*. Grossman's study is penetrating and judicious; I have often been guided by its interpretations. See also the recent collection, *James Fenimore Cooper: A Re-appraisal*, ed. Mary E. Cunningham, especially the papers by David Maldwyn Ellis and by Robert E. Spiller.

to the Democratic party in the Jacksonian years.[2] It was a curious alliance, on the face of it, for the son of a wealthy Federalist squire, a schoolmate of young Jays and Van Rensselaers, heir to a secure place in New York's gentry order. Yet Cooper never felt himself a traitor to his class, or a rebel, or even a critic in any fundamental way; on the contrary, it seemed to him natural that the children of Federalist die-hards should be "almost always decided democrats."[3]

The beginnings of an explanation can be found in Cooper's notion of political locations: "Here," he wrote in *A Letter to His Country-men*, "the democrat is the conservative, and, thank God, he has some-thing worth preserving."[4] If this were a wholly wrong conception of contemporary politics, and thus a case of misdirected sympathy, there would still be reason to inquire how a man of some judgment could make such an error. Cooper found his essential party friends among the Jacksonians, I suggest, because he shared with them an angry sense of loss: the First American Republic—the "Doric" age, to apply his term for Washington's character—was going down before a raw com-pany of the commercial *nouveau riche*, the speculative promoters of paper towns and enterprises, the mock-democrats of the popular press. He was, in short, a variety of Tory Democrat who gave his qualified allegiance to the party engaged in resisting the conspicuous agents of social and economic subversion.[5]

Cooper, one must add, took on many more adversaries than could be found among the Whigs; ultimately his resistance reached a pitch of intransigence which made him seem, in James Grossman's telling phrase, "perversely bent on taking his stand against time itself."[6] Reading Cooper as a straight Jacksonian author would require a rude

[2] Waples, *Whig Myth, passim.*
[3] Cooper, *Notions of the Americans*, II, 222. Cooper's background is neatly sum-marized in Grossman, *Cooper*, pp. 9–17. His social circle included the most exclusive families of New York and Philadelphia. See *Correspondence of James Fenimore Cooper*, ed. James Fenimore Cooper (Cooper's grandson).
[4] Cooper, *A Letter to His Countrymen*, quoted in Waples, *Whig Myth*, p. 147. Parrington's discussion of Cooper's political viewpoint remains in many ways the most convincing. *Main Currents*, II, 222–37.
[5] It is worth noting, too, that the Jacksonian party in Cooper's New York was led by solid upstate citizens, Van Buren, William Marcy, Silas Wright, Michael Hoff-man, and the like; and that in office it produced an honest, prudent, able state admin-istration. When the anti-rent war—which so unsettled Cooper—flared in the 1840's, it was the Whigs who played up to rebel feelings and the Democratic administration which acted sternly in behalf of order. See *infra*, Chapter 11, for further discussion of New York politics.
[6] Grossman, *Cooper*, pp. 263–64.

forcing of the texts. His sympathetic bond with Jacksonian Democracy does not provide an adequate definition for Cooper's point of view; it does prepare one to see in his "contemporary" writings a persistent concern with social ills that troubled the Jacksonians: above all, with the degeneration of republican virtue. Thus Cooper's commentaries on nineteenth-century American society are peculiarly relevant guides to the public sentiment that responded to Jacksonian appeals.

The fictional Effinghams (of *Homeward Bound* and *Home as Found*) are authorized to speak among them the important truths about their country. When Cooper brings them home in the mid-1830's, after a dozen years abroad, he has them confront a society much changed, and all for the worse. No one disputes the judgment of John Effingham, that in twelve years America has experienced the damage of a century to "all that is respectable and good."[7] Cooper's own departure and return correspond roughly to the schedule he gave the Effinghams. Moreover, the observations in *Notions of the Americans*—perhaps Cooper's last generally sympathetic portrait of his countrymen—antedate by about the same dozen years the bitter Effingham report.[8] The Effingham authority, supported by a double coincidence, seems to me a fair basis for maintaining that Cooper saw American society, between the 1820's and the 1830's, in the course of a great moral descent. The rule of the great middle—of middling virtues, talents, possessions, aspirations—had been the last and best hope for a just settlement between the party of the few and the commons; but only so long as the many faced upward toward a natural elite. Now the American middle was feeling its power: following its uninstructed instincts democracy would make a world without moral foundations.

Here I shall examine Cooper's view of the process by contrasting two comprehensive observations of Jacksonian America: *Notions of the Americans* for the 1820's and the Effingham novels for the 1830's. In the general scheme of my study, this version of Fenimore Cooper is intended to provide another suggestive approach to the predispositions of those who heard the Jacksonian appeal. Cooper does not himself consider the connection between the situation he perceives and the

---

[7] Cooper, *Homeward Bound*, p. 223; also Cooper, *Home as Found*, pp. 206–7. For editions of Cooper's works cited in this book, see the Bibliography.
[8] The observations in the *Notions* are dated ca. 1824–28; in the Effingham novels, ca. 1838.

specific Jacksonian response. Yet his Jacksonian sympathies, as I have noted above, led him to look in places where significant indications of this response could be found.[9]

## The Middling Standard: The 1820's[10]

Rarely has there been a foreign traveler so congenial, so educable, as Cooper's made-to-order Continental bachelor in *Notions of the Americans*, or a guide so apt at saving explanations as Cadwallader, the perfect gentle democrat. No doubt Cooper's notions of the Americans were more severe—even in the twenties—than the ones his credulous guest was taught; for Cadwallader took from his creator a strong sense of what was fit for strangers' ears. Yet to call the gathering of *Notions of the Americans* a homely Potemkin tour would be to underrate the evidence of Cooper's stiff rectitude, and to misconstrue the work. The *Notions* takes the ordinary at its best: chooses comfort, decency, order, common sense, and progress as the well-grounded themes of American life in the mid-1820's. The sketch is useful particularly for the definition of a reference point—the middling standard—from which Cooper measured the deterioration of the ordinary in the later social novels.

The revealing scenes of American life, the stranger learns, are often missed by foreign travelers, who, seeking relief from the dullness of "common sense" affairs, develop a "partiality to the woods" and emphasize "the fresher and more vivid tints of a border life."[11] The well-chaperoned bachelor of the *Notions* is led directly to prime sources of understanding: to the countryside of New England and the Middle States, to New York City, to political Washington. New England, taken in a sweeping glance, appears "a succession of fields, sprinkled with houses, and embellished with little groves." The division of the country into modest freeholds—one hundred acres or so, on the average—each with its own house and outbuildings, gives the effect of a used and peopled landscape. Rural society is highly visible,

---

[9] Supplementary sources for Cooper's views on the thirties and after include: *The American Democrat, Autobiography of a Pocket-Handkerchief,* and *New York,* ed. Dixon Ryan Fox. See also *The Monikins, The Crater, The Redskins,* and *The Ways of the Hour.*

[10] The following discussion of the 1820's is based on Cooper, *Notions of the Americans.*

[11] *Notions of the Americans,* I, 99–100. Cooper himself was, of course, an incurable seeker of excitement in the forests.

with its homes crowding upon the roads and its busy traffic along the market routes. The usual village is "beautiful, tranquil and enviable looking"; its qualities are "space, freshness, an air of neatness and comfort."[12]

New England is a touchstone, an influence; but not, of course, a sample of America. The growing points are found in the interior of New York, Pennsylvania, Ohio. Here is more of what the European demands of America—wild woods, burnt-over clearings, "wild-looking memorials of a state of nature"—yet all in curious combination with settlement and domesticity. The Mohawk Valley of New York offers "completely an American scene, embracing all that admixture of civilization, and of the forest, of the works of man, and of the reign of nature." Even "forest" is a misleading term, however, since one sees in fact "a constant succession of open land and of wood" in nearly even proportions. From a hill overlooking the valley, a closer look defines "countless farm-houses" and outbuildings, fields alive with herds and flocks, pyramids of hay, a village with its church spire.[13]

Everything, in these areas settled largely since the Revolution, is newer, fresher, less complete than in New England. Yet the contrast is mainly in stage and degree. The wilderness toward the West may be a route, an incipient settlement, or simply a strange scene between the points of settlement; it is not a stable component of the common social environment. Typically, the new settler occupies the fertile valleys, leaving the mountains under forest. Emigration moves in successive tides toward such favored areas. (A few luckless settlers miscalculate the course of emigration, and face the choice of struggling for years in a rude, half-civilized condition or abandoning their stake. Nine of ten retreat.)[14]

Once the current has set toward a given spot for a time, vestiges of a barbarous life rapidly disappear. Emigrants bring with them the wants, habits, and institutions of an advanced state of society. The artisan's shop rises with the rude farm dwelling. Shortly, log cabins give way to structures of taste, size, and comfort beyond the hopes of ordinary men anywhere in the world. The schoolhouse is built; the

---

[12] *Ibid.*, I, 57, 59, 60.

[13] *Ibid.*, I, 255, 248–49.

[14] *Ibid.*, I, 243–46. The characters in Cooper's novels who remain outside the settlements are never normal American figures. This is obvious in the case of Natty Bumppo. But even men like Ishmael Bush, in *The Prairie*, belong to a special class of border adventurers, not to the regular body of Western migrants.

tavern and the general store appear; the church is raised. The nucleus
of a village has been formed. From fifty or a hundred such "centres
of exertion" spread swarms of men who, in a few years, convert dark
forests into populous, wealthy, industrious counties. Soon the village
store which sells the cleaving axe will stock the luxuries of Europe,
China, and the Indies.[15]

Given thirty or forty years of settlement, a district in the Eastern,
Middle, or Northwestern states will show for its dominant figure the
middling farmer, one of many thousands of the class of "sturdy, independent yeomen." He will be owner of one or two hundred acres
and occupy a substantial frame house. He may be worth between five
and ten thousand dollars. His property will include an orchard, sheep,
cows, horses, oxen, hogs, poultry, and the like. Probably he will fatten
his pork on his own maize, make his cider, kill his beef, raise his own
wheat, rye, and flax; and, in short, live "as much as possible on the
articles of his own production."[16]

Cooper has an exacting standard for the recognition of a city. He
sees only New York, and possibly New Orleans, as something more
than provincial towns. His country center seems to have no strong
character distinct from its environs: the New England village blends
pleasantly into the rural scene; the inland village in newer areas is at
first a "center of exertion" and then an exhibit of rural achievement,
with its surplus goods and moral services. New York is different: not
yet a metropolis in the European sense; hardly a source of standards
and directives for the country; not itself an advance model of a new
order; and yet, somehow, a sign of "the mighty future." Cooper
leaves the traveling bachelor vaguely informed about the peculiar
principle New York represents in American life. It is clear only
that commercial greatness is impending in the twenties, and that extraordinary growth, variety, and mutability are to be the themes of
urban life.[17]

America's great moving principles, as the traveler of the *Notions*
is made to see, converge upon one object: "the improvement of the
species in the mass." Given equality of rights, diffusion of knowledge,
and physical abundance as initial conditions, the object is served by
an active, unrelenting common sense which directs thought and action

[15] *Notions of the Americans*, I, 243–46.
[16] *Ibid.*, II, 154.
[17] *Ibid.*, I, 123–35.

toward utility, feelings and manners toward a plain decorum. Society
is drenched in "the attributes of plain good sense," until Americans
are "not only like each other, but they are remarkably like that which
common sense tells them they ought to resemble."[18]

Thus Americans, whose literature is dull and bare, whose art
scarcely exists, create "more beautiful, graceful, and convenient
ploughs" than one can find in all Europe. In this fact lies "the history
of the character of the people, and the germ of their future greatness."
The American axe is a masterpiece of functional design, wielded with
incredible skill. The continuous flood of inventions, useless and naïve
as many are, demonstrates that immense practical activity of mind
which had its triumph in the production of the steamboat. The Erie
Canal—the greatest such work in Christendom—could be completed
with amazing speed, economy, and accuracy, under the direction of
men trained by "the thousand collisions of active life" to "the utmost
practical knowledge of men and of things."[19]

The same bent toward utility appears in the system of higher education and professional training. The colleges are not organized to
turn out profound scholars; instead they administer a light dose of
general and diversified knowledge to their students, and return them
to the country to mingle in its active employments. The prospective
lawyer enters his clerkship, where he gets a general insight into the
principles of law, a familiarity with practice, and very little in the
way of legal science. His very deficiencies in formal knowledge lead
to a preference for "natural truth" over "quaint follies"; and lawyers
largely trained by experience give the laws themselves a modern dress.
Thus educated, the clever lawyer, following a natural career route into
lawmaking, frames measures "not to harmonize with the other parts
of an elaborate theory" but "to make men comfortable and happy."
Such is the history of thousands; "and it is also an important part of
the history of the country itself."[20]

With each example—the plow, the Erie enterprise, the making of
a lawyer—Cooper moves toward an answer to the stranger's question:
Why has so much been effected so quickly and so well with such limited
means? The unprecedented material progress of America, Cooper
explains, has been the physical record left by a spirit of "activity, enter-

18 *Ibid.*, II, 427–28, 143.
19 *Ibid.*, II, 152–53, 424–27.
20 *Ibid.*, II, 126–28.

prise, intelligence, and skill" that has been abroad since the Revolution. A "natural" social order, based upon equality of rights and protection of property, leaves talent, money, and enterprise free to work their full effects. Space and natural abundance offer liberal resources and, in their undeveloped state, strong incentives to action. A society with no past, no follies, no manners, no legends, wants little diversion from its matter-of-fact material tasks. A modest portion of intelligence, distributed through the nation, becomes a floating fund of informed common sense for the mastery of practical problems. A diversified education, largely the product of worldly experience, enlarges the fund, sharpens its quality, and directs it still more surely toward questions of utility.[21]

In this situation the American is more than self-made according to the usual meaning; he is self-created, out of an image of common sense which all the elements of his past and present suggest to him. With signs of his progress all about him, and a keen awareness of the physical and moral bases of success, the American becomes "sanguine, aspiring, and confident"; he reinforces his nature and bent with a self-approving sense of achievement. He devises even a new measure of time to add dignity to his headlong history: "He sees that his nation lives centuries in an age, and he feels no disposition to consider himself a child, because other people, in their dotage, choose to remember the hour of his birth."[22]

American common sense, as the Bachelor finds it, is an agency of progress; progress is indeed a major theme of American life observed in the twenties; yet progress is not the sole issue of common sense, or the master value in Cooper's *Notions*. Cooper does not lightly buy the well-turned axe at the cost of a threadbare imagination, bold enterprise for narrow minds, wealth for a facile conscience. Some of the costs of American progress he reckons and pays—most easily when he can exchange snob goods for common comforts; but the whole transaction is possible for Cooper, I believe, because progress means an expanding provision for social wants and national growth, under the firm governance of order and decorum. That common sense which grows out of the American condition, acquires vigor, and turns so wonderfully to useful work is precisely the provider of good manners and morals, the preservatives of republican society.

[21] *Ibid.*, II, 422–23, 443, 428–29, 142.
[22] *Ibid.*, II, 441.

Generally in his books Cooper relentlessly presses the old quarrel of Yorkers with Yankees. The best people—Cadwallader, the Effinghams—are almost inevitably his New York neighbors. Thus the tourist of the *Notions* enjoyed a rare privilege in gaining a view of Yankee virtues as germinal American qualities, admirable in their way. Nothing noble, gentle, or inspired can be harvested from those rocks; the staple of the region is a plain people, notable for "enterprise, frugality, order, and intelligence." Thrift among them becomes a "sentiment of deep morality," pursued to secure "private respectability" and, equally, "the interests of the whole." The general tone of the region is pure-middle, with "its air of abundance, its decency, the absence of want, the elevation of character, which is imparted to the meanest of its people." In short, the industrial virtues abound, and they turn out to be not William Graham Sumner's claws-in-cotton—not the combat equipment of the fittest capitalist competitor—but the fundamental decencies merged with a bright self-interest.[23]

Common sense works toward progress and decency in the economic life of the American; the same trait ensures order and decorum in general social relations. Cooper's later writings on America speak ruefully of the social pell-mell which obliterates natural and necessary distinctions among men; in the *Notions* he never ceases admiring the sensible solution Americans have found to the joint demands of equality and quality. The result is not altogether lovely, to be sure: it compresses human experience within a bare middle range; nevertheless, it is salutary.

The stranger notes among the Yankees "an apparent coldness of demeanor" linked to the prevalent kindness of deeds; and among Americans at large a universal "gravity of eye and mien" which marks even the Louisiana French. This cannot be due to climate; surely not to brooding over tragedy or to sullen plotting. Cadwallader provides the answer: this is, again, the touch of common sense, "sovereign guide of the public will," which makes morals "consistent and sound," politics orderly, and manners such only as reason would approve. Saturated with "healthful moral truths," the American must regard "the blandishments and exaggerations of conventional politeness"—"assumed cordiality"—with distrust and distaste. What is lost in grace

[23] *Ibid.*, I, 91.

and gaiety is returned in civility, kindness, naturalness, temperate respect.[24]

Americans refuse, in fact, not the deference due by nature to quality, but servility to mere front. They have a very distinguished body of superiors of their own—a subject I shall return to—and grant them all that sense requires. America has the "conventional castes" which divide all the civilized world. But the barriers are low. The outward marks are faint—it is singularly difficult to rank a person by appearance, especially a woman. And the common traits are many.[25]

The Bachelor finds the perfection of democratic decorum in the conduct of public life, notably at Washington. Here the situation demands that classes associate, and policy demands that quality have its due. It is a critical subject and Cooper turns the commentary back to the reliable Cadwallader. Conducting the traveler about Washington, Cadwallader explains why the American majority do not abuse power in Congress. The relatively poor and ignorant choose representatives of respectable, though not lofty, standing and information. Thus the "middling" exercise power; and the best of them do not use public office as a private entry to the aristocracy, in the English fashion, do not desert their order, but return to it and raise the level. The representatives on view are mostly men of good manners and education, an American "gentry," who associate on easy terms with some few farmers and mechanics, notably self-possessed and decent folk. Of course, through all the public fraternizing, a keen eye can always tell who is who; and of course equal relations cease at the boundaries of private life. Where public and private relations intersect, as at a presidential open house, the Bachelor greatly admires the American capacity for mixing the classes on the strictest terms of

[24] *Ibid.*, I, 165–66, 168, 170, 171–72, 174–77; also pp. 153–55.

[25] *Ibid.*, I, 64–67, 80–81, 156–58, 293–94, 297. Cooper makes some shrewd observations on social typing, especially among American women. Lower-class women seen in public fairly successfully imitate the exterior of the lady. When one reaches the girl of the "second class," it is possible to distinguish her from the true lady not at all by fashion, just perceptibly by quality of material, "and perhaps a little in the air in which it is worn." Already the great and grave American game of taste-hopping is well under way. Eve Effingham, in the novels of the thirties, has discovered how to trim the easily copied frills and affect a rich plainness of dress as well as manner, the most confusing style for the climber to learn. See *ibid.*, I, 178–91.

Cooper further suggests that the diversity of an American's career tends to loosen the hold of special etiquettes and mannerisms of the sort that so plainly set off class and occupational groups in England.

respectability and decorum. Finally, any underrepresentation of the top quality in government—the rich find the road to high office very hard—is well accounted for in the ruling political principle "that the people are left, as much as possible, to be the agents of their own prosperity." The tasks of government are kept within its capacity.[26]

Sound sense has taught Americans to strengthen social decency by another, less obvious arrangement: by treating women of all social conditions with the respect due "the repositories of the better principles of our nature." Because women remain out of the world, men can safely enter into it.

Retired within the sacred precincts of her own abode, she is preserved from the destroying taint of excessive intercourse with the world. She makes no bargains beyond those which supply her own little personal wants, and her heart is not early corrupted by the baneful and unfeminine vice of selfishness. . . . She must be sought in the haunts of her domestic privacy, and not amid the wranglings, deceptions, and heartburnings of keen and sordid traffic.[27]

Thus the husband can "retire from his own sordid struggles with the world to seek consolation and correction from one who is placed beyond their influence." More important:

The first impressions of the child are drawn from the purest sources known to our nature; and the son, even long after he has been compelled to enter on the thorny track of the father, preserves the memorial of the pure and unalloyed lessons that he has received from the lips, and, what is far better, from the example of the mother.[28]

But the master choice of democratic sense has been the willingness to acknowledge and maintain a natural elite. The Bachelor arrives too late upon the scene to meet the ideal American, although he encounters fair copies, and a society still responsive to the example of Washington. Cooper shows in Washington a "Doric" character, with beauty in the harmony of means and purpose, and grandeur in a "chaste simplicity." His massive and enduring achievement was due solely to greatness of character in the face of adversity. Indeed his glory resides

26 *Ibid.*, II, 29–35, 42–45, 72–79, 53–54.
27 *Ibid.*, I, 105.
28 *Ibid.*, I, 105–6. On women and marriage generally, see I, 103–6, 192–99. With the confinement of matrons to a domestic role goes a certain female virtuosity in pursuing the nicer shades of distinction in manners.

not in brilliant deeds but in the whole tenor of his life, and in "the stern lesson of virtue" left to his community.[29]

Somewhere between the peak and the high plateau of American quality the touring stranger finds John Jay, now retired from high official station to a distinguished place in New York society. Jay lives quietly in Westchester, in what might be "a third-rate English country house, or a second-rate French chateau." His farm buildings are a little removed from the house, but still in plain view. The home has the character of "respectable comfort, rather than . . . elegance, or show." Ten or twelve domestics serve in plain dress. The only show of pomp is the "ancient plate" bearing marks of an honorable family name. In the man there is a "happy union of quiet decorum, and high courtesy," a "dignified simplicity." The local yeomanry, approaching respectfully, receive the hand of the Governor in frank and cordial greeting.[30]

The regular rank of American gentlefolk constitute a class of natural superiors, shaped in the image of Washington and the Jays. When money, intelligence, and manners merge in a man, public opinion will concede to him full membership in the national elite, with all the advantages appropriate to a republican aristocracy. Such distinction, earned, has greater meaning than the conventional laying-on of noble rank in Europe. Birth, to be sure, gives some advantage to an American candidate for social honors; yet it is not mere birth, mere money. In the absence of hereditary privilege, the heir must come up to the parent's mark or forfeit his initial claim.[31]

Once in a select circle, the American is by no means forced into "promiscuous association" with his lesser fellows. He has won his choice of company and ought to take it: the country has need of the finer tastes, manners, intellects, and principles cultivated in a kind of social privacy. New admissions are relatively frequent—the marks of aristocracy can be achieved—but not indiscriminate; especially, moral requirements are strict, and social downfall can be more rapid than ascent. Putting social position before every man who can merit it does not level but elevates the nation, inviting all to stretch their aspirations. Cooper dreams of the future nation of one hundred million, graced

---

[29] *Ibid.*, II, 251–59.
[30] *Ibid.*, I, 85–86, 88.
[31] *Ibid.*, I, 88, 153–58; II, 389–92, 415–21.

by some four or five million men of fortune, breeding, and education who would enter full communion with the elect of all nations.[32]

The cultivation of a natural aristocracy demands—permits—no more political provision than the maintenance of a "natural" order: a system of equal rights and security for property. The "gross absurdity" of supposing that any major party in American history has supported radically opposed principles is quickly shown the Bachelor: How could the mass of republican communities be said to entertain the wish to subvert their own authority when, for instance, they supported the Federalists? As early as 1800 it was clear that fierce political rivalries were "essentially, nothing more than two great parties, struggling for place, and who adopted different politics about as much for the purpose of opposition as for any other reason." In the desperation of repeated failure, some Federalists did meditate wild schemes, and thereby destroyed the party.[33]

The current frenzy over Jackson's rise to prominence is, the stranger learns, but another party exercise. This supposedly dangerous general is met and passed as a gentleman of "mild and graceful mien," of "manly and marked features" and "courteous dialogue." Cooper offers to name for the panic shouters one hundred gentlemen in the Middle States—men of education, fortune, and religion—who are warm supporters of Jackson. The question between Jackson and Adams in 1828 "is altogether one of men." That Jackson appears to be Cooper's man is a matter of character judgment; the virile qualities of decision, courage, and patriotism, joined to simple courtesy and stout independence, make the stronger image of the Doric model.[34]

Such is the best face of America in the twenties, as Cooper shows it to his acquiescent foreign visitor. Comfort, order, and decency prevail under the guidance of common sense. Controlled progress issues from every quarter. Politics maintains essential principles and finds a new leader of the old stamp. The quality sits just high enough above the ordinary to raise its level and temper its effects. The social mood is serene and sanguine. If Cooper spares the stranger some of his own doubts and fears, he nevertheless guarantees—through the imposing authority of Cadwallader—the essential justice of this view

[32] Ibid., II, 415–21.
[33] Ibid., II, 443–61, 219–22.
[34] Ibid., II, 242, 243–44, 227–32.

of American democracy, prospering within the bounds of the middling standard.

### The World Without Foundations: The 1830's and Beyond

Cooper did not show the Bachelor mirages. He never suggests that great, strange forces invaded America between the stranger's departure and the Effinghams' (and his own) return. How then did the land of common sense and progress, decency and order, become a place good men cursed, lamented, or abandoned? A change in Cooper's private outlook, only tenuously related to general social trends, is one source of answers: the *Notions* were an antidote for vitriolic British travel notes, like Captain Hall's; harsh personal experiences with unruly neighbors and rude press critics soured Cooper; an extended stay in Europe suggested nobler standards of culture. Perhaps the very existence of Jacksonian Democracy as an embattled political force, disputing the possession of American loyalties, gave a sharper polemical cast to the visible world. All these have some plausibility; and yet I find an essential consistency in outlook.

The ordinary at its best, for all its pleasant aspect, was never taken for the ideal order by Cooper's standards: at best, the sacrifices were real, the achievements limited. More important, society organized by the middling standard was a precarious creation: its mobility could run wild, its naturalness give way to oafishness, its prudence turn to greed, its pragmatism become mere craftiness, its decency decay into an arrant philistinism, its subtly graded order sink into a false equality. The Bachelor of the *Notions* was amazed to see American society functioning so well because he was a European; still he was a European of Cooper's making and his wonder was, in some part, Cooper's warning that a nation self-made in the image of common sense was a most delicate balance of forces. Cooper's line between the good in the middling standard and the evil in the "social bivouac"[35] of the 1830's is thin: a little excess in the parts, a shift in center of gravity, and the ordinary reveals its mangy underside.

I suspect that Cooper's deepest shock came with the conviction that the 5 per cent leaven of natural gentility would never be; that the Effingham-Hawker-Caverly-Cadwallader set—the established fami-

[35] *Homeward Bound*, p. 289.

lies of wealth, breeding, taste, political virtue—was a tiny coterie, locked out of American society; that the rising middle class was fatally anchored to the mass and would rise no higher, or that it would settle, where it could, for a cheap brand of snobbery. In Cooper's explicit analysis the great descent occurs in three main areas: where the rising tempo of mobility disintegrates communal centers of order and decorum; where the related quest for gain turns feverish, despoiling real values in a speculative riot; where false democracy usurps control of opinion and taste, reducing all to a vile cant of equality. Dodge and Bragg are the dominant types of the new order; the Effinghams its vestigial elite; Captain Truck a relic of strong character in the commons, preserved by salt water; and the Leatherstocking its legend of presocial virtue.

"The whole country," John Effingham remarks, "is in such a constant state of mutation, that I can only liken it to the game of children, in which, as one quits his corner another runs into it, and he that finds no corner to get into, is the laughing-stock of the others."[36] Social flux is so far the essence of American life in the 1830's, as Cooper finds it, that he taunts his readers thus: "The author has endeavored to interest his readers in occurrences of a date as antiquated as two years can make them, when he is quite aware, that, in order to keep pace with a state of society in which there was no yesterday, it would have been much safer to anticipate things, by laying his scene two years in advance."[37] What appeared in the *Notions* as a wholesome sign of national vigor must be reviewed in terms of the deepest skepticism.

In a penetrating sociological history of Templeton—the upstate New York seat of the Effinghams, virtually of the Coopers—the writer outlines the pattern of American settlement and its social consequences. Entering a "new country," Americans pass through three standard stages of development. At first society is characterized by strong community feeling and interest. The hazards of settling a wilderness make mutual effort necessary and greatly reduce the social "distance" between men of different habits, manners, education. The gentleman in the first stage of settlement maintains his character and station, but with "that species of good-fellowship and familiarity, that marks the

[36] *Home as Found*, p. 118.
[37] *Homeward Bound*, Preface, p. iv.

intercourse between the officer and the soldier in an arduous campaign." The classes mingle: men—"even women"—break bread together in a way that would be unthinkable in settled circumstances, the hardy adventures and rough living of the forest apparently lowering the pretensions of the man of cultivation and mere mental resources, to something very near the level of those of the man of physical energy and manual skill. In this rude intercourse, the parties meet, as it might be, on a sort of neutral ground, one yielding some of his superiority, and the other laying claims to an outward show of equality, that he secretly knows, however, is the result of the peculiar circumstances in which he is placed.[38]

This primary stage of "mere animal force" is the happiest period in the first century of settlement. Great cares drive out small, good will abounds, neighbors are helpful, and life has the "childhood" qualities of "reckless gayety, careless association, and buoyant merriment." After this era of "fun, toil, neighborly feeling, and adventure" comes the second major phase of settlement: "society begins to marshal itself, and the ordinary passions have sway."

Now it is that we see the struggles for place, the heartburnings and jealousies of contending families, and the influence of mere money. Circumstances have probably established the local superiority of a few beyond all question, and the condition of these serves as a goal for the rest to aim at.

The learned professions take natural precedence—"next to wealth, however, when wealth is at all supported by appearances." At this point, "gradations of social station" multiply and crystallize, in defiance of equalitarian ideas and institutions.[39]
    The least inviting condition of society in a free country above the state of barbarism is met in this transitional phase of settlement. Tastes too crude to accept regulation impose themselves with all the pretension and forced effort of "infant knowledge." Because of "the late *pêle-mêle*" in the "community" stage, the status struggle is particularly sharp: men aspire above their reach, as that reach would be understood in older communities. Manners are at their worst, exposed to the influence of "the coarse-minded and vulgar." Finally, with the arrival of the third stage, "the marshalling of time quietly regulates what is here the subject of strife." Settlement has reached maturity

38 *Home as Found*, p. 162.
39 *Ibid.*, pp. 162–63.

and "men and things come within the control of more general and regular laws." The essential trait of the third phase is not a particular form of civilization but a general settling down: the community assimilates a stable culture conforming to the regional pattern; class distinctions are more or less rigidly established.[40]

In America the first stage of settlement is highly variable in length; often it is quite short. But the second is almost always long, "the migratory habits of the people keeping society more unsettled than might otherwise prove to be the case." Maturity comes only when a great majority of the living generation are regional natives, bred to one cultural standard. Yet: "Even when this is the case, there is commonly so large an infusion of the birds of passage, men who are adventurers in quest of advancement, and who live without the charities of a neighborhood, as they may be said almost to live without a home, that there is to be found for a long time a middle state of society [between the second stage and the third]. . . ." Templeton remains in this ambiguous condition, divided almost equally between the third-generation descendants of the pioneers and a flock of "migratory birds" whose influence "nearly neutralized that of time and the natural order of things." An emerging sense of loyalty to place and tradition among the natives provides the sole restraint upon a "nameless multitude" who briefly occupy real estate and live entirely in the flat dimension of present interest.[41]

Templeton is by no means an extreme example of the social flux which is shaking the foundations of American society. It requires the delicate sensibilities of an Effingham or a Cooper to find the signs of social upheaval in the history of a quiet country village—not one of the boom towns of the period—which has grown at a moderate pace and appears already to be leveling off. New York is the ultimate case: "a social bivouac, a place in which families encamp instead of troops." New York or Templeton, to Cooper and the Effinghams the principle is the same. The gentle Ned Effingham—a natural aristocrat of sound heart and fair but dull mind—does his best to understand and pardon the strange creatures who challenge the proprieties, and the proprietors, of Templeton. He supposes that the unprecedented prosperity of the masses must worsen manners and morals, "by introducing suddenly large bodies of uninstructed and untrained men and women into

[40] *Ibid.*, pp. 163–64.
[41] *Ibid.*, pp. 164–66.

society"—"a body of strangers, birds of passage, creatures of an hour."[42]

But cousin John Effingham, Cooper's angry prophet of the Yorker gentry and a man whose sharp blade always goes to the heart of matters in the novels, excuses nothing. The "vagrants" of Templeton "fancy everything reduced to the legal six months required to vote." John asks his kindly relative to look about him, "and you will see adventurers uppermost everywhere; in the government, in the towns, in your villages, in the country, even. We are a nation of changes." At first this is the expected response of a people engaged in settling an immense forest.

But this necessity has infected the entire national character, and men get to be impatient of any sameness, even though it be useful. Everything goes to confirm this feeling. . . . The constant recurrences of the elections accustom men to changes in their public functionaries; the great increase in the population brings new faces; and the sudden accumulations of property place new men in conspicuous stations. The architecture of the country is barely becoming sufficiently respectable to render it desirable to preserve the buildings, without which we shall have no monuments to revere.

To all this Ned can only mumble something about exaggeration, and patience, and taking the bad with the good.[43]

While the flux sometimes appears a vast dirty trick of history upon the Effinghams, it is more than that to Cooper because the Effinghams are more than private worthies, ornaments. Without the saving remnant of the quality, middling society turns into its ugliest form. The flux turns America loose, brashly to satisfy its natural promptings at the level of its common nature. Above all, that delicate articulation of formal equals according to natural distinctions is lost. Abandoning the Effinghams, society sacrifices itself. The reign of Dodge and Bragg begins.[44]

In the pathology of the great descent, violent economic fevers accompany the social flux. Where nothing is fixed, money is everything. Acquisition becomes the urgent, continuous preoccupation of

[42] *Homeward Bound*, p. 289; *Home as Found*, pp. 117–18, 224. For a later view of New York, see Cooper, *New York*.

[43] *Home as Found*, pp. 225–26.

[44] Evidence of the damage to tastes, manners, and values is considered in *Homeward Bound*, p. 38; *Home as Found*, pp. iv–v, 15, 42–97, 113–17, 120, 150, 156–57, 160, 186, 312–13, 335–37, 375–77. See also *The American Democrat*.

society, until even useful enterprise is forgotten in the universal frenzy of speculation. Although this is not exclusively an urban phenomenon, Cooper finds his richest material in the business district of New York.

Cooper as usual employs the Effinghams as cicerones, this time to introduce their titled English visitor to the improbable wonders of Wall Street in the thirties. The tour begins at the office of one of the greater auctioneers, lately become the genius of the "town trade." Here one can buy villas, farms, streets, and towns of assorted types. As they enter, the auctioneer is presenting a choice offering: the old Van Brunt farm, which had given comfortable support to the family for over a century. It was first sold to "Feeler" for $5,000, resold the next spring to "Search" for $25,000; sold again the next week to "Rise" for $50,000, who unloaded to a company, before his own purchase had been completed, for $112,000. The fifty acres then were divided into lots, which were sold at auction for the gross sum of $300,000. The auctioneer explains that he has many such properties; some have risen 3,000 per cent in five years, some a mere few hundred per cent. These speculative properties are miles beyond town. If the same land were called a farm, it would bring only a farm price, but once surveyed and detail-mapped it reaches what the auctioneer calls its "just value." Well mapped, even ocean bottom sells high. In the auction salesroom a crowd is bidding wildly for rocks, bogs, all on the credit of maps, and all "in the fearful delusion of growing rich by pushing a fancied value to a point still higher."[45]

Such weird affairs are beyond the grasp of Squire Ned—of course he knows that they are wrong—and John Effingham is obliged to interpret the experience. Land mania is but a special instance, for John, of the unlimited extravagance pervading the whole community.

Extravagant issues of paper money, inconsiderate credits that commence in Europe and extend throughout the land, and false notions as to the value of their possessions, in men who five years since had nothing, has [sic] completely destroyed the usual balance of things, and money has got to be so completely the end of life, that few think of it as a means. . . . All principles are swallowed up in the absorbing desire for gain—national honor, permanent security, the ordinary rules of society, law, the constitution . . . are forgotten, or are perverted. . . .

The entire community is in the situation of a man who is in the incipient stages of an exhilarating intoxication, and who keeps pouring down glass after glass, in the idle notion that he is merely sustaining nature in

[45] *Home as Found*, pp. 100–103.

her ordinary functions. This wide-spread infatuation extends from the coast to the extremest frontiers of the West; for, while there is a justifiable foundation for a good deal of this fancied prosperity, the true is so interwoven with the false, that none but the most observant can draw the distinction, and, as usual, the false predominates.[46]

As the tour continues through the warehouse district, John describes the further ravages of the economic fever, when it passes from the extremities of land speculation to the ordinary business of the country.

The man who sells his inland lots at a profit, secured by credit, fancies himself enriched, and he extends his manner of living in proportion. The boy from the country becomes a merchant—or what is here called a merchant—and obtains a credit in Europe a hundred times exceeding his means, and caters to these fancied wants; and thus is every avenue of society thronged with adventurers, the ephemera of the same widespread spirit of reckless folly. Millions in value pass out of these streets, that go to feed the vanity of those who fancy themselves wealthy, because they hold some ideal pledges for the payment of advances in price like those mentioned by the [land] auctioneer, and which have some such security for the eventual payment, as one can find in calling a thing that is really worth a dollar, worth a hundred.[47]

John's hope for the country lies only in the prospect that a disease so violent cannot last. Possibly the inevitable season of repentance will restore a decent economic balance. But one cannot be too confident: not even the great fire in New York's business district, a flagrant providential warning, had been sufficient for a moral awakening.[48]

Cooper's clumsy satire, *The Autobiography of a Pocket-Handkerchief*, contains possibly his most bitter and thorough commentary on the economic derangements of the 1830's. Among a lot of gougers, parasites, confidence men, and touts—the new economic men—the type figure is one Henry Halfacre, land speculator and paper millionaire. He has come from nowhere and built a paper fortune out of town-lot speculations in New York and the newly settled regions of the West. Halfacre's empire rests upon a flimsy pyramid of interlocking credits: he buys and sells on paper promises; manages to make his assets appear in liquid condition by discounting a fraction of the

46 *Ibid.*, p. 103.
47 *Ibid.*, p. 105.
48 *Ibid.*, pp. 105-9.

paper he receives, enough to show a five-figure bank account and meet his current demands. As one of those "who shoot up like rockets, in two or three years," Halfacre supports the illusion of his affluence by maintaining a mortgaged home on Broadway—an address which gives "a sort of patent of nobility"—and a showy style of life, symbolized by the hundred-dollar handkerchief his daughter Eudosia flaunts.[49]

Jackson's removal of the government deposits from the Bank of the United States gives a momentary jolt to the Halfacre career: money becomes scarce, "more especially with those who had none," and Halfacre breaks down in the effort to cover his commitments. "His energy had overreached itself," Cooper writes, "like the tumbler who breaks his neck in throwing seventeen hundred somersets backwards." Temporarily, the Halfacres are crushed, and curse the author of their downfall, "that tiger, Jackson"—"the old wretch." Soon enough the nimble Henry recovers his senses and plots a course for riding out his bankruptcy. The kernel of his plan is to create an illusion of honest character which will divert attention from the lots still in his possession. The family ostentatiously abandon their house, auction the furniture, and—the dramatic climax—return the costly handkerchief, all to the loud applause of the New York press: here is an honest man sacrificing his goods to raise funds for the creditors. In the meantime Halfacre shrewdly liquidates his holdings, paying creditors in much overvalued lots, and reserving his little cash for the few recalcitrants who would otherwise start suit. Finally, he has balanced his books, pocketed half the real value of his holdings, and maintained the reputation of an honorable man.[50]

Thus is common sense in economic life diverted from utility and decency. Enterprise is reduced to a bag of tricks, a fantastic juggling act.

To attempt an interesting *roman de société* with American materials was, in Cooper's mind, a desperate venture which justified all sorts of literary devices to create diversion or entertainment in a drab subject: "more ship" for the Effingham plot, curious characters anywhere. (Indeed, Cooper's long attachment to Natty Bumppo and his Indian comrades stems at least partly from the literary conviction that

---

[49] *Pocket-Handkerchief*, pp. 126–28, 158–60, 128–31.

[50] *Ibid.*, pp. 155, 158–60, 161–67. Another dimension of the tale is the record of the cold exploitation of a poor seamstress by the merchants who cater to the vulgar demands of the newly rich.

fictional interest could be sustained only at the wild margins of American life.)[51] Steadfast Dodge and Aristabulus Bragg cannot be taken for accidents of fiction, however; their appearance in the Effingham novels is determined by grim social reality. Cooper's only literary concession is to do the portraits in the style of caricature. Both Dodge and Bragg are village figures, self-made quasi-gentlemen risen from the mass just high enough to sense its mind and take it where it wants to go. One is a brash Yankee editor, serving his ambition by confirming the provincial mind in all its worst tendencies; the other an adroit upstate New York lawyer, a virtuoso player of all the economic and political angles in the new social pell-mell. Their careers are enmeshed with the critical changes in American life; their character makes them unmistakably new men; even their village situation is typical in a nation still — despite its rising commercial towns — predominantly rural, settled in dispersed clusters.[52]

Steadfast Dodge is without doubt the lowest character in all Cooper's gallery of American defectives. He has not a single good moment in two longish novels, is granted not even the credit for downright villainy: Dodge is a shapeless mass of ignorance, arrogance, cowardice, avarice, envy, vanity, and servility, mixed with a certain low cunning—a subhuman absurdity. Cooper no doubt saw in him the Weeds and Webbs and all that rancorous tribe of Whig editors; the editors at any rate seemed to see themselves and struck back in a long campaign of vilification against the author.[53]

Dodge is the pure product of Yankee community and conformity. In a region where individuality was smothered in conventions, caucuses, public meetings, and associations of all sorts, Dodge "from his tenth year up to his twenty-fifth . . . [had] been either a president, vice-president, manager, or committee-man of some philosophical, political, or religious expedient to fortify human wisdom, make men better, and resist error and despotism." He was a master of "the language of association" and could match any American in his control of such terms as " 'taking up'—'excitement'—'unqualified hostility'— 'public opinion'—'spreading before the public,' or any other of those generic phrases that imply the privileges of all, and the rights of none." (The root phrase of this vocabulary, Cooper remarks in another book,

---

[51] *Homeward Bound*, Preface, p. iii; *Home as Found*, Preface, pp. ii–v.
[52] *Homeward Bound*, pp. 290–91.
[53] Waples, *Whig Myth*, pp. 208–21, stresses the Whig identity.

is "they say." "No one asks 'who says it,' so long as it is believed that *'they* say it.' ")[54]

A habit of speech is in Dodge an element of character. His miserable physical cowardice is compounded always by concealment behind a fabricated committee, or alleged public opinion. He perceives the world entirely in the terms of popular majorities and minorities, of "streaks of public opinion" identified by party labels. "So much and so long had Mr. Dodge respired a moral atmosphere of this community-character, and gregarious propensity, that he had, in many things, lost all sense of his individuality; as much so, in fact, as if he breathed with a pair of county lungs, ate with a common mouth, drank from the town-pump, and slept in the open air." The image is deceptive, however, if it suggests some deep organic bond between Dodge and his fellows. He shares their limitations of mind and spirit, to be sure; but he communicates with them only in a mechanical, manipulative way, seeking favor and fearing rejection. Dodge never took a step "without first weighing its probable effect in the neighborhood." The great question in any public gesture is always "whether it would be likely to elevate him or depress him in the public mind." In political relations, Dodge is an "Asiatic slave" to the majority and a "lion" in defying the minority.[55]

Only in the protective environment of "party-drill," however, has Dodge the nerve to defy anyone; "in all other things he dutifully consulted every public opinion of the neighborhood." Self-distrust bred a "rabid desire" for universal approval, especially for the sanction of his natural superiors; for Dodge did vaguely sense his own deficiencies. His jealous detraction of superior qualities, concealed under "an intense regard for popular rights," expresses just this grudging respect "for everything that was beyond his reach." He would like nothing better than acceptance by the Effinghams; he approaches them full of the "distrust and uneasiness" of the "vulgar and pretending" when faced with "the simplicity and natural ease of the refined." The Effingham set amuse themselves briefly with this windbag, and then dismiss him firmly and without further thought.[56]

Steadfast Dodge is, as I have said, terribly real to Cooper, and so

---

[54] *Homeward Bound*, pp. 38–39; *American Democrat*, p. 175.
[55] *Homeward Bound*, pp. 88–89.
[56] *Ibid.*, pp. 89, 92–100, 195–99.

important that he has not a private gesture, a scrap of dress, an act or word, which is merely for the story: everything goes for evidence in the case against the false democrat. Cooper forgives Dodge nothing, though he pardons America a little for creating him. It is natural that a young and scattered population should be provincial. The moral foundation in America is broad, and supports "a moral superstructure so narrow," because "popular sentiment" rules over domains where it has only "limited and superficial attainments." The Dodges are the inevitable punishment of the people for their vain pretense to omnicompetence. Vapidity, folly, malice, envy, bigotry, arrogance, hypocrisy, ignorance, poured out through the popular press, are the fate of America until maturity—if it ever comes—effects "a greater concentration of taste, liberality, and knowledge."[57]

Eve Effingham, Cooper's candied vision of the good in American civilization, offers a further explanation of "the animal," Steadfast Dodge. Perhaps the prevalence of the Franklin legend is to blame for making every green printer fancy himself a sage and prophet. American boys are taught that they can achieve anything by merit; they conclude that they are in fact fit for everything; and thus the teaching causes "pretenders to start up in all directions." The male Effinghams draw out the consequences: Dodge's type dominates the American press, doing vast damage by shaping the minds of helpless readers. Liberty is confounded with personal envy and "the jealousies of station"; self-interest is installed in place of public duty. The gravity of the Dodge menace is obvious in the United States, where government has become a gross *"press-ocracy."*[58]

Dodge is sheer cant done up into a man; Aristabulus Bragg is a different and better issue of the same social stock. Where Dodge is wholly absorbed in the mirror world of opinion manipulation, Bragg touches the world of real affairs at various points, in a bold, breezy, often skillful way. Bragg is a "plastic character," in Cooper's estimate, "bold, morally and physically, aspiring, self-possessed, shrewd, singularly adapted to succeed in his schemes where he knew the parties, intelligent after his tastes, and apt." If Bragg had had better luck in his early influences, his native gifts could have made him a gentleman

[57] *Home as Found*, pp. 317–18. Some of Dodge's glaring deficiencies are shown in *Homeward Bound*, pp. 183–84, 231–32, 268–69, 367–68.
[58] *Homeward Bound*, pp. 202–4.

and a valuable social servant. It was his misfortune, not his fault, that he was shaped by the common standard of village democracy.[59]

Bragg was a native of western Massachusetts who migrated to upstate New York at nineteen. In two years he had been admitted to the local bar and founded a successful practice. The Effinghams had employed him as agent for their Templeton properties during their long absence, at once a mark of trust and, in John's hard phrase, a calculation "on the principle that one practiced in tricks is the best qualified to detect and expose them." Where Bragg meets Dodge, in the realm of false democracy, he is unequivocally a bad actor. In his general role as a plastic, versatile village careerist Bragg represents an ambiguous quality. He stands at the margin of the middling standard. Cooper calls him the epitome of the good and evil in a very large class of Americans.[60]

Bragg is quick-witted, prompt in action, enterprising when he has no stake and wary when he does. He is ready to turn hand, heart, and principles to anything that offers an advantage. Nothing is above his aspiration, nothing too menial to do. Expert in legal and business affairs, Bragg is also a smooth talker, in accents uncouth and provincial; a deliberate self-improver with his smattering of classics, dancing, medicine, and divinity. One Effingham sees in him "an amusing mixture of strut, humility, roguery, and cleverness"; another finds

a compound of shrewdness, impudence, common-sense, pretension, humility, cleverness, vulgarity, kind-heartedness, duplicity, selfishness, law-honesty, moral fraud, and mother-wit, mixed up with a smattering of learning and much penetration in practical things. . . . Mr. Bragg, in short, is purely a creature of circumstances, his qualities pointing him out for either a member of Congress, or a deputy sheriff, offices that he is equally ready to fill.[61]

Any thought that Bragg deserves to be taken in as apprentice to the real quality, in the old hope of recruiting aristocracy from the middle ranks, is quickly scotched by Cooper and the Effinghams. John Effingham, the most candid of the lot, classes Bragg with "a valuable house-dog." Edward, without insults, maintains a wide distance between client and lawyer. And the perfect Eve involuntarily prolongs

[59] *Home as Found*, pp. 222–23.
[60] *Ibid.*, pp. 9–10.
[61] *Ibid.*, pp. 9–11.

Bragg's cautious suit through the length of a novel simply because she cannot recognize that such a creature could hope for her hand. Whenever Bragg comes too close, he acts the clumsy oaf, to the annoyance or amusement or indifference of the Effinghams. Typically, they "detect" but do not "notice" his *faux pas*. Cooper calls Bragg a gentleman, with an apology, "for we suppose Aristabulus must be included in the category by courtesy, if not of right."[62]

Through Bragg, Cooper collects the attitudes and opinions of the country. He serves as a kind of native informant for his lofty and remote employers, bringing especially the news of ordinary life. Thus Bragg tells of the village lawyers in New York, men like himself, who mix professional business with horse dealing or—the current rage— "dealing in Western cities" and "other expectations." His conversation is burdened with references to good business prospects in milk or sweet potatoes. When John Effingham tries to make him see that these latter at least are "honester and better occupations," Bragg is puzzled, for "with him everything was eligible that returned a good profit, and all things honest that the law did not actually punish."[63]

This conversion of all values into cash equivalents does not exempt the values of home and neighborhood. Poor Sir George, the English visitor, is astounded at Bragg's innocent report of "the Western fever" carrying many New Yorkers away from home, especially the "regular movers." And Bragg in turn is a little touched by Sir George's picture of stationary Old England: "Very poetical. . . . It must be a great check to business operations." He explains that history is no "incumbrance" to mobility in America: one "may do very much as interest dictates." "A nation," Bragg concludes, "is much to be pitied that is weighed down by the past . . . since its industry and enterprise are constantly impeded by obstacles that grow out of its recollections." Bragg assures the company that he and his fellows feel no attachment to a home, a tree, or a churchyard which they would not readily abandon for a price.[64]

What Cooper sees in Bragg, then, is the new man of pell-mell, the perfect adaptive organism for a situation without rules or bounds. Physical and economic mobility make "love of change" the exclusive principle. As Bragg informs Powis (Eve's eligible suitor and, as it

[62] *Ibid.*, pp. 11, 16–19, 138, 299–302.
[63] *Ibid.*, pp. 20–22.
[64] *Ibid.*, pp. 22–25.

happily turns out, her cousin) : "Rotation in feelings, sir, . . . is human nature, as rotation in office is natural justice." Some of his friends suggest it would be healthy if "the whole society be made periodically to change places." Are they all agrarians, then? Powis is quickly reassured on this score by the canny lawyer: "As far from it as possible; nor do I believe you will find such an animal in this country. Where property is concerned, we are a people that never let go so long as we can hold on, sir; but beyond this, we like lively changes."[65]

A last view of Aristabulus Bragg, as he juggles his dual role of Effingham agent and popular favorite in the Point affair, must emphasize his most doubtful qualities. (Cooper drags Dodge back upon the scene quite artificially to make the lesson perfectly obvious.) The episode in the novel is the parallel to Cooper's famous wrangle with his neighbors, which opened a bitter history of legal suits and newspaper polemics. The importance of the incident does not lie in a conflict of substantial economic interests; on the contrary, the case suits Cooper's purpose precisely because the stake is a small piece of scenic property, and the principle alone counts. The "all-powerful, omnipotent, overruling, law-making, law-breaking public" insists upon converting its picnic privileges on Effingham property (the Point) into a legal right. Even the gentle, tolerant Ned Effingham is made to lose his temper over such presumption.[66]

The unfortunate Bragg is caught in the middle of the affair. As lawyer to the Effinghams he must press the case against the invading villagers. As village leader, with some responsibility for instigating the incursion, he must carefully sustain his popularity. As product of his age, he cannot conceive the motives of the Effinghams in defying public opinion on so trivial a matter. When "they say" they own the Point, it must be so: "for it is impossible that everybody should be mistaken." Finally, the Effinghams condescend to show him legal proof for their claim—their word alone should have been enough— but Bragg is no less "aghast" at the "unheard-of temerity" of the family in ignoring organized public protest and even threatening suit against the authors of an insulting public resolution. The sole outright virtue in Bragg, through the entire controversy, is his "profound

[65] *Ibid.*, pp. 323, 145–48.
[66] *Ibid.*, pp. 202–22, 205.

deference for the principles, character, and station of Mr. Effingham, that no sophistry, or self-encouragement in the practices of social confusion could overcome." Bragg respects, at least, what he cannot understand or be.[67]

Cooper winds up the Effingham tale with a series of matches, joining like to like: Dodge gets none; Sir George takes Grace, the imperfect American heiress (about right for a mere English baronet) ; Paul Powis, John Effingham's lost son, alone is worthy of Eve—the perfect match of quality. Bragg wins Eve's French maid, who will be taken for a lady by most Americans, and goes West, where he will practice law, or keep school, or go to Congress, or saw lumber, or do whatever comes to hand, while his new wife will set up as dressmaker and French teacher. In the end, Bragg is perhaps as much a mystery to the Effinghams as they are to him. They know certainly what he is not: one of them. His origin in social pell-mell is clear; his characteristics as a fluid careerist can be described. But what he *is,* and how to come to terms with him, remain a puzzle. As Eve, always so sure in her judgment, confesses: "He seems so much in, and yet so much out of his place; is both so rusé and so unpracticed; so unfit for what he is, and so ready at everything, that I scarcely know how to apply terms in any matter with which he has the smallest connection."[68]

The perspective of the Effingham books is bounded on one side by Ned, on the other by John, with Powis, Eve, and the author comfortably between. Bragg, Dodge, Truck, and the others are just what Effinghams see when, reluctantly, they look out upon America. Each general fault is the contrary of an Effingham virtue. In short, we know the best people from all the previous discussion, and only a little more remains to be said of their traits and of their function.

The Effinghams are everything that the elect of the twenties aspired to, with the added perfection of a cosmopolitan polish. Everything about them—their possessions, their appearance, their style of life, their manners—is a beautiful blend of Continental grace and republican simplicity; everything is keyed to quiet elegance, impeccable dignity, pure refinement. It would be as shocking to discover an Effingham acting in bad taste as it would be to catch Natty Bumppo losing an Indian trail.[69]

[67] *Ibid.,* pp. 208–11, 220, 222, 219.
[68] *Ibid.,* pp. 429–30, 142.
[69] *Ibid.,* pp. 1–8, 12, 17–19, 183–85.

The Effingham men, each in his way, define the possibilities of gentility in America. Knowledge, independence, manners, noble bearing, elevated principles, wealth, habits of refinement, gentle extraction, liberal attainments in every direction, place Edward and John in the first rank of international society. Both are tall, handsome Yorkers of commanding presence. Edward lives on the income of a large hereditary landed estate. He has succeeded to his property at an early age, and so for many years has lived in an "intellectual retirement." In this fortunate situation, he has achieved a notable freedom from prejudice, an even temper, and a just mind. He makes little pretension to greatness; his strength is in his goodness. Almost by instinct he manages to "hit the line of truth" in all questions; and he is never thrown off by excitement or interest: "Independence of situation had induced independence of thought." Toward America, Ned is loyal, just, tolerant: he neither betrays his country abroad, in the fashion of the touring *arriviste,* nor gives it mawkish flattery at home. "He loved his native land, while he saw and regretted its weaknesses."[70]

Ned's cousin, friend, and traveling companion, John Effingham, is a gamier dish of gentility. Dorothy Waples, in her effort to identify strict party lines in Cooper's work, has placed John in the enemy camp: a gentleman conceded to the Whigs. Yet on every important count— principles, manners, taste, position—John belongs with the family. If John votes Whig—a dim possibility, though I doubt whether he troubles to vote at all—he would despise his party, in no wise represent them, and remain in mind and character solely Effingham. He is severe and cynical where his cousin is winning and kindly; but then he is acute and knowing, and his judgments of America express the Effingham mind in hard, clear truths, explaining often what Ned can only vaguely sense. By the end of the Point affair, there is little difference in the views of Ned and John.[71]

James Grossman has appraised the Effingham function brilliantly. They are perfect, passive, almost disused ornaments of the republic. They hold their example before a society which is at least envious, at most awed, but on no account inspired to imitation. They will enforce the laws and remind the presumptuous that the power of the "re-public" is still more awful than the power of the public. But no substantial force in American life runs in their direction. Nor do they entertain

[70] *Ibid.,* pp. 181–83; *Homeward Bound,* pp. 53–56.
[71] *Ibid.,* pp. 53–56.

ambitions for entering the life of their time. The Effinghams exist in retirement, live on income, and cultivate graces and virtues in privacy. Indeed, a good deal of their positive effort is expended precisely to maintain privacy. The mating of Effingham cousins is Cooper's final stroke, to isolate the vestige of American quality in purity, and concede the active world to the rising Braggs.[72]

It is true that the Effinghams win their Point battle and prove that some common sense, common honesty, and prudence remain in the public when it can break loose from the demagogues of false democracy; and yet it is hard to find a hopeful figure anywhere beneath the Effinghams. The best in the commons is Captain Truck, and he is as much a relic as the Effinghams: a bluff original of an obsolete breed, raised on catechism and piety, deeply respectful to his betters, whose virtue has been preserved by ship's discipline. Significantly, Truck and a still crustier remain, the old "commodore" of Lake Otsego, are the only links Cooper provides to the one social hero deemed worthy of the republican succession, Andrew Jackson. The antique captain agrees with the superannuated Commodore that Old Hickory is a man's man: "Tough, sir; tough as a day in February on this lake. All fins, and gills, and bones."[73]

Even in the *Notions* of the twenties, Jackson appeared not as the leader of masses but as an impressive personal figure in the Doric style, as the rugged gentleman patriot of simple commanding ways. Jackson's direct appearance in the *Pocket-Handkerchief* satire, although it involves the policies of the Bank War, is made to seem a personal encounter between the champion of the republic and the Halfacre frauds. Of necessity Cooper places Jackson in the midst of life, but only to preserve the old decencies, as an individual figure of authority. Dodge and Bragg may be Whigs, yet essentially they represent the widely prevalent social type, the false democrat, bred by the changing American climate. Against them Cooper masters only two old oddities to vote for Jackson, and the seceded Effinghams to place their veto on the whole mess.

The Effingham element is a frozen vestige; Jackson is a distant individual champion of the Doric republic. Cooper's last resort for a sign of American nobility is the passing echo of a Yorker legend. The gentlefolk of Templeton, taking in the natural beauties of Lake

72 *Home as Found*, p. 219; Grossman, *Cooper*, pp. 114–24.
73 *Home as Found*, p. 222; *Homeward Bound*, p. 242; *Home as Found*, p. 285.

Otsego, come upon the old site of Natty Bumppo's hut. Each in turn reaches out his hand to acknowledge another, long-extinct strain of virtue. To the refined Eve, Natty was "a man who had the simplicity of a woodsman, the heroism of a savage, the faith of a Christian, and the feelings of a poet. A better than he, after his fashion, seldom lived." Sophisticated John Effingham is, in a rare moment, almost tenderly affected by the reminiscence: "Alas! . . . the days of the 'Leather-Stockings' have passed away. He preceded me in life, and I see few remains of his character in a region where speculation is more rife than moralizing, and emigrants are plentier than hunters."[74]

This brief encounter with legend is more, I think, than a quaint interlude in the tale. That it immediately precedes the eruption of the Point affair at least suggests an intention to juxtapose primitive virtue and present degradation; and the Effingham remarks confirm the purpose. In one respect, Natty is the masterpiece of the presocial democracy of the woods: natural experience has trained him to perfection in active competence and moral purity. The democracy of the clearing shows no capacity for shaping his successor. For active duty society must turn to Aristabulus Bragg. As always in his novels, Cooper does not permit the Effingham elite to weigh the merits of its own brand of cultivated excellence, perfected in retirement, against the natural and active virtues of the Leatherstocking.[75] Both are worthy models for America; both have been banished from the settlements, one to the remote prairie, the other behind the walls of privacy.

Long before the Effinghams made their *pro forma* stand against the invasion of their picnic grounds, satisfying their principles and changing nothing, Natty Bumppo had abandoned Lake Otsego. As settlers infested his woods, Natty—according to local legend—would notch a pine for each arrival, until "reaching seventeen, his honest old heart could go no further, and he gave the matter up in despair." The eccentric ancient, the "commodore" of the lake, delivers the final judgment: "They may talk of their Jeffersons and Jacksons, but I set down Washington and Natty Bumppo as the two only really great men of my time."[76]

[74] *Home as Found*, pp. 196–97.
[75] Henry Nash Smith has made this point most effectively in his Introduction to Cooper, *The Prairie*, pp. v–xx.
[76] *Home as Found*, pp. 199–201.

## On Cooper as a Source

I have suggested at the outset that Cooper's America is neither a Jacksonian projection nor a transcript of reality, but something between: the product of a probing for the moral strains which Cooper felt, in common with Jacksonian allies, in the changing social environment of the thirties. Cooper demanded more of America (especially a directive role for the quality) and regretted more in the change (including the new modes of democratic politics which Jacksonians had largely developed). Indeed he presents only two eccentrics from the class beneath the Effinghams with the moral sensitivity to feel the great descent and react against it. Nevertheless, he helps us to define the temporary equilibrium of the Old Republic which Jacksonians remembered (with a good deal of selection) as an ideal past; and to feel the painful pressures of flux and fever which predisposed Jacksonians to condemn the agencies of social change. The conservatism of Cooper and the conservatism of the Jacksonians crossed a wide gap to meet in a common resistance; while the Braggs—and Whigs—plunged into action.[77]

Unfortunately, Cooper will take us no further into the political life of his generation. He had given his sympathy, as a citizen, to the measured and modest, the vigorous and decorous, democracy of common sense; and America had betrayed him. Cant democracy, fevered avarice, and blind mobility were everywhere beyond the Effingham gate. Unlike Tocqueville, Cooper neither explored with understanding the feelings of a people so circumstanced, nor looked curiously for a "new science of politics" to fit the new condition of Americans. The

[77] How Cooper steeled himself to choose the lesser evil is a subtle biographical question which I cannot resolve here. His dilemma had much in common with that of other intellectuals—men like Hawthorne, Melville, Paulding—who came to a similar Jacksonian choice: men who could not expect Jacksonian Democracy to realize their own essential values. I have been content to find in Cooper a useful intermediary, a cicerone whose inflamed sensibilities reported the climatic changes of an era, and whose intelligence gave some order to the process. From Cooper's enigmatic bond with the Jacksonians I would derive no more than this: to an agrarian conservative of that age the last faint image of the Doric order could be found in the virile old patriot of the Democracy and in the cause of moral restoration. The tenuous connection will not sustain an independent argument either on the nature of Fenimore Cooper's convictions or on the character of Jacksonian Democracy. Interestingly, Cooper's home county in New York, Otsego, was firmly Jacksonian; but this only compounds the difficulty, for the local Democratic leaders had enough of Dodge and Bragg in them, I judge, to discourage Cooper's sympathy.

American democrat in retreat is more rigid than the resigned French aristocrat, perhaps because he asks more for his country: a share of both the democratic and the aristocratic goods, in just the right proportions.

Nonetheless, Cooper—with his closer vantage point, his briefer perspective, and his more intimate involvement—adds to Tocqueville's findings on Jacksonian society. On fundamental facts there is broad agreement: that equality is the salient public value; that majority opinion rules the state and dominates the minds of its individual citizens; that acquisitiveness is the master motive; that rootlessness and continuous practical improvisation define a way of life. Tocqueville, with his systematic understanding of democracy, unquestionably makes his findings count for much more, yet Cooper does have his points as a historical witness. If America had been drifting from the start on the great tide of the universal democratic revolution—Tocqueville's view—still the events of a decade which could sap Cooper's faith in the republic were peculiarly significant. The outsider took what he saw in 1830 as a matter of course—for the Americans. The insider felt with much of his generation the shock of change from one to another stage of middle-class democracy.

Again, the outsider with a telescopic view, Tocqueville, could not take seriously the limited social stratification which persisted within a radical equality of condition; although he could write brilliantly of the insatiability of the popular equalitarian passion, even in the leveled democratic universe. Cooper, with something of John Adams' nose for the eternal aristocrat in plain dress, flushed the business and financial upstarts, and the self-made opinion manipulators of press and party, who had displaced the Washingtons and Jays and Effinghams and Coopers as notables and leaders of American society. Neither Tocqueville nor Cooper effectively explores the curious alternations of jealousy and envy and esteem which Americans expressed in politics toward those who now took the prizes in the democratic market place. Perhaps the most arresting single insight on this score is still Tocqueville's: in Jacksonian times the new elite would keep their pride and vanity and ambition behind closed curtains, and act the plainest of common men upon the public streets. Much of Cooper's hatred for the *nouveaux* arose precisely here: the offense of their grossness and provincialism was compounded by that cold hypocrisy which let them play their political game through Steadfast Dodge, the mere dirty tail of an American democrat.

The great descent of the common-sense republic meant, for Fenimore Cooper, the turning of democracy from its better to its worse nature. Representative Jacksonians shared neither Cooper's demands for a gentle, decorous democracy nor his fear of an equalitarian society and culture. For this reason, perhaps, they rarely inquired so far as Cooper did into the workings of a democratic social system. Jacksonians did sense a social turning which would bring corruption to the manners and morals of their beloved republic; and, like Cooper, they found a major source of evil in new economic ways. The Bank became their Monster, symbolizing forms and powers hostile to the commonwealth of virtuous producers. In the following discussion, I shall examine the economic processes behind the Monster of Jacksonian appeals, in order to identify more clearly some of the actual changes experienced by this generation.

# 5

## BEHIND THE MONSTER

### A VIEW OF ECONOMIC PROCESSES

❧

The twelve-year reign of Andrew Jackson and his man, Van Buren, left a mixed record of triumph and failure. A regime sustained by heavy electoral majorities was forced on critical occasions to act the opposition in its own house. An irresistible democracy which seized Washington from the remnant of the republican elite was drummed out twelve years later, in the final travesty of a democratic campaign. Most important, after the Monster Bank was cornered and destroyed, the country experienced first a frenzy of private and public speculation (with a vast proliferation of the hated paper-issue banking), then panic and severe depression lasting through Van Buren's term and several years beyond. Jacksonian Democracy could both conquer and persuade, and yet not rule according to its deepest purposes.

Defections within the regime could frequently be managed by fresh appeals to the electorate, as in the smashing reelection of 1832. Even the political turnabout of 1840 appears a transient irony: depression, Little Van's unhappy personal reputation, accumulated local, personal, and special grievances of a long regime, all were caught up in a carnival campaign to give the Whigs not quite 53 per cent of the popular presidential vote. (The early death of Harrison, exposing the instability of the successful coalition, made Whig legislative and executive control almost ineffectual.) Jacksonian Democracy soon recovered its political force and restored its favorite issues to the political center. It could claim a greater conquest in recreating the styles and institutions of democratic politics, even in dictating to its opposition standards of availability and permissible limits of policy variation.

The power to conquer and persuade, and to define the modes of doing so, remained with the Jacksonians for a decade or more after the politically faceless Harrison arrested Van Buren's public career. No such accounting will put away the flagrant contrast between Jacksonian policy aims and their social consequence. Indeed, the recurrence of political success in the face of a fundamental failure to shape the course of social and economic development presents a paradox that may lead to fuller understanding of Jacksonian Democracy. Major social changes were not of the sort which lie secret in the census returns until a great crisis or a great historian discovers them; they were the more or less open and direct concern of public discussion. Nor did the contrast lack occasion for sharp definition, for the most dramatic events of the Jacksonian regime—Bank War, boom, and slump—succeeded in short order, and made together an explicit theme for political debate. Jacksonians won preferment in the teeth of failure —in part, one may suspect, because of failure—and used power as a platform to denounce evils which seemed to multiply with blows.

Assuming that political rhetoric responds to, though rarely corresponds to, reality, and plays back into reality, I want initially to sketch the economic background of Jacksonian politics in a way which is at once relevant to the themes of political discourse and consistent with the shape of economic reality as economic historians have reconstructed it. I anticipate my later discussion to propose that the bank-boom-bust sequence was the primal experience of Jacksonian life, which fixed the content, tone, and terms of politics for as long as Jacksonianism counted in America. And I further suggest that this sequence of events exhibited, in exaggerated relief, the salient features of economic change in the Jacksonian era. What follows is neither an original history of the events, nor a rounded economic portrait of the age, but a selective sketch of dominant traits which will serve as context for the discussion of the Jacksonian persuasion expressed in political appeals.

### The Very Monster: BUS 2[1]

The Second Bank of the United States grew out of the chaos of war finances and was designed like its Hamiltonian predecessor to restore the national credit and currency and, not incidentally, to secure

---

[1] Fritz Redlich's analysis of central banking appears in his *The Molding of American Banking: Men and Ideas*, Part I, pp. 96–181. Some of Bray Hammond's im-

the interest of great holders of the public debt. In another light, the Bank was the great aberration of Democratic Republicanism, heedlessly indulged with a twenty-year term, and rediscovered with a shock as Jefferson's old monster only when a Tennessee patriarch gave second thought to renewing its charter, arched his back, and struck.

Mr. Biddle's bank had, and has, an army of persuasive supporters, equipped with arguments of every kind: economic, constitutional, fiscal, political. None, however, could imagine casting the Bank in the pathetic role Daniel Webster wrote for Dartmouth College: the beloved little corporation seeking only to live out its perpetual life in quiet service. The Bank was a giant, immensely powerful even on the political side, where it was most exposed. Economically, it was the greatest corporation in the country, by far the leading single domestic agency in the currency and credit system, and accordingly in business affairs. Upon its conduct depended the fiscal routine of the national government and, potentially, the national credit. An ambitious master enterpriser, perhaps a business genius, ruled over the Bank from his Greek temple on Chestnut Street, directing a tightly disciplined organization which, through numerous branches, reached into every consequential place of commerce in the country. The prestige of the national government and a monopoly charter were at the Bank's disposal.

Thus, when one speaks of the Bank as a symbol of corporate power, monopoly privilege, complex credit economy, and so on—as I shall do at length in later sections—the symbolic relationship is more nearly that of the powerful king to his state than that of the flag to the sentiment of loyalty. That is to say, the part is in fact a substantial element

---

portant contributions on this subject are in his "Jackson, Biddle, and the Bank of the United States," *Journal of Economic History*, VII (May 1947), 1–23; and "Banking in the Early West: Monopoly, Prohibition, and Laissez Faire," *ibid.*, VIII (May 1948), 1–25. Ralph C. H. Catterall's *Second Bank of the United States* remains the basic history; it has been supplemented by the work of students like Redlich and Hammond mainly in the sense that a fuller understanding of central banking functions informs the later analyses, and that a deeper appreciation of the Jacksonian animus has modified Catterall's accented portrait of the Bank War. A judicious modern summary of BUS affairs, in a general discussion of American financial institutions from 1815 to 1860, occurs in George Rogers Taylor's *The Transportation Revolution*, pp. 301–11. Here, as elsewhere in this chapter, I have often relied on Mr. Taylor's balanced judgment where expert testimony conflicts. Valuable statistical data appear in Walter Buckingham Smith, *Economic Aspects of the Second Bank of the United States,* together with an able narrative of economic events. William Graham Sumner, *A History of Banking in the United States,* contains a shrewd analysis of public policy toward banking.

of the whole; the leading case of a class; the advance guard of a tendency.

Among recent interpreters of Biddle's bank the most sympathetic as well as the most astute, Bray Hammond and Fritz Redlich, take the institution at its greatest valuation: as a commercial bank, a source of currency, a government fiscal agency, and especially as an embryonic central bank. Both writers, following modern conceptions of the strategic role of monetary and credit policies in the determination of general economic movements, exceed perhaps the Jacksonian critics themselves in attributing actual or potential economic power to the Second Bank. When Biddle is defended against the Jacksonian charge that the Bank failed to provide a uniform circulating medium, the answer is that the Bank did succeed in that task, that a semiprivate corporation had the power and capacity to establish an effective national currency. Again, Biddle's boast that he had not used the Bank's economic power to destroy a single state bank is received as a wholly credible, though politically naïve, assertion of the Bank's capacity, from its persistent creditor position, to discipline most local banks at will. Under Biddle, the Bank had achieved the leading position in the domestic and foreign exchange business, and in the domestic specie market; it became the great holder of the nation's specie and exchange reserve—with all the power implied. Further strengthened by a large holding in the federal funded debt and an exclusive use of the national deposits, free of interest, the Second Bank was indeed the formidable "money power" of Jacksonian times.

The cases Hammond and Redlich cite for illustration of the Bank's influence over general economic movements are impressive. Redlich recounts Biddle's masterful intervention in 1825 to avert a crisis: first strengthening his own position, then putting firm but gentle pressure upon the state banks, collecting and conserving specie for an ultimate reserve, and, when the threat of crisis passed, cautiously expanding loans while keeping the Bank in its creditor relation to other banks. Again, in 1828, Biddle could anticipate a worsening foreign exchange situation, direct a cautious contraction through his New York branch, and thus gradually impose a prudent course upon unheeding New York and Philadelphia banks, concluding the operation as before with a gentle expansion of the Bank's credit on minimum-risk transactions.[2]

[2] Redlich, *American Banking*, pp. 135–38.

Although Biddle's motives in directing Bank policy during the later stages of the Bank War are not absolutely clear, his large responsibility for precipitating the crisis of 1834 by a policy of sharp contraction is certain. For both Redlich and Hammond, the crucial demonstration of the Second Bank's controlling influence is a negative instance: destruction of the Bank, and Biddle's fierce refusal to concede defeat, "ruined an excellent monetary system"; "delivered the private banks from federal control and . . . [the] people to speculation"; and "left a reckless, booming anarchy."[3]

Here begins another twist in the problem, and Hammond is the best guide. The Bank under Biddle had a great influence upon the economy, which was used primarily before the Bank War to discipline an explosively dynamic system. It performed, indeed, a restraining function over currency and credit which conscience-Jacksonians sought in hard money and a free-trade credit system. Its absence meant "a reckless, booming anarchy." What but suicidal ignorance could explain an anti-Bank policy which achieved nothing but the utter defeat of its ends? Hammond plays the paradox to the limit: "wringing their hands," as he says, the Jacksonians helped an "acquisitive democracy" take over Hamilton's conservative system of bank credit and "limber it up to suit the popular wish to get rich quick."[4]

Yet Hammond senses that this is not the real point of the tangle. Jacksonians on principle—men like Benton, Blair, Kendall, and Bancroft, Silas Wright, Van Buren, not least Andrew Jackson—spoke for an agrarian idealism in which

America was still a land of refuge and freedom rather than a place to make money. Its aim was to clip the wings of commerce and finance by restricting the credit that paper money enabled them to obtain. There would then be no vast debt, no inflation, no demoralizing price changes; there would be no fluctuant or disappearing values, no swollen fortunes, and no grinding poverty. The precious metals would impose an automatic and uncompromising limit on the volatile tendencies of trade.[5]

But, Hammond remarks in another connection, "Their austere and simple ideals were ecologically impossible in a land of wealth and individualism."[6]

---

[3] Hammond, "Jackson, Biddle, and the Bank," *loc. cit.,* pp. 9, 20.
[4] *Ibid.,* p. 10.
[5] *Ibid.,* p. 6.
[6] Hammond, "Banking in the Early West," *loc. cit.,* p. 4.

Possibly the Jacksonians—again, the believers, not the Hunkers—
should have seen Biddle's bank as their lesser evil; certainly it is no
wonder they refused the choice. Omitting even the questions of monopoly privilege, of private economic power, of a political *imperium
in imperio,* and taking the Bank on its best public-service behavior, one
sees in the institution a master organizer of a complex market economy
resting on a flexible monetary and credit system; the thirty-five million
dollar corporation acting under the centralized direction of (as Redlich has it) "the prototype of the modern [big] business executive":
a brilliant entrepreneur and administrator with bold previsions of
modern central banking, a private lord of creation who heard every
whisper in the land and commanded patronage and influence in the
highest places of business and politics, a man who came to see himself
in the ambitious role of regulator of the currency, public financier, and
economic empire builder.[7] If Jacksonians took the Bank for the sign
of "the coming economic order (capitalism),"[8] they stumbled on the
master fact, as informed economists now define it, through all their
folklore economics and archaic dreams. If their resistance was worse
than futile, it was in an important sense necessary.

### Progress and the Circular Malady

The Second Bank died two deaths: the first, a political martyrdom;
the second, a sudden economic collapse during the great depression of
1837–43, when Biddle audaciously—recklessly, most scholars agree—
tried to reconstruct the Bank's empire without the federal base, to
resist the deflationary turn against the prevailing judgment of the
great commercial bankers, and fell at last in disgrace. The end of
Biddle was not, of course, the beginning of a Jacksonian economic
world, in banking, currency, or any other field. As Hammond says,
the new situation was quite the reverse: "a reckless, booming anarchy."
During the 1830's a steady process of economic development—in westward expansion, in urban and industrial growth, in trade, transport,
and finance—turned into a wild boom. Whether Biddle, left un-
molested in possession of his quasi-public bank, could or would have

---

[7] Redlich, *American Banking,* pp. 110–24; Hammond, "Jackson, Biddle, and the
Bank," *loc. cit.,* pp. 20–23.
[8] Redlich, *American Banking,* p. 171. See also: *ibid.,* pp. 162–63, 180–81; Hammond, "Jackson, Biddle, and the Bank," *loc. cit.,* p. 8.

arrested the boom is a moot question. In any case, Jackson's condemnation of the Second Bank and the allocation of the fast-rising government deposits among selected state banks accentuated the inflationary movement.[9]

The flagrant signs of the boom were the speculative indexes, showing startling rises in bank loans and liabilities, land sales, and state debts. The Bank had itself discovered the vast possibilities in credit expansion, building its average bank note issues from $4,500,000 in 1823 to $19,000,000 in 1831, with corresponding increases in deposits, loans, discounts, and other branches of its business. The state banks, which had grown steadily since the close of the 1819–21 depression, suddenly released a flood of credit in the thirties with the aid of the newly dispersed government deposits. Between 1830 and the first crisis year, 1837, their loans and discounts rose over two and one-half times, while deposits and circulation more than doubled. Very little of this sudden credit infusion could be traced to capital accumulation within the business community; nor was its main purpose to service normal commercial transactions. Such vast sums were scarcely more than book and paper anticipations of bright dreams. The subsequent deflation meant a ruthless retrenchment of credit facilities until, in 1843, deposits and circulation were reduced almost to the 1830 volume. But new expansions and contractions of credit were to follow in the 1840's and 1850's, in part the fever readings of a profoundly unstable and unstabilizing banking system.[10]

In the harshest view, the expansionist post–Bank War system of currency and credit caused such severe shocks to the economy that it substantially reduced the net increment of economic progress. The extreme wildcat phase of the system, Hammond thinks, contributed nothing but disturbing effects to the development of the West. Yet a different basic emphasis prevails in modern discussions. For no writer is the system an ideal choice; but most concede it a capacity to stimulate a highly wasteful whirlwind development of capital resources,

[9] Hammond, "Jackson, Biddle, and the Bank," *loc. cit.*, pp. 4–5. Cf. W. G. Sumner, *Jackson,* pp. 311–15, 397–401; Smith, *Economic Aspects,* ch. xi. The viewpoint of the conservative New York banking community toward Biddle's later policies is well represented in Albert Gallatin, *Banks and Currency,* pp. 10–46.

[10] Taylor, *Transportation Revolution,* p. 305; Walter B. Smith and Arthur H. Cole, *Fluctuations in American Business, 1790–1860,* p. 305; Taylor, *Transportation Revolution,* pp. 324–25.

ascribing this effect to the forcible transfer of purchasing power "from the economically less active to the more active part of the population."[11]

Schumpeter certainly surpasses every serious interpreter of Jacksonian banking history in his insistence upon the constructive achievement of "reckless banking" in America. Granting all the flaws in the credit mania of the thirties, and the inevitability of a stern reckoning for them, he nevertheless maintains that this is not the main point: inflationary banking, and the common "inflationist mentality" which sustained it, was essentially a rational response to a profound economic need. "It was the financing of innovation by credit creation—the only method available . . . in the absence of sufficient results of previous evolution—which is at the bottom of that 'reckless banking.' " The significance of this function can be seen in Schumpeter's very definition of capitalism as "that form of private property economy in which innovations are carried out by means of borrowed money, which in general, though not by logical necessity, implies credit creation." All that Schumpeter neglects is a matter beside his purpose, but central to mine—the Jacksonian reaction: the shock which the miracles of credit creation induced, and the anxiety over the ensuing flood of "innovation" that was rapidly transfiguring their familiar and valued world.[12]

A large share of the credit created in the thirties financed a land bubble of staggering proportions. Revenues from the sale of public lands (and acreage sold) multiplied over tenfold between 1830 and 1836. At the same time, fantastic private speculation in the lots of cities, old, new, prospective, and purely imaginary, prevailed from the Atlantic seaboard to the Western limits of settlement. In Manhattan, to take a single case, one estimate indicates a doubling of the value of land and buildings from 1833 to 1836, and then a drop in 1838 to one-third of the peak figure. Titles flew from hand to hand, credits piled upon credits, book fortunes rose and vanished overnight, until in the

---

[11] Harold M. Somers, "The Performance of the American Economy—1789–1865," *The Growth of the American Economy*, ed. Harold F. Williamson, pp. 331–33; Hammond, "Banking in the Early West," *loc. cit.*, pp. 23–25; Hammond, "Jackson, Biddle, and the Bank," *loc. cit.*, pp. 9–10; Redlich, *American Banking*, p. 66; Harold F. Williamson, "Money and Commercial Banking," *American Economy*, ed. Williamson, pp. 253–55.

[12] Joseph A. Schumpeter, *Business Cycles*, I, 294–96, 223.

sad reckoning brought by panic and depression the whole mad structure fell apart.[13]

Yet the element of solidity in the bubble ought to be recorded. New York City, for example, was in the midst of a tremendous expansion which raised its population from about 123,700 in 1820 to over a million by 1860. By 1851 (according to the Manhattan land series cited above) real estate values had again equaled the speculative peak of 1836; through subsequent fluctuations, each succeeding trough was well above the last. In short, the wild speculations in city lots reflected a real promise in New York, and elsewhere: the national rate of urban population growth in the 1830's was twice the growth rate for the total population, and this in turn was part of a major population trend which, between 1820 and 1860, raised the proportion of urban (2,500 plus) dwellers from about 6 per cent to nearly 20 per cent of the total population. Moreover, many of the pipe-dream cities of 1836 did materialize by 1860. Chicago is a sensational case, but only part of a general proliferation process: in 1820, twelve cities were in the 10,000-plus class; in 1860, 101 cities had reached this size, and eight exceeded 100,000.[14]

Similarly, those who gambled on the future rise of public lands in the West were madmen only in the short-run business sense—only in thinking that future prospects could be realized all at once by means of an infinitely expansible credit system—and not in their basic sense of direction. Thus, between 1830 and 1840, the population of the North Central section—a major site of the public domain—more than doubled: hectic land-office scenes in Illinois, Michigan, or Wisconsin could be related to the remarkable tempo of settlement in a new country. As Turner emphasizes, a new section was created, holding by 1850 nearly one-quarter of the national population. Pretty clearly the land bubble of the 1830's was a high-flying exaggeration of a real upsurge in urban and Western settlement: economic absurdities, encouraged by an undisciplined credit system, passed over into real achievements in remarkably short order.[15]

13 United States, Bureau of the Census, *Historical Statistics of the United States, 1789–1945*, pp. 11–12, 120. See also: Taylor, *Transportation Revolution*, p. 340; Reginald C. McGrane, *The Panic of 1837*, pp. 43–69; Thomas Ford, *A History of Illinois*, pp. 181–82; Hone, *Diary*, I, 145, 201–2, 399.

14 *Historical Statistics*, pp. 11–12, 25; Taylor, *Transportation Revolution*, p. 388.

15 Frederick Jackson Turner, *The United States, 1830–1850*, chap. vii; *Historical*

The boom of the mid-thirties was fed from many sources: from the frenzied creation of credit by the banks ("more or less out of nothing," as Redlich remarks) ; from the heightened construction activities involved in new settlement; from the effects of a government surplus, "banging about the money market," Sumner observes, "like a cannon ball loose in the hold of a ship in a high wind." Related in different ways to all of these expansionist tendencies, and a powerful force in its own right, was the headlong venture in deficit spending undertaken by many of the state governments, old as well as new. European, especially British, investment capital was attracted by the wholesale issuing of state bonds to finance canals, railroads, banks, and other large-scale enterprises. Inspired by the magnificent success of New York's Erie Canal, state legislatures projected the most ambitious schemes of internal improvement in the faith that growing, or rechanneled, trade and settlement would pay the costs and something over. In the years 1820–30, bond issues by eight states totaled $26,500,000, almost one-third of that for New York's uniquely prosperous ventures. Between 1830 and 1838, eighteen states issued bonds to the amount of $147,800,000, with even sparsely settled states like Illinois and Indiana participating subtantially. By 1838 the outstanding aggregate state debt was more than $170,000,000 and rising. Well over half of this figure represented investment in transportation improvements.[16]

Again, the instinct which prompted ambitious internal improvement schemes strikes one as sound, the mode and tempo of execution as audacious, often reckless, sometimes (as in Illinois) absurd. The negative judgment, at least, is readily confirmed by reference to the financial disasters experienced by most of the enterprising states after the boom finally collapsed in 1839, and to the many failures of particular projects. The positive judgment is perhaps too easily ignored amidst the wreckage. The more than 3,000 miles of canals built be-

---

*Statistics*, p. 27; Joseph Schafer, *Four Wisconsin Counties: Prairie and Forest*, pp. 56–81, 123–24, shows the mixture of speculative activity and real growth in the early Wisconsin settlements; see also Theodore C. Pease, *The Frontier State, 1818–1848*, pp. 173–88.
    [16] Redlich, *American Banking*, p. 66; Sumner, *Jackson*, p. 316; Taylor, *Transportation Revolution*, pp. 372–75. See also: John B. McMaster, *A History of the People of the United States*, VI, 340–49; Louis Hartz, *Economic Policy and Democratic Thought: 1776–1860*, pp. 129–80; Francis P. Weisenburger, *The Passing of the Frontier, 1825–1850*, pp. 90–104; Pease, *Frontier State*, pp. 194–233; Ford, *Illinois*, pp. 182–396.

tween 1816 and 1840, about two-thirds of this total in the thirties alone, and the equal railroad mileage created from scratch during the same decade, were at once the response to a rapidly expanding community, a self-fulfilling prophecy of future growth, and an all-important means for the development of a national market economy. After all the casualties are mourned, the bankrupt enterprises and the bankrupt states, one still sees reason in the improvement madness of the 1830's, and results of unlimited importance. Here, too, Schumpeter's judgment of American inflationism is relevant: that bold creation of credit, for all its follies, was the key to innovation, i.e., creative economic development. One cannot dismiss his observation that the American price level never remained far out of line with the British, since increasing national product consistently caught up with the immediate inflationary effects of credit expansion. With some time, and not a little pain, the economy exhibited a capacity to make good its long-shot bets.[17]

It appears inevitable that the gaudy mid-thirties dream of sudden fortune should have collapsed. The credit inflation flowed from a highly vulnerable banking system lacking resources and techniques to sustain its commitments. The land bubble was balanced precariously upon a shaky credit structure, and had to fail as soon as a hard reckoning of values was enforced. The bond issues of the states created large immediate obligations against doubtful, sometimes hopeless, revenue prospects; a process of liquidation could not long be avoided. Briefly, the very excesses of the boom, inherently unstable, defined the necessity for a crisis as soon as faith faltered and bets were called.

This is not, however, all that can be learned from Jacksonian economic troubles. Just as the boom phenomena present exaggerated signs of fundamental growth and change, so the experience of panic and depression may point beyond particular flaws in that development to the general character of the emergent economic order. In the widest view, the vulnerability of the American economy to panic and depression was related to the high-pressure growth process which made instability the natural condition of American life, and to that flaring passion for acquisition which could carry clerks and shopkeepers into

[17] Taylor, *Transportation Revolution*, pp. 52–55, 79; Schumpeter, *Business Cycles*, I, 295.

city-lot speculations and ordinary farmers into the quest of the un-
earned increment on Western acres. Somewhere between the largest
workings of growth and spirit, and the precise flaws in antecedent
actions, one can identify changes in economic structure and routine
which the 1837–43 disturbances throw into high relief.

Recent economic historians seem fairly well agreed on the proposition that Americans underwent a revolution in the organization of
their economic lives between 1815 or 1820 and 1860. Formulations
of the change vary considerably in emphasis and direction, according
to the principles of the writer and the point of departure for his analysis. Redlich, looking first at Biddle and his financial entrepreneurship,
then at the stubbornly uncomprehending Jacksonians, sees the emergence of "the coming economic order (capitalism)"—essentially, the
"modern credit economy." From similar materials Hammond derives
a comparable analysis, although he is inclined to make the emergent
process rather more specific: not the modern credit economy as such,
but expansionist laissez-faire finance, reflecting the "bullishness" and
"energy" of "an acquisitive democracy," especially of "the new generation of businessmen, promoters, and speculators." Hammond, in
short, is most impressed by the triumph of unlimited and undisciplined
acquisitiveness over *both* the conservative agrarian ideals of Jackson
and the sound, integrated financial system promised by the Bank at
its best.[18]

Louis Hacker attempts a comprehensive stage-by-stage analysis of
American capitalism through the nineteenth century, and draws his
main conclusions in different terms. The period from 1789 to about
1843 he views as the last, expansive phase of mercantile capitalism,
which, released from colonial dependence, took on the large tasks of
opening the West, building a national transportation system, developing overseas and domestic commerce, and financing trial ventures in
manufacturing. By the terminal date, Hacker argues, consistently
profitable opportunities for the merchant capitalist were declining, his
great constructive role was pretty well fulfilled, and his characteristic
weakness for get-rich-quick speculations in land, canals, and railroads
was partly cured. A conversion to industrial capitalism became the
"order of the day" after 1843, and proceeded with such haste in the

[18] Redlich, *American Banking,* pp. 162–65, 170–71 ; Hammond, "Jackon, Biddle,
and the Bank," *loc. cit.,* pp. 23, 9–10, 6–7.

1850's that the new order required only "control of the state" to complete its triumph.[19]

Thomas Cochran comes at the change from the institutional side and discovers a similar result by 1860: "The Industrial Revolution had come to America, and created the modern world of business." That conclusion, taken literally, runs ahead of his detailed argument. Cochran's meaning is seen more clearly in his statement that "almost all the varied forms and functions" of the twentieth-century business world had evolved by 1860, and were in the course of establishing their dominance; i.e., a new controlling pattern had entered unmistakably, although the texture of economic life remained very much a mixture of old and new elements. Again, in terms of an industrial discipline, Cochran finds down to 1860 not of course the general prevalence of large-scale factory industry, but the new appearance of a competent industrial labor force, a reserve of unskilled immigrant labor, and in general the "forms and functions" of an emerging industrial order, together with such remarkably advanced models as the miniature twentieth-century world created by the Boston Associates in eastern Massachusetts.[20]

A major clue to the change lies, for Cochran, in the gradual displacement or transformation of the traditional sedentary merchant who, from a small shop in downtown Boston or New York or Philadelphia, had done business with the wide world as wholesaler, retailer, shipper, and anything else that came to hand. The transfer of mercantile capital to internal ventures between 1812 and 1830—to banking, transportation, Western lands, manufacturing—was the initial phase of business change. Then the increasing adoption of the corporate form brought an irreversible commitment to modern business organization: a move toward bigness, specialization, administrative coordination, impersonality, and a wide-marketing orientation.[21]

A prudent authority on all these matters is George Rogers Taylor, whose comprehensive economic history of the 1815–60 period, *The*

[19] Louis M. Hacker, *The Triumph of American Capitalism*, pp. 16–27, 199–200, 208–14.

[20] Thomas C. Cochran, "Business Organization and the Development of an Industrial Discipline," *American Economy*, ed. Williamson, pp. 279–80.

[21] *Ibid.*, pp. 279–95. For statistical data on the spread of corporate organization, see George H. Evans, Jr., *Business Incorporations in the United States, 1800–1943*, pp. 10–30.

*Transportation Revolution,* incorporates the important results of recent scholarship with a minimum of theoretical elaboration. Obviously, Taylor is discussing more than a transportation revolution, yet the case for making this set of changes central is persuasive. Drawing from his evidence and scattered conclusions, one might assemble this series of propositions: (1) the construction of a national transportation-communication network was the great economic preoccupation of the 1815–60 era; (2) by 1860, the task was accomplished in broad outline and in some details for the major settled regions of the United States; (3) significant innovation recurred continually through the period (canals, steamboats, railroads), transforming the structure and operation of the transportation system itself; (4) in aggregate, these innovations stimulated a sequence of economic adaptations of the largest consequence, notably a rapidly advancing intersectional division of labor; (5) this in turn sustained a marked development toward specialization and integration of commercial, financial, and industrial functions; (6) the strong population current into the West and into towns was facilitated directly by the new means of transportation, indirectly by the broad economic changes noted in (4) and (5) above; (7) the scale of transportation enterprises involved a general trying-out of corporate organizations employing other people's money; (8) positively, this provided not only useful experience and precedents, but a favorable atmosphere for popular acceptance of a doubtful instrument apparently required to meet important communal needs; (9) even negatively, the initial involvement of most states as promoters and builders of internal improvements, ending often in financial disaster, provoked a popular reaction in favor of applying laissez-faire principles to big corporate as well as little "private" enterprise.[22]

That the concentrated and radical process of development defined by these historical interpretations helped to create a highly sensitive economy is made plain in Arthur H. Cole's expert analysis of American business fluctuations between 1820 and 1845. Like Taylor and others, Cole takes 1820 as the approximate dividing line between the

[22] *Ibid., passim.* See also Hartz, *Economic Policy and Democratic Thought;* Oscar and Mary Handlin, *Commonwealth: A Study of the Role of Government in the American Economy; Massachusetts, 1774–1861;* Hammond, "Free Banks and Corporations: the New York Free Banking Act of 1838," *Journal of Political Economy,* XLIV (April 1936), 184–209; Carter Goodrich, "The Revulsion Against Internal Improvements," *Journal of Economic History,* X (November 1950), 145–69.

colonial and national periods of economic relations. The end of colonial economic status does not in the least suggest to Cole an effective declaration of independence: he finds the close resemblance of American to English price movements a fair index to the continuing importance of external influences. The indispensable foreign market for American staples, the large opportunities for American overseas shipping, the decisive role of the London money market in supplying commercial and investment credit, all made the American economy highly responsive to British conditions. What had changed substantially was the system receiving such influences, perhaps most significantly in these respects: (1) American business steadily transferred its attention, energies, and resources (including resources borrowed from abroad) to tasks of internal development; (2) "Local independence and self-determination in business affairs—though, of course, almost always qualified in various ways since the settlement of the country —were steadily losing what potency they had once possessed."[23]

Thus the scope of internal economic relations was greatly extended with the rise of the West and its incorporation into a system of intracontinental commerce. A growing national division of labor supplied a growing intersectional trade through the new transportation channels, with a resulting increase of interdependence among sections and economic groups. A substantial manufacturing industry in the North Atlantic states was called into existence by the possibilities of new, and newly linked, markets of the West. At the same time, the rapid expansion of credit facilities and resources provided means for settlement, internal improvements, new industries, and extensive commercial relations. Cole makes clear the importance of the integrating functions which accompanied expansion and diversification. Thus the Second Bank and—of lasting significance—the rising New York financial and commercial center exerted a powerful influence upon the whole network of domestic and foreign exchanges. This meant, among other things, a much heightened sensitivity throughout the economy to disturbances in any one sector or area.[24]

---

[23] Smith and Cole, *Business Fluctuations*, pp. 37–43. In the 1850's Edwin T. Freedley guessed that two-thirds of American production was geared to an exchange system. *A Practical Treatise on Business*, pp. 95–97.
[24] Smith and Cole, *Business Fluctuations*, pp. 37–43.

## Behind the Monster

It has been enormously difficult for modern scholarship to take
the Jacksonian political appeal seriously on its own terms: at one
extreme its message is discounted as the largely meaningless babble
of demagogues; at the other, it is blown up into the prophetic utter-
ance of a modern welfare ideology. Perhaps on the basis of the
preceding sketch one might justify a fresh start: a view of Jacksonian
political discourse as a response to events and institutions perceived—
however dimly or instinctively—in much the way modern analysts
see them, i.e., in the shape of signs and portents revealing profound
changes in the American condition. Behind the Monster lay a central
chunk of economic reality, realized and in the making.

# 6

# THE JUDGES AND THE JUDGED

## A VIEW OF ECONOMIC PURPOSES

❧

I have thus far treated economic processes as somehow external to the Jacksonians who experienced and judged them. If, however, I am right that the Monster Bank of Jacksonian rhetoric represented —in fact and vaguely in perception—pervasive qualities of an altered economic life, then the case is far more difficult. The favorite notion of Jacksonian spokesmen, that a few powerful and enterprising agents imposed alien ways upon an innocent society, is scarcely credible. The rapid economic transformations owed much, certainly, to innovating genius, call it evil or creative; yet the innovations took hold in a society where economic choice was decentralized and within broad limits free. One sees the work of many hands for a singularly receptive nation. Americans who followed the Jacksonian persuasion with their votes, a number varying from just under to more than half, were in some degree censuring their own economic attitudes and actions.

Here within brief limits I shall try to indicate from contemporary reports something of the spirit of work among Americans. My purpose is to see economic processes from the inside, in relation to the prevalent attitudes of working citizens.

American history overflows with the evidence of a growing, moving people, improvising their social world as they transformed resources into goods and utilities. For contemporary witnesses these were marvelous doings, and their pages abundantly record the instances of growth and change which the statistics of population and economy generalize. The world seemed spinning wildly: how, Francis Lieber wondered, could a people endure feeling "all the time as if tied to the wing of a windmill"? "Ten years in America are like a century in Spain," he felt.[1] Everywhere the observers of Jacksonian society discovered violent motion: in the continuous migrations; in the rise and transformation of communities; in the perpetual revolution of technics, trade patterns, and business organization; in wild business fluctuations, monetary instability, and the rapid rise and fall of private fortunes. Harriet Martineau saw a whole people boldly venturing upon "the process of world-making."[2] Adam de Gurowski supposed that a "devouring mobility" must be "one of the most salient and all-absorbing features of the popular character"; in effect, an independent master motive.

Domestic ties, the affections of home and hearth, are powerless over the immense majority. Action carries them away, and they change with wonderful facility spots, abodes, regions, and states. . . . Mobility urges the American incessantly to work, to undertake, to spread, create, produce.[3]

To these witnesses Americans were not the victims but the makers of their fate. Fabulous growth and change were seen as the product of vast human energies devoted to work with an intensity, audacity, and flexibility quite unknown to Poor Richard or the economic man of Adam Smith. The tempo and direction of economic development were, in short, general expressions of the goals and styles of citizens at work. Special qualities apart, the sheer concentration upon gainful work in the American becomes the great dominating fact for most observers. "The sleeping fox catches no poultry," Poor Richard said. "Up! up!"[4] By common report Americans of Jackson's time were eternally on the prowl. To Francis Grund: "Business is the very soul of an American: he pursues it, not as a means of procuring for himself and his family the necessary comforts of life, but as the fountain of all human felicity." He saw the same high pitch of business involvement in town and country, in all classes. The pursuit began in childhood and continued "till the very hour of death."[5] A few decades later Gurowski found no slackening of the drive: "Production, activity are enjoyments, and existence becomes a burden, and deteriorates morally and materially without a serious pursuit, without daily work

---

[1] Francis Lieber, *The Stranger in America*, II, 186–88.
[2] Harriet Martineau, *Society in America*, I, 156.
[3] Adam G. de Gurowski, *America and Europe*, p. 151.
[4] Nathan Goodman (ed.), *A Benjamin Franklin Reader*, p. 287.
[5] Francis J. Grund, *The Americans in Their Moral, Social and Political Relations*, pp. 202–4, 206.

and occupation."⁶ Thomas Low Nichols, commenting on his experience as a member of the Jacksonian generation, recalled that farmers, businessmen, all conceived their working tasks as endless and totally exacting. By internal more than external necessity: "The harvests press upon the reapers."⁷

The pervasive mood encountered by many witnesses matches the evidence of enormous preoccupation with work. Met at the public dinner table, at the evening party, at loose ends, where the demand is for the free play of sociability, Americans commonly appear as Dickens saw them: "Such deadly leaden people; such systematic plodding weary insupportable heaviness."⁸ "Jonathan is a very dull boy," groaned Mrs. Trollope.⁹ Leisured gentlemen of liberal attainments, gracious and charming ladies, were accounted precious curiosities among a nation of grubs. But Horatio Greenough—an expatriate sculptor whose words often were more gifted than his works—suggested a deeper understanding in his phrase contrasting Jacksonian America with Vienna: "We hoist the sail and are seasick; they anchor and dance."¹⁰ The grim, gulping dinner company were in other settings still a serious sort—as several accounts relate—yet their qualities were not reducible to mere lower middle-class vulgarity. One writer notes the prevalence of the wrinkled brow; another finds a dusky, nervous look in American faces. Within the limits of an essential seriousness, the reported mood is variously, or alternately, restless, excited, tense, anxious, severe, even sad.¹¹ "In all the years of peace and plenty," Nichols writes, "we were not happy." And he adds: "In no country are the faces of the people furrowed with harder lines of care. . . . Work and worry eat out the hearts of the people, and they die before their time."¹²

⁶ Gurowski, *America and Europe*, p. 368.

⁷ Thomas Low Nichols, *Forty Years of American Life, 1821–1861*, p. 194. For similar impressions see also: James Silk Buckingham, *The Eastern and Western States of America*, I, 94–99; II, 3; Gurowski, *America and Europe*, pp. 371–72; Charles Fenno Hoffman, *A Winter in the Far West*, I, 58–59; Frances Trollope, *Domestic Manners of the Americans*, pp. 36–45, 303.

⁸ Charles Dickens, *American Notes for General Circulation*, p. 355. See also *ibid.*, pp. 431, 433–34, and Dickens' bitter American caricatures in *Life and Adventures of Martin Chuzzlewit*.

⁹ Trollope, *Domestic Manners*, p. 305. See also *ibid.*, pp. 122–23, 209.

¹⁰ Quoted in John Kouwenhoven, *Made in America*, p. 101. See also the comment of Oliver W. Larkin in *Art and Life in America*, p. 183.

¹¹ Hoffman, *Far West*, I, 89–90; Lieber, *Stranger*, I, 283.

¹² Nichols, *Forty Years*, pp. 193–94. See also Gurowski, *America and Europe*, pp. 64, 378–79; Martineau, *Society in America*, I, 156.

The mood cannot be completely captured without more intimate details than these reports provide. Here, however, we need only take a broad suggestion of the emotional state associated with the economic attitudes of Jacksonian Americans. Americans, say the witnesses, committed their energies, their concern—their lives—to work. They could swing from tense excitement to brooding severity; but they could never be less than wholly serious. They had unlearned to play, to reflect, to rest: to detach themselves in any important way from the urgent business of the day. And all their purposes were immediately focused on one subject: the "almighty dollar."[13]

The lines of caricature are evident: significant qualifications and variations can be learned from the same books and from other contemporary materials. If the point, however, is not to do comprehensive justice to any one American, or to every one, but rather to seize characteristic and decisive traits for social action, then these crude impressions of the American as worker deserve further examination.

Dickens and Mrs. Trollope are simply disgusted with American dollar worship: they have quickly found the goal of work, and found it mean and boring. Mrs. Trollope is satisfied that she has seen the archetypal "hard, dry, calculating character" of the American in Nick, a ragged brat of ten who plies a thriving chicken and egg trade near Cincinnati, hoarding his gains in his pocket like "a young Jew."[14] But the "prevalent desire of gain" so often noticed by the witnesses—the "universal and everlasting struggle for wealth," the "giddy passion of money-getting"—demands more curiosity than one finds in the acid English lady who could not retail her notions of luxury and culture to Ohio customers. America was a world in which, as Thomas Nichols noted: "Money is the habitual measure of all things."[15] The dollar was almighty because, within a vast range, it could purchase what men wanted. Said Freeman Hunt, preceptor, advocate, and reporter to New York's business community: "the feeling is universal, that to be anybody, or to do anything, one must have wealth."[16] If, in James Hall's terms, "the use of money . . . controls and regulates everything," then working furiously for gain, as Americans were seen to do, meant getting the means for satisfying wants not yet named.[17]

---

[13] Dickens uses the phrase. *American Notes*, p. 211.
[14] Trollope, *Domestic Manners*, pp. 122–24.
[15] Nichols, *Forty Years*, p. 195.
[16] Freeman Hunt, *Worth and Wealth*, pp. 182–83.
[17] Quoted in Hunt, *Worth and Wealth*, p. 224.

Mrs. Trollope had indeed proposed an interpretation of the money goal in her sketch of the grubby little miser; but her view is rare among contemporary observers. Still admired in Jacksonian times, by common report, and still hard to find was another model lad, Poor Richard's earnest 'prentice, slowly coining his security out of patient drudgery, tactful manners, and rigid self-denial. (Dick himself had noticed, after a quarter century of maxim-izing, that the people "heard it, and approved the doctrine, and immediately practiced the contrary, just as if it had been a common sermon.")[18] A much stronger lead for understanding economic purposes is given by Miss Martineau, who thought the "prevalent desire of gain" had "more of the spirit of competition and of ostentation in it, than desire of accumulation."[19] Americans work passionately for wealth, said Nichols, because "it is the only thing needful; the only secure power, the only real distinction." In his view: "Every one is tugging, trying, scheming to advance—to get ahead. It is a great scramble, in which all are troubled and none are satisfied."[20] Francis Lieber saw everywhere a "striving and driving onward"; a "diseased anxiety to be equal to the wealthiest, the craving for wealth and consequent disappointment, which ruins the intellect of many" and contributes to an "appalling frequency of alienation of mind" in America.[21]

Thus a major theme of work appears: acquisition for ascent. This is quite clear of the imagery of the miser fondling his coins, or of the shopkeeper building his fortress of secure respectability. Observers meet with intense upward striving among farmers, mechanics, operatives, even servants, as well as merchants and professionals. The drive asserts its dominance early in life and never eases. "An American," Grund remarks, "is, almost from his cradle, brought up to reflect on his condition, and, from the time he is able to act, employed with the means of improving it."[22] Tocqueville, Lieber, Gurowski, Buckingham, Martineau: all note the early training in independence, the remarkable precocity of American boys, especially in their assumption of adult economic roles and aspirations.[23] Freeman Hunt, himself an

[18] *Franklin Reader*, pp. 301–9.
[19] Martineau, *Society in America*, II, 144, 175.
[20] *Nichols, Forty Years*, pp. 194–95.
[21] Lieber, *Stranger*, I, 68–69; II, 29–30.
[22] Grund, *The Americans*, p. 18.
[23] Tocqueville, *Democracy in America*, II, 192–97; Lieber, *Stranger*, I, 121–22; II, 173–76; Gurowski, *America and Europe*, pp. 46–49; Martineau, *Society in America*, II, 188–89, 271, 273, 277; Buckingham, *Eastern and Western States*, II, 194.

enthusiast of the active business life and a noted success counselor, is disturbed to find "youth robbed of its sunshine and taught to ape manhood."[24] A New Hampshire schoolboy of the twenties recalls later how his generation was whipped into feverish ambition: "our teachers constantly stimulated us by the glittering prizes of wealth, honours, offices, and distinctions, which were certainly within our reach"— "there were a hundred avenues to wealth and fame opening fair before us, if we only chose to learn our lessons."[25] (Gurowski shrewdly notes the significant role of the young teacher in the district schools, still confident and energetic, and merely pausing on his way to greater things; this in contrast to the withered drifter or the narrowed martinet of European lower schools.)[26]

As young men were inspired to make themselves, so were they taught to feel their own guilt for failure. Two large assumptions brought the judgment home and undermined the victim's effort to protest his innocence or withdraw his effort: that opportunities for success were rich, various, and available on equal terms to all; that failure was an individual responsibility, due mainly to defective character and remediable by self-improvement. An important element here is the measurement of success or failure over the long course of a career, not by the outcome of a single effort. In the highly volatile Jacksonian economic world the incidence of failure was necessarily high, and the community developed an impressive—to many, shocking —degree of tolerance for the "honest bankrupt." There was nothing soothing in such tolerance, however; its cold touch could only signify that the chance and the responsibility remained for a new trial. If failure was not final, neither was success definitive. The endless "striving and driving onward"; the "great scramble, in which all are troubled and none are satisfied"; these qualities of Americans at work indicate a highly elastic notion of achievement which could find failure even in success arrested. As Grund commented: "A man, in America, is not despised for being poor in the outset . . . but every year which passes, without adding to his prosperity, is a reproach to his understanding or industry. . . ."[27]

24 Hunt, *Worth and Wealth*, pp. 486–87.
25 Nichols, *Forty Years*, p. 37.
26 Gurowski, *America and Europe*, pp. 291–92.
27 Grund, *The Americans*, p. 173. Also: Willard Phillips, *A Manual of Political Economy*, pp. 75, 153. The notions of open opportunity and personal responsibility are to be found throughout the sources. For a Jacksonian view see my discussion of

Miss Martineau, it will be recalled, paired "ostentation" with "competition" as controlling aims in the "prevalent desire of gain." Wherever one touches the contemporary record there is good evidence of the almost instantaneous conversion of economic gains into conspicuous improvements in the living standard (and of buying on credit in anticipation of future gains). "Silks and satins put out the kitchen fire," warns Poor Richard.[28] On the contrary, they were seen to light the fires of ambition and mark the upward path of striving workers. To James Buckingham, touring America in the 1830's, "a large house, fine furniture, and costly dresses for the female portion of the family . . . seem the first objects of every man's ambition."[29] A radical Ohio Jacksonian, when taunted publicly for stopping at a luxury hotel, declared what must have been a very common conviction: "that it is one of the first ideas of a democrat to live upon the best which the country offers"—even, added Mr. Reemelin, if he is "a poor one."[30]

Sedgwick and Rantoul in Chapters 8 and 10. Opportunities as perceived by observers and observed are reported in: Grund, *The Americans*, pp. 232, 236–38, 258–59, 288–91, 329; Buckingham, *Eastern and Western States*, I, 232, 237, 296–97; Martineau, *Society in America*, II, 61, 99–100; Trollope, *Domestic Manners*, pp. 116–18, 120–21; Lieber, *Stranger*, II, 165; Ole Munch Raeder, *America in the Forties*, trans. and ed. Gunnar J. Malmin, p. 68; Patrick Shireff, *A Tour through North America*, pp. 348–49, 398–99.

Apart from the heavy toll of the business cycle, the incidence of failures and new starts was high. For illustrations see Jeremiah Church, *Journal of Travels, Adventures, and Remarks of Jerry Church*, pp. 8–41; Thurlow Weed, *Autobiography*, ed. Harriet A. Weed, pp. 1–210; Horace Greeley, *Recollections of a Busy Life*, pp. 36–141; William C. Howells, *Recollections of Life in Ohio from 1813–1840*, pp. 1–195. But the sheer record of physical mobility is testimony enough to the erratic course of careers and fortunes. A startling rate of urban business failures is reported: see Hunt, *Worth and Wealth*, pp. 78–80; the survey by Edwin T. Freedley in *A Practical Treatise on Business*, pp. 211–18; Greeley, *Recollections*, p. 96; Martineau, *Society in America*, II, 145.

Certainly the successful broadcast the lesson of private moral responsibility. See, for example, *Extracts from the Diary and Correspondence of the Late Amos Lawrence*, ed. William R. Lawrence, pp. 25–26, 31, 82; Weed, *Autobiography*, pp. 43–44, 58–59; *Autobiography of Amos Kendall*, ed. William Stickney, p. 444. Success counselors like Hunt and Freedley preserve a good deal of Poor Richard's emphasis upon character as the key to success. With them, however, business strategy and tactics assume a more central role; and their recognition of the great frequency of failure makes their judgment of the victims just a little hesitant. Thus Freedley doubtfully concludes: "We must hope that it was by departing from the plain and well-established maxims of common caution that men invited disaster upon their enterprises." *Practical Treatise*, p. 216. It is almost a relief to encounter some Americans resigned to failure, if only where the case is obviously hopeless. See John H. Griscom, *The Sanitary Condition of the Laboring Population of New York*, pp. 2–38.

[28] *Franklin Reader*, p. 287.

[29] Buckingham, *Eastern and Western States*, II, 3–5.

[30] Speech by Charles Reemelin, in J. V. Smith (reporter), *Report of the Debates and Proceedings of the Convention for the Revision of the Constitution of the State of Ohio, 1850–1851*, II, 264–65.

And it was natural for an American economist to assert: "Almost all articles used and consumed in living, have the character of both necessaries and luxuries."[31]

Among the countless references to progressive consumership one might usefully notice two reports made at opposite social extremes. Observing the habits of the seaboard rich, the New York journalist Freeman Hunt was sickened by "the really wicked personal extravagance, which at present forms the most prominent social feature of our Eastern cities." Fashionable ladies pay without a thought fantastic sums for gowns and scarves and bonnets, extravagances which would have sent chills of horror through their prudent grandmothers of equal social rank. Out of "miserable personal vanity," simply to out-lace or out-jewel a rival at some grand soiree, such "painted triflers" drive their husbands to overwork and early death, to speculation and ruin. Although they are a small minority, their pretension to social superiority is widely accepted: "They are thus enabled practically to give a tone to society at large." In simpler city circles, in villages and farm homes, these vain indulgences are copied until half the women of America have learned to dress beyond their means.[32]

So the consumption achievements of the more ambitious and successful groups, notably the urban business and professional elite, communicate an incitement to the rest of society to work, to gain, to imitate. But it is important to see the process from the broad end; and Thomas Ford contributes an invaluable account of value conversion at the fringes of settlement—Illinois in the twenties. Ford witnessed in his life the stages in the transformation of Illinois from raw frontier to relatively settled commonwealth, and the parallel changes in manners and motives. With the instinct of a gifted anthropologist he tracked the passage through turns in the habits of dress. By 1830, Ford recalls, the old territorial costume was almost obsolete: the outfit of coonskin cap, buckskin breeches, and moccasins, with butcher knife and tomahawk ready at the belt; for the women, homespun frock striped with blue and turkey-red dye, bare feet, and cotton kerchief. Rapidly after 1818 the men of Illinois had turned to cloth coats and pantaloons, wool hats, boots and shoes; the women to gowns

---

[31] Willard Phillips, *Political Economy*, p. 30. Also: *Recollections of Samuel Breck, with Passages from His Notebooks (1771–1862)*, ed. W. H. Scudder, pp. 181, 275–76, 298–301; Shireff, *Tour*, p. 25; Trollope, *Domestic Manners*, pp. 116–18.

[32] Hunt, *Worth and Wealth*, pp. 282–84. See also Freedley, *Practical Treatise*, pp. 223–28. The sales records of Midwestern country stores indicate the demand for luxury goods: Lewis Atherton, *The Pioneer Merchant in Mid-America*, p. 45.

of silk and calico, bonnets of straw, silk, or leghorn, slippers of kid or calf. And thereon hangs Ford's tale: "With the pride of dress came ambition, industry, the desire of knowledge, and a love of decency." The old folks futilely denounced "these new trappings"; they preferred to live in the old cabins, go barefooted, and eat hog and hominy, while prophesying ruin in the silence of the loom, in the waste of good scarce money on such wanton finery.[33]

Rather persuasively Ford associates the change, much of it, with the establishment of churches and the growing practice of church-going. Not that he credits the flowering of the vanities to backwoods brimstone; Ford has a nice eye for unintended consequences. Rather the local church brought young men and women together regularly and so accustomed them to admire impressive appearances, to wish for admiration: soon they came well-dressed and clean on finely out-fitted mounts. The demands of making an appearance created the will to exert greater industry,

and taught them new notions of economy and ingenuity in business, to get the means of gratifying their pride in this particular. This again led to settled habits of enterprise, economy and tact in business, which once ac-quired and persevered in, were made the cause of a thriftiness unknown to their fathers and mothers.[34]

Observation of frontier life over thirty-five years confirmed Ford in his impression that youth felt no pride and yearned for no improve-ment where churchgoing was not regularly established. Young men would rarely change their rough everyday dress and dirty linen, would go about with hair uncombed and beards unshorn, spend Sunday hunt-ing, at the races, at the grocery, or lounging sullenly at home. The girls were surly drudges who would end their week in "sleepy stu-pidity." Such young, "without self-respect," felt "a crushing and withering sense of meanness and inferiority mingled with an envious malignity towards all excellence in others." In their neighborhoods were bred "a rough, vicious, ill-mannered and ill-natured race of men and women."[35]

The sources run too thin, once more, to sustain a confident analysis

[33] Ford, *History of Illinois*, pp. 94–96.
[34] *Ibid.*
[35] *Ibid.*

of consumer goals and their relation to the spirit of work. One can be fairly sure that great numbers of Jacksonian Americans spent liberally for comfort and display, taking their fashion cues from the metropolitan elite. The leaders were quick and nimble; and the led, it seems, were pressed hard to find the means for emulation. Perhaps two major interpretations of the chase, roughly convergent, emerge most clearly from contemporary reports. There is first the notion of a fluid, expanding equalitarian society, which encourages every man to assert his right "to live upon the best which the country offers." Few are so miserable or servile that they will not think each good thing they see potentially their own; few so fully and securely provided that they will not find new objects to covet. But emulation as reported has another, sharper tang: if the American democrat reaches for his share of the fat of the land, he nevertheless often seems a peculiarly joyless citizen, a man obsessed with the pursuit and never satisfied by his reward. Thus some observers see a long chain from work to money to goods to status. Where formal signs of rank have blurred, the infinitely expandable counters of consumption reflect achievement and so express relative standings on a sliding scale. An American must run to work and then to market just to keep his place; to "go ahead" he must sustain a killing pace.[36]

No doubt one country girl in Paris silks meant more to the observer's eye than a dozen seen in homespun. Always one suspects that witnesses tended to report what seemed strange and striking to a European, or to an older or disaffected American, neglecting the sleepy places and stolid types, as perhaps, in reverse, the American abroad would feast on ruins and quaintness. Nonetheless, the substantial consistency of impressions seems to indicate an actual, salient pattern. The high visibility of the pattern suggests that it characterized at least the more successful population of the more interesting (growing, changing) places. Distorted emphasis becomes, too, an indirect assertion of novelty in the object encountered: testimony in the present case for the rising importance of the heavily reported attitudes toward work. Exact and reliable knowledge of the distribution of attitudes would be immensely valuable; but at least we can be reasonably sure

[36] Tocqueville's penetrating analysis of equality and mobility is considered in Chapter 3, *supra*.

we have seen here, through the eyes of witnesses, a prominent—I think the dominant—theme.

Now a grave omission comes to mind: Was there no active use for that conspicuous assumption and prescription of republican ideology, the preference for land and moral independence? Land was, of course, the most abundant and available resource in Jacksonian times, and agriculture was by far the first pursuit. Necessarily land and farm would figure largely in men's economic schemes. Land was important as a production resource, as a commodity in the real estate business, as an object of consumption, as the point of entry to a new community. Miss Martineau saw, partly in imagination, a vivid image of land as the American's sovereign good: a source of solace, a refuge, a social springboard; a sort of validation and ultimate reward for a life's work. Thus:

The possession of land is the aim of all action, generally speaking, and the cure for all social evils, among men in the United States. If a man is disappointed in politics or love, he goes and buys land. If he disgraces himself, he betakes himself to a lot in the west. If the demand for any article of manufacture slackens, the operatives drop into the unsettled lands. If a citizen's neighbors rise above him in the towns, he betakes himself where he can be monarch of all he surveys. An artisan works, that he may die on land of his own. He is frugal, that he may enable his son to be a landowner. Farmers' daughters go into factories that they may clear off the mortgage from their fathers' farms.[37]

It matters little that Miss Martineau adds some doubtful flourishes to her account. Land served a variety of important needs, economic and noneconomic; unquestionably land hunger was powerful and general. The meaning of land to Jacksonian Americans is an intricate and fascinating subject. Here, however, we are concerned only with a single comprehensive question: Did land evoke an image of bucolic life which wakened and directed industry in a unique way? Testimony varies considerably, yet the major emphasis is clearly negative. Land served primarily the purposes of acquisition and ascent; it was a medium of production, consumption, and exchange distinguished mainly by its abundance and convenience. The republican yeoman on his hundred acres, building his farm and character together and taking his reward in self-sufficient independence, populates the speeches of Jacksonian Democrats but not the countryside that observers viewed.

[37] Martineau, *Society in America*, I, 292.

Miss Martineau is probably right that agriculture, compared with industrial pursuits, was still considered "the more honorable occupation."[38] The farmer claimed his honors as the traditional bearer of republican virtue, as the bone and sinew and sound heart of the nation; he pursued his work, as Tocqueville and others remark, in much the same spirit and toward much the same ends as the generality of his countrymen.[39] In the course of making a different point, Lieber insisted that the American farmer "forms no class by himself"; he is in status and broad attributes simply a full citizen.[40]

Thus most comments on the American approach to work make no special case for farmers and give no peculiar role to landed property. "The mercantile genius of the country," Grund finds, "pervades all classes of society, and by its universal influence unites them effectually to a large homogeneous whole."[41] With few constraints of law, sentiment, or custom predetermining economic choices, Nichols observes, men act from day to day according to pecuniary prospects. Every man becomes an independent businessman in spirit. "Nearly all Americans trade and speculate. They are ready to swap horses, swap watches, swap farms; and to buy and sell anything. . . . Money is the habitual measure of all things."[42] The broad impression, comprehending town and country, focuses upon a national order of instinctive traders and shoestring enterprisers in free pursuit of maximum returns. There are only odd corners for the ideal yeoman in the record of Americans who change places and careers to find the quickest and the largest reward; who adapt business and industrial practices to the shifting

[38] *Ibid.*, II, 38.
[39] Tocqueville, *Democracy in America*, II, 157. See also Buckingham, *Eastern and Western States*, II, 261–62.
[40] Lieber, *Stranger*, II, 157–61. The absolute and relative increase in urban population suggests—even when the effect of foreign immigration is allowed for—a strong counterattraction to land and farm. The lure of town life and work for ambitious country boys is clear, especially in the case of Yankee strivers determined to escape unfruitful farms and static villages. See, for example, Greeley, *Recollections*, p. 60; Nichols, *Forty Years*, pp. 37–38. But some observers insist that the trend is much more general, indeed alarming. See Buckingham, *Eastern and Western States*, II, 82–83; Freedley, *Practical Treatise*, pp. 208–10; Hunt, *Worth and Wealth*, pp. 36–37, 93–94, 233, 487–89; also Cornelius Mathews, *The Motley Book*, pp. 18–19. It is certainly revealing that Freeman Hunt, who glorified the urban businessman as a modern knight or prince, should have thought it necessary to stress the moral and economic perils of the city, and to preach the dignity and solid rewards of country work. Hunt, *Worth and Wealth*, pp. 42, 56–59, 317, 387–88.
[41] Grund, *The Americans*, pp. 293, 295.
[42] Nichols, *Forty Years*, pp. 194–95.

requirements of efficiency and profit; who force their new communities into the market current while the wilderness still surrounds them;
who treat land "like any other kind of merchandise," freely mixing
real estate with farming interests.[43]

Indeed terms like flexibility and adaptability often seem too tame
to capture the reported ways of work among Jacksonian Americans.
The cool calculation and then the prudent pursuit of advantage assume
the aura of an old-fashioned style. The central economic figure is not
the classic trader who offers his extra spear for your surplus fish, but
the speculative enterpriser who scents distant opportunities and bor-
rows or invents the means for grasping them. A preference for high-
risk, high-gain transactions is found at all economic levels: everyone
is ready to place his bet on the future rise of the market, to borrow
on his hopes. Thus the American, in his urgent quest for gain and
advancement, becomes to many witnesses the very opposite of the
sturdy, stable citizen-producer; becomes an adventurer steered only
by a bold imagination. The Easterner who leads his family into the
Michigan wilds, the country boy who tries his fortune in the "mael-
strom" of New York, are fairly common types. The reckless speculator in land or business is a familiar figure to contemporary observers.
Perhaps nowhere is the wildcat spirit more vividly expressed than
in a bit of conversation heard in a Chicago hotel. Time: the forties.
The hotelkeeper is discussing wildcat notes:

Why, sir, . . . this hotel was built with that kind of stuff. . . . I will take
"wild cats" for your bill, my butcher takes them of me, and the farmer from
him, and so we go, making it pleasant all around. I only take care . . . to
invest what I may have at the end of a given time in corner lots. . . . On
this kind of worthless currency, based on Mr. Smith's [the issuer's] supposed wealth and our wants, we are creating a great city, building up all
kind of industrial establishments, and covering the lake with vessels—so
that suffer who may when the inevitable hour of reckoning arrives, the
country will be the gainer, Jack Rossiter [the speaker] will try, when this
day of reckoning comes, to have "clean hands" and a fair record. . . . A
man who meddles, my dear sir, with wild-cat banks is on a slippery spot,
and that spot the edge of a precipice.[44]

[43] Among countless illustrations, see: Gurowski, *America and Europe*, p. 372;
Hunt, *Worth and Wealth*, pp. 82–83; Nichols, *Forty Years*, pp. 60–64; Lieber,
*Stranger*, I, 71–72; II, 65–71; Hoffman, *Far West*, I, 124–33, 184–91; Trollope,
*Domestic Manners*, pp. 120–21; Shireff, *Tour*, pp. 81–82; Raeder, *The Forties*, pp.
148–49.

[44] John L. Peyton, "Over the Alleghenies," in *A Mirror for Americans*, ed.
Warren S. Tryon, III, 603–6. See also Grund, *The Americans*, pp. 258–60, 264–65,

If the shared impressions of observers can be accepted even partially, Americans in their approach to work were mighty sinners against Jacksonian commandments. Perhaps if we knew more about the distribution of attitudes and party preferences among distinctive social groups, the seeming conflict would be reduced. There is inconclusive evidence that groups least involved in the economic attitudes reported above—and least likely to succeed by acting on them—were especially responsive to Jacksonian appeals. Western "huge-paw boys" and low-status city dwellers are commonly cited examples. There are corresponding indications in the sources that the Jacksonians were relatively weak among the most successful, ambitious, enterprising groups: among men whose roles and prospects and achievements tended to support the attitudes I have discussed. Merchants, bankers, promoters of various kinds, and the rich generally appear to have been disproportionately anti-Jacksonian in political preference. But the evidence is limited and far from consistent; more important, it could not prove enough at best. Nationally and in many local areas party preference alternated or remained quite closely divided. In social composition America was predominantly middle-class: a nation of farmers, mechanics, and shopkeepers, with a growing but still largely outnumbered permanent wage-earning class. And finally the observers of America at work insist upon the substantial uniformity of economic attitudes throughout the population, and report exceptions mainly for small ethnic, regional, or occupational clusters: for German immigrants, at the start of their American farming careers; for the remnant of the old French population in the West; for loggers, coal miners, sailors; for slum dwellers and isolated borderers. On these several

---

292–93; Hunt, *Worth and Wealth*, p. 130; Greeley, *Recollections*, p. 96; Martineau, *Society in America*, II, 142, 145; Nichols, *Forty Years*, pp. 57–58, 104–5; Hoffman, *Far West*, II, 41–44; Hone, *Diary*, I, 45, 107, 111, 408; II, 107; Lieber, *Stranger*, I, 68–69. The *Journal* of Jeremiah Church is perhaps unique in recording the frank sentiments of an adventurer. Jerry concluded early in life that "I must go into a speculation of some other kind, for hard work did not agree with me; it hurt my feelings." He ridiculed the Jacksonian view "that the speculator is the man who ruins the country." "Every man," thought Jerry, "is a speculator, from a wood-sawyer to a President, as far as his means will go, and credit also." *Journal*, pp. 7, 45, and *passim*. Freedley, *Practical Treatise*, pp. 165–71, reprints an anonymous letter telling "How to Get Rich by Speculation." The writer's sly message: " 'Never speculate; but when you do, be sure to mind our rules.' " *Ibid.*, p. 171. If the record of a notorious thief of the period can be credited, a good many respectable-seeming folk throughout the country were ready to speculate on either side of the law. Sile Doty, *The Life of Sile Doty, 1800–1876*, Foreword by Randolph G. Adams.

grounds one returns to the initial proposition: that in significant measure the Jacksonians were at once the judges and the judged.[45]

The political analysis of Jacksonian Democracy would be simpler and clearer if this were not so: if the Jacksonians could in fact be taken for innocent—still better, struggling—victims of external social changes. Accepting the notion of their deep involvement in the process, however, one begins to believe in the reality of this Jacksonian society with its vast energies and driving hungers; with its vertiginous changes and its vertigo; with its brilliant hopes, its backward longings,

[45] Examples of nonconformity in economic values are found in: Buckingham, *Eastern and Western States*, I, 119; Hone, *Diary*, I, 93–94, 189–90; Trollope, *Domestic Manners*, pp. 17–18; Grund, *The Americans*, pp. 220–21; Hoffman, *Far West*, I, 108–19; Ford, *Illinois*, pp. 35–38, 94–96, 279–81. Ford suggests that continuous migration into Illinois tended to dissolve unique harder qualities and make the population "just a slice off the great loaf of the old States." *Ibid.*, pp. 228–31. Hard and comprehensive evidence on the social traits of party constituencies is difficult to come by. There are interesting ecological proposals in Turner, *The United States: 1830–1850*. The Jacksonians, of course, insistently identified their main following with farmers and mechanics; their opposition with the rich, the merchants and bankers, the privileged. Simply by asserting the classification loudly and often, they helped to make it real. Although Whigs seldom boasted of their social superiority, in the old Federalist fashion, they were still inclined to portray Jacksonians as a party of ne'er-do-wells, foreigners, vagrants, and the like, under the control of incendiary demagogues. Again, the image had consequences in political behavior. See, for example, Martin Van Buren, *An Inquiry into the Origin and Course of Political Parties in the United States*. Contemporary observation tends strongly to confirm the notion of a class influence on party preference, along lines suggested in the text. See, for example, Ford, *Illinois*, pp. 198–201; Gustave Koerner, *Memoirs of Gustave Koerner, 1809–1896*, ed. Thomas J. McCormack, I, 440–43, 589; Nichols, *Forty Years*, pp. 311–12; Weed, *Autobiography*, pp. 476–78, 502–4; Greeley, *Recollections*, pp. 108, 136; Hone, *Diary*, I, 120, 139, 141–42, 189–90, 197, 230–31, 235–36, 284, 352–53, 427–31; II, 652, 655, 714, 717, 936. See also Grund, *The Americans*, pp. 222–23; Thomas C. Grattan, *Civilized America*, I, 303. Jerry Church expressed the speculator's dislike for "Jacksonianism" in its opposition to paper-money banks and easy credit and in its tendency "to pass laws to keep a community poor, for the object of trying to make them honest." *Journal*, pp. 440–46.

The anti-Jackson leanings of important Eastern businessmen are noticed often in the secondary materials. More striking is Atherton's finding that 70 per cent of a sample of Western merchants (primarily storekeepers in country towns) were Whigs. *Pioneer Merchant*, pp. 23–26. Revealing, but special and highly inconclusive, studies of class followings include: Dixon Ryan Fox, *The Decline of the Aristocracy in the Politics of New York*, chap. xiv and Appendix, pp. 440–49; Walter E. Hugins, "Ely Moore: the Case History of a Jacksonian Labor Leader," *Political Science Quarterly*, LXV (March 1950), 105–25; William A. Sullivan, "Did Labor Support Andrew Jackson?" *Political Science Quarterly*, LXII (December 1947), 569–80; Edward Pessen, "Did Labor Support Jackson?: The Boston Story," *Political Science Quarterly*, LXIV (June 1949), 262–74; and the rejoinder to the last in Robert T. Bower, "Note on 'Did Labor Support Jackson?: The Boston Story,'" *Political Science Quarterly*, LXV (September 1950), 441–44.

and its raw conscience. The ambiguities in Jacksonian appeals and policies—the mixed themes of liberty, equality, and republican virtue —express the disturbed reactions of many citizens to the processes behind the Monster, reactions intensified and confused by a common participation in responsibility. Here in particular one approaches the large meaning of the corporate monster in Jacksonian politics: a gigantesque figure in a moral drama, detached from ordinary experience, upon which men could focus their discontent with society, and with themselves. In the plainer language of Poor Richard: "Mankind are very odd creatures: one half censure what they practise, the other half practise what they censure; the rest always say and do as they ought."[46]

46 *Franklin Reader*, p. 295.

# 7

# OLD HERO AND SLY FOX

## VARIATIONS ON A THEME

❧

Old Hero and Sly Fox should be adversaries in a morality fable. In fact they were natural and intimate allies. That Martin Van Buren finally went down in a din of gold-spoon libels and log-cabin fictions, leaving behind the image of the Little Magician, the Red Fox of Kinderhook—these are facts of one order. But first he came in, legitimate heir to the leadership of the national Democracy, trusted friend and lieutenant to the old chief: an authentic voice of the movement and no midnight thief. His autobiography does not tell all—not even all we have a right to know—and still it serves quite wonderfully to elucidate the relation between the old chief and his practical administrators, between the Jacksonian persuasion and the organized Jacksonian movement.

### Confessions of the Second Leader

In some respects Van Buren has higher claims than the General to stand as the representative figure of Jacksonian Democracy. He was the product of a long line of plain Dutch farmers who cultivated their own soil and maintained a position of modest respectability in local New York society. His regular education, like Jackson's, was scanty, and he qualified for the law by way of an office apprenticeship. None of the spicy flavor of racecourse, cockpit, and dueling ground, which marks Jackson's youth, attaches in the least to the personal history of Van Buren. Both men used law practice as a springboard into public office; but in comparison Van Buren would appear to have risen more directly from the rough-and-tumble of democratic politics, Jackson to have relied for his start upon the patronage of the magnates of early Tennessee society. While Jackson launched his public career under the sponsorship of the great, soon joining them as full member of the planter–merchant–land speculator aristocracy of western Tennessee, Van Buren early antagonized the powerful rival families in his locality and won his professional success against their opposition.[1]

When there was material enough to make of Van Buren the Plain Dutchman or the People's Advocate, why could he earn no better name than Red Fox or Little Magician? Half-consciously Martin Van Buren embodied a Jacksonian paradox. His lifelong delight in the excitements of party magic was almost smothered by a stern contempt for the mere manipulator in the fluid enterprise of party politics. The bitter pain he felt from the fox-magician reputation came precisely out of this sympathy with the attitude of his detractors. Van Buren understood very well why the curse had fallen upon his head, and at least suspected that it might be warranted. Neither pride in his self-made success nor a conviction of the rectitude of his political course could silence his doubts about the worth of such gifts and traits as the courtroom and the caucus honored.[2]

Whether indignantly, sadly, or ironically, Van Buren omits no opportunity to throw off the charges of partisan intrigue. In New York State politics, for instance, he denies all responsibility for removing DeWitt Clinton from the Canal Board, a crude Democratic blunder which aroused popular resentment strong enough to give Clinton the governorship—a case, Van Buren comments, of *"killing a man too dead."* When Van Buren appeared at the polls to vote, the crowd set up a taunting chant of "Regency! Regency!" He was too thoroughly identified with the party machine to escape the consequences of any of its operations: "I left Albany for Washington as completely broken down a politician as my bitterest enemies could desire."[3]

Again, early in the administration of John Quincy Adams,

---

[1] Martin Van Buren, "The Autobiography of Martin Van Buren," ed. John C. Fitzpatrick, in *Annual Report of the American Historical Association for the Year 1918*, II, 7, 13–16, 21. On Jackson, see Abernethy, *From Frontier to Plantation in Tennessee*, pp. 115–26. An important corrective to Abernethy is Charles G. Sellers, Jr., "Banking and Politics in Jackson's Tennessee, 1817–1827," *Mississippi Valley Historical Review*, XLI (June 1954), 61–84. The still valuable old authority is Parton, *Life of Andrew Jackson*, I, 96–309. See also Edward M. Shepard, *Martin Van Buren*, pp. 14–87.

[2] See "Autobiography," pp. 11–13, 71–73, 79–80, 169–72, 179–80, 379–99.

[3] *Ibid.*, pp. 143–44, 149.

Van Buren was blamed—unjustly, he maintains—for walking tiptoe around the new administration until his own election to the Senate had been secured. This charge of "non-committalism" became "the parrot-note of my adversaries" through his public life, and *"Van Buren-ish"* came to signify self-interested evasiveness. How deeply the accusation hurt him is plain from the tone of injured innocence in which he pleads his invariable desire to have his opinions on public questions known to all. Van Buren became a standard target for the malice of the rival party wits. For example: a man allegedly asks Van Buren, does he believe that the sun rises in the east? The Sly Fox is made to reply "that I presumed the fact was according to the common impression, but as I invariable [*sic*] slept until after sunrise I could not speak from my own knowledge."[4]

In self-defense, beyond the point-by-point rebuttal, Van Buren portrays himself as the always reluctant candidate, whose official preferments came only through "the well understood wish of the great majority of the political party of which I was a member." (This reticence, he adds, was "inexorably demanded by the habits and feelings of Northern people.") He must repeatedly rehearse the record of support given him by the party and "the democratic masses"; explain the opposition to him as the product of political intrigue. At one point, he would cut down the oppressive reputation by denying his gifts: "If I had possessed a tithe of the skill in subtle management and of the spirit of intrigue, so liberally charged upon me by my opponents, and upon the strength of which they gave me the title of 'magician,' I could have turned aside the opposition." Throughout the "Autobiography" Van Buren takes particular satisfaction in maintaining the personal respect of his political opponents; he reports a remarkable number of deathbed scenes in which formerly bitter party rivals pay tribute to his decency and ability.[5]

The very tone and frequency of his protests indicate an awareness of his special vulnerability to the attack on his public character. When Van Buren does not speak of himself directly, another dimension of his implicit self-knowledge appears. Thus, in his English notes, he observes nothing of the common life or the bottom side of politics; he records a strong distaste for such a liberal as Brougham, who seemed

[4] *Ibid.*, pp. 196–99.
[5] "Autobiography," pp. 224, 226 n., 225–28. In fact he was respected by even so jaundiced a Whig as Philip Hone. See Hone's *Diary*, I, 136, 244, 410–11.

to carry his newly won dignities with the spoiled, haughty, assuming air of the *arriviste*; but Wellington stirs him. The staunch, blunt, reactionary Duke recalls the Old General: "In moral and physical courage, in indifference to personal consequences and in promptness in action there was little if any difference in their characters." Generally the visiting American is impressed by the character of the English upper classes, who can assume power without preening or grubbing, without petty partisanship or crafty opportunism. This does not make Van Buren a waverer on the principle of aristocracy; his public record will acquit him fully. It does suggest his sharp sense of the unworthiness of the shoddy operator in public life, a sense sharp enough to drive him across a basic line of political principle in search of praiseworthy character models.[6]

A final instance of the same sort is too tempting to neglect: Van Buren's personal relations with that political terror, Randolph of Roanoke. In the relationship, Van Buren is the humble partner—"I was a good listener, a character which Randolph liked." The erratic, vitriolic brilliance of the Virginian, who could dub Jefferson "St. Thomas of Cantingbury" and credit Clay with the brilliance of a dead mackerel by moonlight, worries Van Buren, and yet fascinates him. Long hours are spent drinking in monologues on English life, on the old heroes of Virginia, on the magnificence of the old Virginia establishments, on Virginia pride and hospitality. It is an impressive display when the very model of party regularity obtains the Russian embassy for the almost pathologically proud Virginian, who, in Henry Adams' estimate, "would probably have horsewhipped any man who dared tell him he must obey his party." The diffident admirer accepts, in some confusion, a token of John Randolph's gratitude: a fine blooded horse.[7]

This sort of evidence safely supports only a modest thesis about Van Buren: that the character of career politician was for him a doubtful and precarious identity, one which led him to admire, perhaps to envy, the courage, solidity, and decisiveness of a Wellington, the poise and flair and proud idiosyncrasy of a Randolph. Far above these political types, however, stood Andrew Jackson, the very pattern of the morally complete politician. There is an almost pathetic eagerness

6 "Autobiography," pp. 464, 473–74.
7 *Ibid.*, pp. 430, 418–31; Henry Adams, *John Randolph*, pp. 195, 537.

in Van Buren's assurances that his relations, political and personal, with "that noble old man" were "cordial and confidential" to an extent never surpassed among public men. To be chosen by the Old Hero enhanced his own worth. Yet it gave an uneasy sort of satisfaction, for Van Buren could not help calculating "how far the political capital thus furnished—the greater, all things considered, than had been possessed by any previous Administration—might be successfully employed in the acquisition of public advantages which under less potential auspices I would have justly regarded as hopeless."[8]

The portrait of Jackson in the "Autobiography" projects the wavering ego of the author. This is the "gallant general"—"no politician" —whose character reveals "strong sense, perfect purity and unconquerable firmness." His name was "in very deed, a tower of strength." "His strength lay with the masses and he knew it"; for his willingness to spend himself in their service, to sacrifice ease and comfort, even to hazard his life for their security, "could not escape their knowledge or fail to secure their love and gratitude." Such faith in the integrity of the people and "in their fidelity to those who are faithful to them" not only secured his popularity but strengthened him in his political course. "He hated concealments. There was no trait in his character more obvious to others or more proudly and justly asserted by himself than his fearlessness in declaring his opinions and his readiness to bear any responsibility attaching to the avowal of them." Certain "peculiar circumstances in his condition" made Jackson naturally "one of the people"; "they were his blood relations—the only blood relations he had." Not that he lacked dignity or distinction; his "simple yet kindly old-school manners" disarmed the most snobbish of the foreign diplomatic corps. He was deeply persuaded that "to labor for the good of the masses was a special mission assigned to him by his Creator."[9]

Although Van Buren confesses few outright sins in the "Autobiography," and conceals none of the virtues of his own character, he does not imagine that anyone could publish such a portrait of him and be credited. In his inaugural address (March 4, 1837) Van Buren submits what is almost an apology for his appearance in the presidential office. His predecessors, who founded and perfected our "inestimable institutions," were humbly grateful for the honor of the

[8] "Autobiography," pp. 232, 397–98.
[9] *Ibid.*, pp. 229–30, 232–33, 253, 255, 262, 327.

presidency; how then should one feel who only inherited what others had fought for? While he contemplates "with grateful reverence that memorable event, I feel that I belong to a later age and that I may not expect my countrymen to weigh my actions with the same kind and partial hand." To "dare to enter upon my path of duty" Van Buren must recall the quality of his co-magistrates and the "patriotism, the intelligence, and the kindness of a people who never yet deserted a public servant honestly laboring in their cause."

The closing note suggests much of what I have been trying to say about Van Buren's political self-image: he cannot hope to equal his "illustrious predecessor"; but from his participation in Jackson's counsels, his observation of Jackson's public conduct, his agreement with the principles and sentiments Jackson represented, his possession of Jackson's confidence—from these gifts Van Buren "may hope that somewhat of the same cheering approbation will be found to attend upon my path." Finally, he turns from Jackson to God, in asking that the ways of our beloved country may be the "ways of pleasantness and all her paths be peace."[10]

Old Hero and Sly Fox. Where did the difference lie? A simple answer is, I think, the best, and the autobiographical clues point toward it. Martin Van Buren was one of the new young career men of American politics, men whose reputation and success had grown largely within the bounds of organized party activity. Americans liked party maneuvers as they liked heady, precarious ventures in land and business; they deeply honored neither. In Van Buren for the first time a president appeared who had no ennobling ties with the Founding Fathers, who had not lost or shed blood in the national cause, whose remembered past included no battlefields but the courtroom and the back room. A second-rate old man beat him in 1840 with a contrived log cabin and a real battlefield.

The Jacksonian political leader faced a baffling task. As leader, he could not simply impersonate the plain republican character of one of his ideal constituents. Votes had to be won, names had to be known. But how? Close identification with the mere mechanics of political organization operated as a major handicap. In accounting for the failure of his sometime rival, DeWitt Clinton, to sustain the sympathy and respect of the masses, Van Buren discovers sources of contempo-

10 Richardson, *Messages and Papers*, III, 313, 320.

rary popular judgment which must have shaped his own political reputation:

In this matter of personal popularity the working of the public mind is often inscrutable. In one respect only does it appear to be subject to rule, namely, in the application of a closer scrutiny by the People to the motives of public men than to their actions. When one is presented to them possessed of an ardent temperament who adopts their cause, as they think, from sympathy and sincerely regards their interests as his own, they return sympathy for sympathy with equal sincerity and are always ready to place the most favorable constructions upon his actions. . . . But when a politician fails to make this impression—when they on the contrary are led to regard him as one who takes the popular side of public questions from motives of policy their hearts seem closed against him, they look upon his wisest measures with distrust, and are apt to give him up at the first adverse turn in his affairs. . . . Feeling has of course more to do with it than reason, yet, though sometimes wrong it must be admitted that they are much oftener right in their discriminations. Jefferson and Jackson were favorites of the character I have described, and justly so. Clinton was not.[11]

Van Buren became Sly Fox and fell to the Old Farmer of North Bend:

> We've tried your purse-proud lords, who love
> In palaces to shine;
> But we'll have a plowman President
> Of the Cincinnatus line.[12]

### The Voice of the Second Leader

Martin Van Buren must be registered as a victim of Jacksonian Democracy. And yet his presidential voice does not betray the accent of Sly Fox; on the contrary, the presidential papers are Jacksonian in the full sense hypothesized before. By my examination of the "confessions" I hope to have established at least this much: that Van Buren's service to Jacksonian values was loyal in intent, and was even favorably received at first, but finally was turned against him because of certain real and reputed aspects of his character and career. So much granted, one can make something of the political messages as testimony about the meaning of Jacksonian Democracy.

The general thesis proposed in Chapter 2 remains my point of reference. Van Buren's tone and manner vary from Jackson's, of

---

[11] "Autobiography," p. 168.
[12] A. B. Norton, *Tippecanoe Songs of the Log Cabin Boys and Girls of 1840,* bound with A. B. Norton, *The Great Revolution of 1840,* p. 21.

course; and some differences necessarily turn upon the changing shape of common problems. The mere fact that the Bank War has been won diffuses the focus of debate, softens polemical edges. The national government has done almost all in its limited power to promote hard coin at the expense of paper. The onset of depression draws out more of the general Jacksonian economic position. The successor is rather more inclined toward personal meekness and seeking comfort in neutral patriotic themes. Interestingly enough, the one subject on which Van Buren does make a significant extension of the Jacksonian position is not exposed in the presidential papers. An explicit analysis and defense of political party organization, within the terms of Jacksonian ideology, occurs only in works written during retirement and posthumously published.[13]

The most arresting of the contrasts in the official discourse of founder and successor may be indicated by a story told in Van Buren's "Autobiography." Returning from an assignment in England, Van Buren called upon the General and found him ill and bedridden, a spectral figure. Jackson passed a hand through his long white locks and gripped his friend: "The bank, Mr. Van Buren, is trying to kill me, *but I will kill it!*" Not, the witness certifies, a burst of rage or bluster, this was the deep, intense conviction of a man for whom the war of principles was embodied in two great personal adversaries. When Martin Van Buren inherited the presidency, the Bank Monster was dead or dying and its worshipers were to be met in scattered remnants, under the diffuse countenance of a credit system. And the second leader, bred in a political atmosphere of personalities striving for preferment, had not the faith in his own calling which would nerve him to personify the struggle with evil.[14]

Yet, the reputed Fox speaks the Jacksonian language unmistakably. Indeed, his words express the values of republican simplicity and their contraries with a fullness hard to find in Jackson's public papers.

Whatever might be expected of Van Buren, in virtue of his reputation and career, the language that issued from his presidential office resists easy interpretation in the mode of the leading schools referred to in the Introduction. Reporting upon the state of the union in 1839,

[13] *Inquiry into the Origin and Course of Political Parties in the United States,* pp. 165–66, 179, 224–25, 232.
[14] "Autobiography," p. 625.

Van Buren recalls a year in some ways dark: there have been fire and epidemic and trade embarrassments. And yet the nation has maintained a fundamental kind of prosperity, revealed in

the exuberant harvests which have lavishly recompensed well-directed industry and given to it that sure reward which is vainly sought in visionary speculations. I can not, indeed, view without peculiar satisfaction the evidences afforded by the past season of the benefits that spring from the steady devotion of the husbandman to his honorable pursuit. No means of individual comfort is more certain and no source of national prosperity is so sure. Nothing can compensate a people for a dependence upon others for the bread they eat, and that cheerful abundance on which the happiness of everyone so much depends is to be looked for nowhere with such sure reliance as in the industry of the agriculturist and the bounties of the earth.[15]

All the revealing value terms are here exhibited. The steady devotion of the husbandman stands in strong contrast to the visionary speculations of the commercial world. The reward is sure, the pursuit honorable. Palpable harvests are the measure of success; the seasons set the pace; and the ends are the sure comfort and independence bred by honest, self-reliant industry.

Such convictions do not stand apart from the substantial issues of politics and economy. Van Buren's special message, dealing with the economic crisis of 1837, distinguishes present distresses from the permanent prospects of national prosperity: severe embarrassments have arisen mainly from the transactions of commerce, and the effects have fallen mainly upon commercial enterprise. The "great agricultural interest," as if by a show of providential favor, has suffered relatively little in many areas. Van Buren finds that "in direct contrast to the evils occasioned by the waywardness of man, we have been blessed throughout our extended territory with a season of general health and of uncommon fruitfulness." The ultimate security of American business is above question, because the debts so recklessly incurred are guaranteed by the resources and industry of the country, especially by the production of the great staples which will furnish means for liquidating debt, restoring credit, and reviving commercial activity.[16]

Such is the foundation of the true economy and such the source

[15] Richardson, *Messages and Papers*, III, 530.
[16] *Ibid.*, p. 345.

of the false. Van Buren's great agricultural interest cannot be confounded with the drifting enterprisers at the frontier, because he denies the identification in so many words. His terms of praise for the "husbandman" already cited are important clues: "sure reward," "steady devotion," "sure reliance." But there is more explicit evidence. Outlining his public land policy, Van Buren endorses the traditional approach based upon a desire to dispose of the lands at moderate prices to actual settlers: "Thus has been formed a body of free and independent landholders with a rapidity unequalled in the history of mankind." The reform most needful in 1837 (since the curtailment of credit purchases has already been accomplished) is a system of graduated land prices. Under the uniform-price arrangement, large tracts in older areas remain unclaimed since better lands are available ahead. Thus "a desirable compactness of settlements in the new States" is lost; instead, we encourage migration "up the almost interminable streams of the West to occupy in groups the best spots of land." The major end of public land policy—"converting the public domain into cultivated farms owned by their occupants"—is conditioned by the requirement that, in the penetration of the wilderness, "rudeness in the social condition" be avoided, settlement be compact, and communities be formed which are distinguished by prosperity, widespread intelligence, internal tranquillity, and wise political institutions.[17]

Nor does Van Buren's cold eye for squatters and preemption laws convey any sense of sympathy for the border adventurer. Congress has, to be sure, passed retroactive preemption laws from time to time, on plausible grounds: that the lands were empty, that squatters could not afford to buy, that they added value to adjacent public lands, that they intended ultimately to pay the government's price. Grudgingly, Van Buren will allow just one more such law to pass, since the previous legislation has raised hopes in the squatters which it would be unfair to disappoint. But, as a matter of public policy, the legal system of cash sales ought to be enforced: "This course of legislation [preemption laws] tends to impair public respect for the laws of the country." There is no more honor for the frontier primitive than there is for speculator, squatter, promoter, or monopolizer.[18]

"Soil" and "farm" are substantial components of the Democratic

---

[17] *Ibid.*, pp. 384–87, 484.
[18] *Ibid.*, pp. 388–89.

ideal, yet not entirely for the actual objects they denote; perhaps more important are the social traits and norms they suggest. That is to say, the specific praise of agriculture and the specific advocacy of land policies do not dominate Van Buren's presidential papers in any quantitative sense; rather, they establish the tone of a moral appeal.

Jackson's principles put banking and currency issues at the center of national politics; his policies forced certain necessary consequences upon his successor; and a depression facing Van Buren at the outset of his administration set the issues burning. Van Buren's public discussion of banking and currency unfolds in standard form the Jacksonian view of the good economic society and the perils it must face. Remembering that the Biddle Monster has been expelled—and something of Van Buren's character and role—one will not expect a duplication of Jackson's anti-Bank rhetorical style. The substantial moral effect is the same, however, conveyed in broader, flatter terms.

The immediate policy focus for Van Buren's presidential statements is the independent government treasury scheme: a plan for locating securely the federal deposits withdrawn from the Bank of the United States and perilously lodged with the "pet" state institutions. In the perspective of this study, the scheme as a practical contribution to national financial policy is not of large importance; what is important is how it was interpreted in relation to Jacksonian values. Indeed Van Buren has very little to say specifically and technically about the independent treasury and national financial policy. For a government which limits expenditures to actual wants, and revenues to necessary expenditures, an independent treasury would be a secure and effective agent for the deposit, transfer, and disbursement of public funds. That is about his whole case. But it is not the whole meaning; the treasury issue opens into broad questions of economic good and evil. There is an economic crisis; government funds on deposit with state banks are imperiled. The danger of public loss resulting from improper dependence of the government upon irresponsible agents is noticed, and then displaced in Van Buren's discussion by the general evil of a banking and credit system which induces economic crises and is encouraged in its mischief by the receipt of government deposits.[19]

[19] *Ibid.*, pp. 224–25, 325–38.

In his analysis of the crisis of 1837 Van Buren identifies the nature of the evil with a sure Jacksonian hand. Since about 1834, the American economy has experienced "overaction in all the departments of business," a condition brought to dangerous limits by the excessive issue of bank paper and the reckless expansion of credit facilities. This redundancy of credit has engendered "the spirit of reckless speculation": vast loans have been drawn from Europe; credit has been extended in domestic trade far beyond the point warranted by solid demand for goods; purchases of "unproductive" public lands have multiplied wildly; speculative plunges have been taken at absurd prices in lands in or adjoining existing or anticipated cities and villages— again "unproductive"—and immense sums have been sunk in internal improvement projects, often "ruinously improvident." In the course of the bubble craze, much labor "that should have been applied to agriculture" has been directed to less sound pursuits, and the nation has been reduced to the shameful necessity of importing grain from Europe in large amounts. The disease has corrupted character owing to "the rapid growth among all classes, and especially in our great commercial towns, of luxurious habits founded too often on merely fancied wealth and detrimental alike to the industry, the resources, and the morals of our people."[20]

The role of banks in the disaster is for Van Buren nearly self-evident. "Proneness to excessive issues has ever been the vice of the banking system," he argued, and banking in any form inevitably serves "to stimulate extravagance of enterprise by improvidence of credit." A new national bank would differ from the local institutions only in raising the additional menace of "a concentrated moneyed power, hostile to the spirit and threatening the permanency of our republican institutions." His is not, Van Buren insists, an unlimited attack upon credit as such: "The credit bestowed on probity and industry is the just reward of merit and an honorable incentive to further acquisition. None oppose it who love their country and understand its welfare." But, he adds,

when it is unduly encouraged; when it is made to inflame the public mind with the temptations of sudden and unsubstantial wealth; when it turns industry into paths that lead sooner or later to disappointment and distress, it becomes liable to censure and needs correction. Far from helping probity

[20] *Ibid.*, pp. 325–26.

and industry, the ruin to which it leads falls most severely on the great laboring classes, who are thrown suddenly out of employment, and by the failure of magnificent schemes never intended to enrich them are deprived in a moment of their only resource.[21]

After the crisis eased, Van Buren did not relent in his attack upon the still uncorrected evil of leaving public funds at the disposal of agencies whose very nature prompts them to overextend credit and so "[to seduce] industry from its regular and salutary occupations by the hope of abundance without labor, and [to derange] the social state by tempting all trades and professions into the vortex of speculation on remote contingencies." The prospect moves the second leader to one of his angrier attacks: such encouragement of expansionist banking tends to create "a concentrated moneyed power" with powerful political ambitions, imperiling "the community at large." Here again Van Buren would war not upon banks as such—"[I] never doubted their utility when properly managed in promoting the interests of trade, and through that channel the other interests of the community"—but upon their exclusive privileges, their dangerous economic tendencies when they are tempted by large deposits of public funds, and their evil inclination "to control the legislation of the country and pervert the operations of the Government to their own purposes."[22]

After 1838, when Van Buren faced a recurrence of crisis conditions, notably a second suspension of specie payments by the banks, he was enraged by the behavior of "a bloated credit system," "that delusive system of credits." This second suspension he found unwarranted by any failure in public confidence; the banks chose to suspend when the economy was thriving, for the sole purpose of preventing curtailment of credits to one narrow section of the community. Not only must the independent treasury measure be pressed with fresh urgency; but an alarming threat should be opened to the public view. Recent trends in banking practice have gone far toward undermining "the former course of business in this country," with attendant disasters for banks and individuals alike. Foreign trade, for example, once rested upon the exchange of real economic objects, including specie. Now, "mere credit has become too commonly the basis of trade," and foreign debts mount. Many banks have moved directly into the conduct of foreign commerce and "usurped the business, while they impair

[21] *Ibid.*, pp. 328, 331, 334.
[22] *Ibid.*, pp. 494–96.

the stability, of the mercantile community." They establish agencies abroad, deal extensively in stocks and merchandise, encourage the issue and sale of state securities until the foreign money market is glutted. Through large foreign loans they acquire additional means for inciting all sorts of domestic speculation. As long as foreign creditors remain credulous, and United States agricultural exports are sufficient to service the debt, all looks well. But with the first hesitation abroad, or any failure of the domestic economy to provide the means for servicing the debt, down comes the whole flimsy structure. Specie takes flight, domestic loans are drastically contracted when business can least bear the shock, solid property goes up for forced sale, banks suspend, and an impoverished community is left with a "fluctuating and depreciated currency."[23]

This sorry history of ruin reveals no chance misfortune but "the results of the irresistible laws of trade or credit." There is "a chain of necessary dependence" among all banking institutions, extending upward from the small local concern to the chief banks in domestic trade centers, and finally to the powerful London bankers. "It is thus," Van Buren argues, "that an introduction of a new bank into the most distant of our villages places the business of that village within the influence of the money power in England; it is thus that every new debt which we contract in that country seriously affects our own currency and extends over the pursuits of our citizens its powerful influence." In consequence, any "policy, necessity, or caprice" which prevails among the masters of English credit can determine the conditions of economic life for the ordinary American. The usual disclaimer—this is after all the sober, soothing voice of a political craftsman—appears respectfully in the margin: of course Van Buren does not mean to arrest "fair commercial dealing" between England and the United States "based on reciprocal benefits"; he seeks only to avoid the consequences of "the resistless law of a credit currency and credit trade."[24]

For the guidance of national policy, Van Buren's conclusions are simple: withdraw the deposits from state banks; establish the independent treasury; prevent the rise of a new national bank; conduct all federal transactions in specie. Through the hard-money policy, above all, the government should "hold erect the principles of morality and

23 *Ibid.,* pp. 615–16, 542–44.
24 *Ibid.,* pp. 544–47.

law, constantly executing our own contracts in accordance with the provisions of the Constitution, and thus [serve] as a rallying point by which our whole country may be brought back to that safe and honored standard." Beyond this limited circle of example, caution, and indirect restraint the national government, in Van Buren's view, has no power to move. Something more in the way of banking regulation is left to the governments of the states. But the essential malady and remedy lie out of the reach of political power.[25]

Thus Van Buren shifts his argument to broader ground. Credit-mongers have learned to play expertly upon the "sanguine, energetic, and industrious character" of the American people, and have almost persuaded them to stake everything upon "gigantic banking institutions and splendid, but in many instances profitless, railroads and canals absorbing to a great extent in interest upon the capital borrowed to construct them the surplus fruits of national industry for years to come, and securing to posterity no adequate return for the comforts which the labors of their hands might otherwise have secured." Hope therefore lies only in a change of public feeling which will cause people to pause and think of the means to retire debts before contracting them, to cease running heedlessly into debt, to practice "buying less and selling more," to exercise "strict economy and frugality." Once we have removed the present burden—and we must pay in full for all we owe—the rule must be "retrenchment and reform" if ever America is to have "security for the future."[26]

However their motives are viewed, the opponents of this prescription must finally be judged as serving "to gain for the few an ascendancy over the many by securing to them[selves] a monopoly of the currency"; "to produce throughout society a chain of dependence which leads all classes to look to privileged associations for the means of speculation and extravagance"; and thus

to nourish, in preference to the manly virtues that give dignity to human nature, a craving desire for luxurious enjoyment and sudden wealth, which renders those who seek them dependent on those who supply them; to substitute for republican simplicity and economical habits a sickly appetite for effeminate indulgence . . . , and at last to fix upon us, instead of those equal political rights the acquisition of which was alike the object and supposed reward of our Revolutionary struggle, a system of exclusive privileges conferred by partial legislation.

[25] *Ibid.*, pp. 547–52.
[26] *Ibid.*, pp. 552–54.

Even among a people so "enlightened and pure" as Americans the struggle against such profound evils demands a full measure of "the self-denial, the intelligence, and the patriotism of our citizens." No other nation could hope to meet the danger without bloodshed and immense sacrifice.[27]

"Dismantling" and "restoration" were the key terms in my analysis of the moral posture of Andrew Jackson *vis-à-vis* the Jacksonian economic world. Martin Van Buren, it seems to me, clarifies and extends the Jacksonian view. In Van Buren's rhetoric, land and farm hold their *thematic* preeminence; i.e., they represent the norms for the good republic. Evil rises again from elements in the economic order which are forced and artificial, chancy and restless, complex and insubstantial, avaricious and privileged, soft and luxurious. In the evaluation of economy and society, the primary categories continue to be private character and political order, both in the distinctive sense established by Jackson's usage. The image of the Old Republic still provides the end and measure of private action and public policy.

[27] *Ibid.*, pp. 554–55.

# 8

# A PURITAN VERSION

## THEODORE SEDGWICK

❧

The Yale man as Jacksonian now seems a jarring notion, and the old Federalist in league with upstart Democrats borders on paradox. To men familiar with the times this juxtaposition of labels would not perhaps seem quite so queer. Federalism came to offer, after Jefferson's "revolution" of 1800, pretty slim and slick footing; after the notorious Hartford Convention affair it offered nothing to discourage spirited young men from taking off on a variety of political adventures. In New York a whole school of the "high-minded" Federalists entered a tricky and uncertain alliance with Tammany Democrats; some of their names persist into the Jacksonian era. There were comparable alliances in New England and Pennsylvania. Indeed the Whigs of 1840, transported by their acquisition of a log-cabin candidate, sang twelve verses on the subject, beginning this way:

> When this old hat was new, the people used to say,
> The best among the Democrats were Harrison and Clay;
> The Locos now assume the name, a title most untrue,
> And most unlike their party name when my old hat was new.[1]

Of course the Jacksonians did not inherit bodily the principles or the following of the defunct Federalist party. Scattered evidence shows several Whig Philip Hones for each Theodore Sedgwick making his passage from the Yale of Timothy Dwight, through the high-Federalist lawyers' circle at Albany, to a final place among the

---

[1] Norton, *Tippecanoe Songs*, bound with *The Great Revolution*, pp. 85–86. On ex-Federalists among the Democrats, see Jabez D. Hammond, *The History of Political Parties in the State of New York*, I, 487, 528–31; II, 254–55, 325; and Arthur B. Darling, *Political Changes in Massachusetts, 1824–1848: A Study of Liberal Movements in Politics*, pp. 40–45, 60–71.

Jacksonian Democrats in his native Berkshire County, Massachusetts.
The point of interest here is not that Sedgwick's Democratic desti-
nation was fixed by his beginnings—it surely was not—but that a
Jacksonian affiliation was possible for such a man, and not unique.[2]

Following my interpretation of Jacksonian values, one can recognize some continuity of mood, at least, between the Federalist seeking
to stabilize the order of the Founders and the Jacksonian seeking to
restore the solid virtues of the Old Republic. Fenimore Cooper, as
discussed above, found the transition natural enough. When another
country gentleman of Federalist background, Theodore Sedgwick,
son of a prominent Federalist of the same name, set down his views
of private economic conduct, he had no need to invent novel economic
or moral principles in order to sustain Jacksonian political conclusions.
Out of Poor Richard he could draw a blend of the acquisitive spirit,
the prudential virtues, and the tempering obligations of stewardship.
The puritanical code of the western Massachusetts township, crossed
with the squire's creed which had given a non-Hamiltonian component
to the old Federalism, could speak again in Sedgwick's guide to *Public
and Private Economy*. A Whig of similar origins would have argued
many of the same propositions concerning property and poverty: the
brotherhood of rural Yankees outweighed a great many transient
associations. Nevertheless, it is important that Sedgwick made his
version of the case congruent not with Henry Clay's American system
but with Andrew Jackson's stern defense of Old Republican values.[3]

Designed as a contribution to the popular understanding of economic matters, Sedgwick's work takes up the Jacksonian economic
position where high political policy leaves off: where government has
abandoned improper powers, dissolved its illegitimate ties with individuals and associations, mastered its few essential and simple public
tasks, and returned the control of economic affairs substantially to
responsible individual enterprisers, under the "laws of trade." Thus
Sedgwick provides informal, nonpolitical directives for economic be-

---

[2] See the Sedgwick family sketches in the *Dictionary of American Biography*,
XVI, 549–52; and Dorfman, *Economic Mind*, II, 650–52.

[3] Theodore Sedgwick [II], *Public and Private Economy*, Part I. A second part,
reporting observations in England, appeared several years later: *Public and Private
Economy. Illustrated by Observations Made in England in the Year 1836*, Part II.
His travels taught him that he had been entirely right in his previous economic judgments, and added to his store of knowledge some further horrible examples of intemperance and wasteful extravagance.

havior. His is not the only code compatible with Jacksonian loyalty. Yet Sedgwick in fact joined this code and this loyalty; there is a broad streak of logical consistency in the association; and so we may examine Sedgwick's book as an extreme version of the Jacksonian persuasion, which isolates a few themes common to the movement and develops them almost to the final limits—to the point where they would split the party creed into its diverse parts.

Incidentally, the inquiry will suggest the indispensability of the Jacksonians' dramatic symbolism for converting a statement of traditional social values into a belligerent partisan creed. For Sedgwick's book is a moral treatise on household economy, a puritanical Jacksonian's home companion. To give his maxims the force of a social protest, one must superimpose the missing figures of party rhetoric—the Bank, the paper aristocracy, the treasury leeches—that defined the conflict of good and evil for Jacksonian Democrats.

### Property: Reward and Punishment

Property, Sedgwick writes, is power; it is also happiness, the means toward economic progress and individual mental improvement, a necessary condition of social virtue and personal political independence.[4] Nevertheless, he warns: "It would be a poor task indeed to spend time in showing how property is to be gained and preserved, unless with a design, that a noble use should be made of it."[5] This reservation applies particularly to the happiness which property may bring. Wealth taken for itself, or for the uses of sensual indulgence, pomp, and pride, is not a source of happiness. Nor is property to be counted a blessing when it represents "ill-gotten, *disproportioned wealth*"—"wealth obtained by unfair dealings, by fraud, by oppression, by monopoly, by which I mean *legal privileges given to some, and denied to others.*"[6]

When the intended use of property is good and the means of acquisition are legitimate, then all blessings will flow plentifully. Persuasive as these beneficial consequences of property may be, there is further reassurance to be found in the reflection that God has implanted in men a "universal passion" for property, which must

[4] *Ibid.*, pp. 14–22.     [5] *Ibid.*, p. 13.     [6] *Ibid.*, p. 15.

therefore be good. God further demonstrates the value of property "by making the virtues of order, diligence, and temperance, essential to the acquisition of it."[7] Thus it is that political economy may be accounted "a beautiful science," teaching us to manage our affairs so as "to diffuse happiness by spreading plenty among the whole people."[8] The forbidding mysteries of economics reside not in the nature of the science but only in an unnecessarily esoteric vocabulary: "If learned writers would use the words, or any thing like them, that the common man employs . . . the mystery would disappear" and all could profit from their plain truths.[9]

Sedgwick's solid regard for the advantages of property gives his work its dominant theme. His survey of the life of the poor in America thus becomes a negative documentation for the blessings of property. Property and poverty are conceived as fixed states of reward and punishment, between which people move according to personal traits: their habits, their virtues and vices. Sedgwick offers little institutional analysis of poverty, less on economic principles; little comfort and less compassion for the poor. Americans, he seems to say with his minute account of the impoverished condition, are too blithe, too thoughtless: the pit of poverty even here is wide and deep, and ready for all who neglect the proper ways of getting and spending.

In Sedgwick's survey the American poor experience all the classic misfortunes of their kind: excessively hard labor; lack of leisure; poor food, home, fuel; a forced reliance upon costly credit purchases —all summed up on the material side in a higher mortality rate, and on the spiritual side in lowered defenses against vice. His class of the poor includes not only paupers but the day laborers of city and country; many small farmers; the manufacturing population of the Northeast; journeymen mechanics, the "fashionable, expensive poor," and Western migrants. The lowest of these is the class of "day-labour," those whose bodily labors are hardest, whose privations are greatest. Generally they own no property, live hand to mouth, and must resort to charity to meet their emergencies.[10]

So intent is Sedgwick upon revealing the full toll of poverty in America that he gives the problem a scope and gravity incommensurate with any mere array of individual failures. In teaching by terrible

---

[7] *Ibid.*, p. 20.      [8] *Ibid.*, p. 29.      [9] *Ibid.*, p. 153.      [10] *Ibid.*, pp. 77–87, 95–96.

example the need for self-help, Sedgwick defines a situation almost beyond relief. The poor of New York City, for example—meaning here the day laborers—live, several families together, in noisome tenement apartments. Children may go about almost naked, and in some tenements they must remain in bed all day during the winter to stay warm. Living standards are further depressed by the poor man's being forced to buy in small quantities on exorbitant credit terms. The tenements are in many instances leased by their owners to jobbers, who in turn "underlet" to the poor at "the most screwing bargains that can be made."[11]

Among the country poor—again, the day-labor class—perhaps no more than one in eight or ten may own a strip of land, and many are involuntary vagrants. One-half or more lack one of the necessities of rural life, a cow; few have a garden to augment their food supply. Rural day laborers are in their own fashion as poorly clothed and housed as their urban counterparts. Poverty denies them the plainest comforts, even the simple pleasures of having neat children and of being helpful to their neighbors. Probably one-half of these rural day laborers do not even take a country newspaper. Liquor becomes their sole escape from a harsh and meager existence; they are "beyond all others the drinking people of the United States."[12]

Above the line of misery but still within the bounds of poverty are many of the small-farm proprietors. Farmers of the Northern states live mostly in old wooden houses, many of them comfortless and decaying. Their children are "wretchedly educated" in the common schools. Their land deteriorates for lack of manure and clover seed. Gardens are rare, livestock are largely of the scrub variety. The case grows desperate for the many farmers who sink deep in debt to storekeepers, and permit their farms to be "fatally mortgaged" to banks and insurance companies.[13]

The census of poverty extends to the "manufacturing classes" of the North. They consist in considerable part of "poor broken-down people with large families" who "resort to the manufactories" as a last chance for livelihood. Most of this class lack houses of their own, as well as gardens and cows, or other domestic animals. In rural areas, the factory population live huddled together in company houses, often six to a room. The prevalence of "store-pay" imposes "a dead weight

[11] *Ibid.*, pp. 97–99.    [12] *Ibid.*, pp. 100–104.    [13] *Ibid.*, pp. 106–9.

upon poor people." The hard lives of the manufacturing population can be seen in "the pale faces, sunken eyes, and emaciated figures" of so many of them.[14]

And so on through the remaining varieties of poverty in America. The total report gives alarming dimensions to poverty in Jacksonian society—a far grimmer picture than most other contemporary sources reveal. So broad a curse, so many victims, suggest a damning judgment upon the whole economic order as it is coming to be. Sedgwick's diagnosis of poverty as a punishment for private vice or weakness, and his prescriptions following from this, would seem indeed a skimpy product of the evidence he details so relentlessly. Why, then, does Sedgwick not conclude that a transformation of the social structure itself has destroyed individual opportunity and personal accountability?

Sedgwick finds the source of growing poverty not in new institutional patterns but in the general corruption of men's ways. The troubles of the times (evidenced by the depth and spread of poverty) reflect a falling off in virtue and prudence, morals and character. Thus Sedgwick can amass the details of poverty until he approaches the dimensions of a grave social problem, and at the same time hold to a case method of diagnosis and cure. His poverty report should be read as a summation of discrete instances of social malady, and as a prescription for the restoration of a wholesome people, man by man.

The initial lesson drawn from the record of poverty is unmistakable: the class of day laborers "has one lesson to learn, in common with all poor people, and that is, if they expect to improve, they must put their own shoulders to the wheel."[15] Again, with special reference to the rural poor: the simple pleasures of life may be enjoyed by all "when the people come to care for, and to work in earnest mainly for these things."[16] The "shocking and disgusting" aspect of poverty among the manufacturing population in a naturally abundant nation prompts the reflection that poverty will disappear "when the people at large shall have acquired any just ideas of economy, and of the true value of riches."[17] The people "must work out their own salvation."[18] Always the double moral: salvation is individual; and it consists first in the recognition of the value of property.

The first and perhaps the most fundamental sign of individual

[14] *Ibid.*, pp. 110–12.     [15] *Ibid.*, p. 96.     [16] *Ibid.*, p. 103.
[17] *Ibid.*, p. 109.     [18] *Ibid.*, p. 113.

recognition of the worth of property is evidenced in spending habits. The case of the "fashionable, expensive poor" provides a prime negative instance. This is a group recruited from no one distinct class, but from all foolish souls with a propensity for "following the fashions" of the rich. They see everything through the eyes of the rich, but have the pocketbooks of the poor. While they suffer for want of good, substantial, necessary garments which might be made at home, they run to fashionable milliners and tailors. And so with everything: personal and household finery draws them into debt when they have not a pot to cook in.[19]

The case is similar with those farm women who run to the stores for "fashionable gewgaws, and prefer fine ribbons to fine farms."[20] Journeymen mechanics rarely own homes or save a penny, yet their women are "running after capes, feathers, ribbons, flounces, and ten thousand gew-gaws, which consume the substance of so many poor people."[21] A view of the hardships of poor settlers in the West suggests that a small part of "the millions, fooled away yearly both by rich and poor, would if saved by each individual, ward off many of the evils" of poverty.[22] Sedgwick is dismayed that Americans consider it the height of "gentility and fashion" to consume large quantities of champagne; it flows freely in the West-bound boats, and, in the interior of Illinois or Michigan, there is—he says—hardly a village of forty houses where champagne cannot be found.[23] One central theme runs through the entire set of nine "practical lessons" yielded by the record of poverty in America: that if men will stop making and selling gewgaws and produce and buy only useful things, wealth will accumulate and spread through society, all will work, and capital will be fully and effectively used.[24]

The immediate economic point of Sedgwick's commentary on foolish spending is, of course, that private incomes are wasted which could otherwise satisfy the simple necessities of life, and, more significantly, could form a capital to elevate the saver to a more responsible and rewarding economic station.[25] The farming family's "mere neglect and want of economy," especially the running after finery, deprives it of good buildings, good fields, good gardens, good stock; briefly, runs the property down, puts the family in the hands of

---

[19] *Ibid.*, pp. 113–15.    [20] *Ibid.*, p. 106.    [21] *Ibid.*, p. 113.    [22] *Ibid.*, p. 120.
[23] *Ibid.*, p. 126.    [24] *Ibid.*, pp. 130–31.    [25] *Ibid.*, pp. 106–9.

creditors, and finally forces it to sell out at half value and drift West.[26] If the journeyman mechanic would learn to save at least half his annual wages, he could secure economic independence, with all its blessings.[27] Most of the distresses of the poor Western settler could be avoided with "a little independence, a little fortune, perhaps a small sum of money" such as "almost any of our young manufacturers, mechanics, or farmers' sons may lay up in a very few years" by avoiding sensual indulgence, the craze for gewgaws.[28] The great reform of the age would be teaching the "common people" a "wiser way of spending their money."[29]

Sumptuary reform attacks not only wasteful consumption but wasteful production as well. The people must determine to avoid "the soap bubble business"; to buy and to *make* only useful articles. It is within the power of the laborers to cultivate "productive" industry, less by influencing public policy than by enforcing their own private veto power as consumers, and by exercising the "independence" of the worker who commands capital.[30] The workingmen can overcome their individual poverty, and thus relieve communal poverty, "by labouring for what they . . . want or ought to want, and then expending the produce of their labor for what they want, or ought to want."[31] The soap bubble business should be left to the class of "idlers": to lackeys, servants, lazy sons of the rich, mere men of fashion, "lottery people," and a few "gentlemen" who occupy themselves with breeding race horses.[32]

Plain and simple habits of consumption, then—with their corollaries, tenacious (seemingly miraculous) saving, prudent investment, and useful production—constitute the likeliest ways out of poverty toward property. Gewgaws and fancy things, champagne in Illinois and hard drink everywhere, are marks of a spending folly that condemns the poor to lasting failures. For Sedgwick, temperance reform, especially in the rural areas, has been "the greatest moral and intellectual reformation that ever took place in the same time in the world,"[33] and "one great cause of the present unparalleled increase in the wealth of the country."[34] Finally, education, as it reveals the value of property and augments the capacity for acquisition, completes

[26] *Ibid.*, p. 113.     [27] *Ibid.*, p. 124.     [28] *Ibid.*, pp. 225–26.     [29] *Ibid.*, p. 161.
[30] *Ibid.*, pp. 183–84.     [31] *Ibid.*, p. 217.     [32] *Ibid.*, p. 183.
[33] *Ibid.*, p. 176.     [34] *Ibid.*, p. 177.

the round of essential changes:[35] a reform mainly in the realm of customs, usages, and fashions; aimed primarily against "trinkets, finery, gew-gaws, fashionable trifles, dainties, and poisonous drink";[36] to be achieved by means of individual self-improvement. There is, for Sedgwick, "but one *true* way—it is in the acquisition of property, virtue, and education."[37] The rock is property.

### Producer and Idler: Grading Scales

Several schematic notions emerge from Sedgwick's poverty-property discussion and both underline and qualify its meaning. When the sketches of poverty have been finished with certain useful lessons, given above, Sedgwick proposes a fundamental distinction between the consumer, identified with the idler, and the producer, identified with the industrious.

The consumer-idler is one of the very few Americans who consume without working, or whose productive efforts yield nothing useful—lackeys, gamblers, men of fashion, and the like.[38] A respectable representative of the type is the gentleman farmer—"a man who is not obliged to work on his farm"—but he is a figure very rare in America.[39] More generally, persons who live upon their incomes are too few in the United States to constitute a social class.[40] For example, in Sedgwick's home county of Berkshire, in western Massachusetts, he can find not more than two persons who live so; more might, if they chose, simply consume their means, but in America "to live without some regular employment or industry is not reputable."[41] Finally, some consumer-idlers do live and thrive by "lucky speculation, fortunate trade, or inheritance"; but again "there is no *class* that is not compelled to work."[42]

What remains is "the whole people"[43] less a few eccentrics. "It is true, then, in the best and strictest sense," Sedgwick concludes, "that the great body of the people of the United States are *working people.*"[44] Farmers, mechanics, manufacturers, and in general "labourers" are obviously "producers of wealth." So too are judge, lawyer, sheriff, artist, and an indefinite list of others, despite some lamentable prejudices to the contrary.[45]

[35] *Ibid.*, pp. 153, 227–28, 239.      [36] *Ibid.*, p. 244.      [37] *Ibid.*, p. 225.
[38] *Ibid.*, p. 183.      [39] *Ibid.*, p. 229.      [40] *Ibid.*, p. 232.
[41] *Ibid.*, p. 240.      [42] *Ibid.*, p. 232.      [43] *Ibid.*
[44] *Ibid.*, p. 221.      [45] *Ibid.*, p. 235.

In summary, Sedgwick casts out of grace only a few uncommon types whose occupations offer neither the best chances for material success nor any hope of honor under the reigning standards of social esteem. These irregulars aside, Americans earn their incomes, and almost every calling confers the honorific title of workingman and producer of wealth. The contrast between consumer-idler and industrious producer thus does not indicate a *problem* for Sedgwick, but a fundamental and favorable condition of American society. The situation becomes problematic only when public institutions and measures intrude upon the natural state of affairs, imposing false distinctions and special privileges; or when private character and morals are defective and so render workingmen incapable of sustaining their proper creative role. Hence Sedgwick's concentration upon the individual and the private as source and remedy of substantial social evils.[46]

The special esteem in which Sedgwick holds the farmer suggests some further distinctions within the all but universal working class. Among creative men the farmer represents a peculiar center of virtue and perhaps the highest embodiment of productive labor.[47] Sedgwick's "common farmer" is half manual laborer—"a *working* man," doing the same tasks as his hired hands, dirty work and chores included—and half "mental labourer," the lord of his soil, planning and directing its uses, counting the profits and losses. Like the greatest in the land, he has responsibility for "maintaining his rank," for it is a deep disgrace to lose the paternal acres to a bank or a speculative conniver and so be forced westward into exile.[48] The farmer's worth is reflected in his political position: in many states "the farmers are clothed with more power . . . than any other class, and probably more than all others."[49]

Given a political system which denies special privileges—"there shall be no institutions *by law* that shall make men unequal"—"*self-elevation*" operates as the grand American principle. "This, then, is the great consolation in the United States to every working man, that nearly every other man is a labourer also; and that all, without distinction, have many opportunities of elevating themselves, of passing from one business to another, from one class to another."[50] In one respect, then, Sedgwick presents a society of equals (both before the

---

[46] *Ibid.*, pp. 225–28, 232.      [47] *Ibid.*, pp. 221–22.      [48] *Ibid.*, p. 229.
[49] *Ibid.*, p. 230.      [50] *Ibid.*, p. 225.

law and in their shared distinction as producers) freely rising and falling according to private habits and virtues. But there is more to his class divisions.

Providence, Sedgwick believes, assigns men places in higher or lower classes.[51] Self-elevation involves not an undifferentiated motion toward property but a rise through class levels invidiously distinguished. There is a "scale of labourers" rated according to the relative dominance of mental labor in the occupation. This reflects a "real distinction in nature," a distinction founded upon "individual character" and expressed in the desire of men to cultivate their minds. Thus there always will be "high and low, rich and poor, masters and servants, officers and their men, masters of ships and their crews, farmers and their labourers, master mechanics and journeymen, manufacturers and their workmen." In urging the Eastern farmer to hold rank by maintaining the paternal estate, Sedgwick seems to suggest a traditional basis of social status; but perhaps he is simply applying here the notion, long common among Yankees who stayed home, that the West was a barbarous country unfit for Christian settlement.[52]

Sedgwick can stretch his class-scale notion almost to meet the idea of station. In this light, many of the sumptuary restrictions noted earlier appear as censorship, not only upon living beyond one's means or wasting resources and energies, but upon living beyond one's place in life. Factory workers, for example, who are bidden to the astounding feat of saving one-half or more of their annual wages, receive assurance that they may "still live in a manner becoming their station."[53] Gewgaws and finery *for journeymen mechanics,* champagne *for poor clerks and Western settlers,* and generally the conspicuous consumption of the "fashionable poor" are sources of poverty, signs of imprudence and waste; and beyond these, damning evidence of the vice of impersonating a social superior.[54]

Mobility, according to Sedgwick, should be legally free and practically possible; yet it must be a passage between established stations, high and low, conducted with due respect for the proprieties of place along the social scale. Graded natural differences in gifts and character lend their distinctions to the trades of men, requiring various ranks, rewards, and codes of social conduct.[55]

[51] *Ibid.,* p. 224.    [52] *Ibid.,* pp. 227–28.    [53] *Ibid.,* p. 225.
[54] *Ibid.,* pp. 113–15, 126, 229.    [55] *Ibid.,* pp. 224–36.

*A Sort of Jacksonian: The Restoration Theme
Reviewed*

Sedgwick, then, falls in-bounds of the Jacksonian persuasion but falls, so to speak, intact and on his own feet. A random set of family traits shared by Sedgwick with Jackson and Van Buren would include: hostility toward privilege as a distortion and corruption of natural social arrangements; aversion to the ways of chance and cunning; contempt for softness and sensual indulgence; praise for the active and productive as against the passive and manipulative economic roles. All three consider debt a cardinal sin, and spun-out credit a kind of devil's lure. More systematically, they share a view of politics as a system of defense for the good private life. They take private life first in its economic aspect, in terms of property and occupation; and these in turn as sign and source of character and morals. The last terms convey both the things of worth which politics defends and the proper ground for worthy politics. All three men see a falling off from a better past in the decisive realm of character and morals, and predicate their hopes for wholesome progress on the return to a prior base of values.

In Sedgwick, strains of Yale, Federalism, Berkshire County, and railroad promotion are grafted on good Jacksonian stock: the result shows necessarily some unique features. Distinctions between his argument and the appeals of the national party leaders are reducible in part to differences in the context of discussion: thus Sedgwick writes about private economic conduct and he can largely *assume* the Jacksonian political framework, within which private economic fates determined by individual character form his center of concern. Again, he has not the direct responsibility for winning party battles and so can more freely sermonize the errant members of the almost boundless "working class" and barely notice the stained fringe of gambling, idling elements. In contrast, Jackson and Van Buren discuss precisely the question of establishing the political framework by correct public policy, and most readily assail social evil in the ways and purposes of classes who may be linked with rival parties.

Attributing to casual circumstance some force in determining Sedgwick's deviations from the line of Jackson and Van Buren, one yet finds much to be explained. Starting from a common view: there is substantial unity in the high place given to property-in-the-clear, to tangibles owned and controlled, to the debt-free and masterless man; briefly, to economic independence. Jackson and Van Buren root property, the good sort, in concrete conditions (finally, in the soil), and see their moral code as a natural expression of the habits of worthy occupations. Independence, for them, is best signified by the economic role of the independent farmer, who instinctively knows and follows the moral directives inherent in independent farming. From that source come rules and standards for a wide range of behavior, and for the use of the larger community.

In Sedgwick's divergent interpretation, independence seems to mean an abstract measure of means sufficient to permit private determination of economic behavior. The *kind* of property is not rigorously prescribed, if only it is not useless. Property is a neutral currency which can purchase responsibility; or, in terms more real for Sedgwick, it is a generalized way out of the hole of poverty and up to the level of accountable conduct. Jackson and Van Buren infuse a sound morality into property at the productive source and consequently tend to favor the older and simpler trades and rules of trade, whereas Sedgwick's search for the warrants and limits of abstract property leads him to prescribe a separate code of private conduct governing the attainment and right use of propertied independence. The God of the Puritans has made "the virtues of order, diligence, and temperance, essential to the acquisition of [property]";[56] His steward Sedgwick teaches "that a noble use should be made of it."[57]

The central terms of Sedgwick's case — property, the work-prudence-parsimony code, productivity, mental labor, self-elevation —point toward a broad acceptance of the rising economic order. Why not simply take the Sedgwick book as an authentic guide to success in the contemporary economic world? No doubt he thought it would serve that end.

Recall Tawney's portraits of the conscientious Protestant wrestling with new economic lures, swaying between apologetics and anathema. Sedgwick, by turning property into a uniform currency, appreciating the value of mental labor (the more flexible and free pursuits), exhorting men to acquisition, clearly edges out into his own economic age. Yet he cannot really see it: when he says property, he talks incessantly of grim poverty; when he says acquisition, the

56 *Ibid.*, p. 20.    57 *Ibid.*, p. 13.

talk is all of wicked spending; when he says producers, he talks of savers and wastrels. Essentially what Sedgwick wants of the new world is an endowment for the old church school.

The reduction of communal authority over economic affairs, as a principle, releases men to seek property according to their lights; so much is good laissez-faire doctrine and Sedgwick's view as well. For certain purposes this may be a sufficient sign of doctrinal accord; but pursued further, it leads to ambiguities. We are concerned here with the individual seeker: how he seeks, what he finds, and how he uses what he finds. Men may pursue a neat self-interest, taking cues from an automatically self-regulating market, and putting other matters in another universe of choice; or they may regard each transaction as an affair of conscience and the market as the meetinghouse of moral agents talking in a quasi-economic language.

For Sedgwick, I believe, the market may be the arbiter of prices, never of values, even economic values. It is surely of some importance that he will not discuss economic matters in the market idiom, will not weigh choices by the impersonal mechanism of the price system. In the place of self-interested competitors matching wants and skills under standard economic rules, Sedgwick sees each man bringing his virtue, wisdom, and character to market for a reward which is strictly economic only for the brief moment necessary to convert it into better goods—the wholesome goods of home and family life, the intellectual pleasures, the good of doing good. "It is by labouring for what they . . . want or ought to want, and then expending the produce of their labour for what they want, or ought to want," he says, that men obtain optimum satisfactions from their economic actions.[58] The invisible hand of Adam Smith turns private interest into general material welfare by way of maximum efficiency. The rather more obtrusive hand of Sedgwick turns excellence of character and conduct into general welfare (i.e., widespread excellence of character and conduct) with the interim aid of a property endowment.

If one could reduce these ambiguities in the relationship between Sedgwick's views and the standard rationale for a fluid market economy, there would still remain other distinctions of a more concrete sort, notably in Sedgwick's notions of mobility and station. Again, his surface theme would satisfy a variety of economic judges, in-

[58] *Ibid.*, p. 217.

cluding the conventional laissez-faire advocate: upward or downward motion in economy and society is essentially the private affair of responsible free agents. Neither the conspiracies of the money power nor the sufferings of injured innocence assume any serious importance for Sedgwick; indignation and compassion are not his style. And yet it is not the cool omniscience of the market place which guides and measures private progress through the economic ranks.

How far removed he is from the ordinary context of economic discussion appears in his incidental commentary upon one of the most portentous of the rising economic institutions, the factory. Like some of his contemporaries, Sedgwick can neither condemn out of hand the factory system of industrial organization nor come to terms with it. In his atomistic, moralizing view of the world, factories are the accidental work *milieu* of one contingent of the unpropertied poor; they represent no powerful economic principle. His emphasis is on the "poor broken-down people" who are reduced by desperation to seeking factory employment.[59] How the factory came to be there as a refuge, what changes it portends, are not his questions.

The "pale faces, sunken eyes, and emaciated figures" that people Sedgwick's industrial scene do not point to the cold indifference of capitalist greed, nor are they natural marks of the machine upon its operatives; neither remediable abuses nor inevitable by-evils of a system, they are simply one more form of punishment for propertylessness. And so he does not dispose of the system one way or another, except to spirit away its labor force by urging workers to raise a ransom from their wages and be off to greener fields. By fierce self-denial—putting aside a major portion of his income—the worker can purchase a property stake (perhaps in Western land) and with it a chance to lift himself to the dignity of economic independence. Presumably a prior exercise of prudence, industry, and self-denial by the nonmanufacturing population would keep them from the factories in the first place; i.e., prevent them from becoming economic outcasts ripe for recruitment.[60]

Progress for the unsuccessful, debt-bound farmers—the propertied poor—is a matter of digging in, not pulling out, but the purposes and even the devices are very much the same. The family farm is the family heritage, and it is to be saved by a fresh dedication to

[59] *Ibid.,* p. 110.      [60] *Ibid.,* pp. 110–12, 124, 225–26.

the old virtues. Dimly, perhaps, there may be a farm market and a greater economy in the background of the discussion; but in focus there is only the single farm enterprise under the rule of its master. The fate of the farm is the direct and almost exclusive consequence of his character. If he will mend his buildings, tend his garden, work his fields, save manure, breed better stock, and above all curb the buying fancies of his womenfolk, he will secure his honorable station in society.[61]

The West is a retreat for improvident failures, and a point of entry for surplus farmers' sons, young factory workers, immigrants, and others who by parsimony have raised the means to establish themselves as farm proprietors. Nothing about Sedgwick's West has the air of pioneering enterprise. The rewards of land speculation are ruled out (not even mentioned) : the land is seen never as alienable real estate, always as so many actual or potential independent farmsteads. He makes no bid to adventurers or squatters; he appeals rather to prudent, serious young men whose savings are an earnest of respectable intentions and a guarantee of their prospects. When this Yankee Jacksonian has finished taming the West, there is not even an innocent drink to be had.

Up From Poverty is the driving maxim of Sedgwick's work, and it may be partly for this reason that he has so little economic counsel for those who have arrived. Above the crucial property line, all is conservation and morality. His commandments are : do not squander, do not waste, hold on. His promises : comfort of a spare, simple sort, suited to station; improvement of mind and character; a life of independence disciplined by virtue. "Mental labour" is his nearest equivalent for the managerial and entrepreneurial skills, and this is exemplified most clearly by the half of the farmer that exercises *responsibility for decisions,* with full emphasis upon responsibility and little upon acumen, inventiveness, audacity, and drive. The positive directive for, say, mechanics who by force of character have assumed responsible command over their tools is that they produce "what they want or ought to want" (essential, useful things) ; and even these things are known best through their opposites (baubles, finery, gewgaws). Credit appears in Sedgwick's book only as the farmer's burden, the day laborer's Shylock, the fatal trap for the improvident.

[61] *Ibid.,* pp. 105–9.

In effect, partly by indirection, Sedgwick's economic code projects a world of small proprietors in which the objects of ownership would be single and simple, the rules of conduct timid, steady, retentive, conservative. Does this take him by a back road to the land of family farms, petty craft, and petty trade? Perhaps. More significantly, Sedgwick's sovereign remedy of property ownership leads him to fix a vacant stare upon the detailed surface of the actual economy; condemning little, he incorporates nothing in his value scheme from the side of venture, risk, novelty, and complex dealings. His final object is to make a general man of property, a steward in some ways like the old Puritan model and in others like the estate manager, whose task is to stock and guard the supplies, keep meticulous accounts, and manage an income that accrues as bounty and support for a life of virtuous industry.

# 9

# A FREE-TRADE VERSION

## WILLIAM LEGGETT

☙

For readers of the New York *Evening Post* and *The Plaindealer* during the 1830's, William Leggett provided a Loco-Foco version of Jacksonian Democracy, combining in their elemental simplicity the core ideas of Jeffersonian liberalism and free-trade economics. Out of the mixture he derived somehow an exciting class appeal, in which the ever querulous Philip Hone could find "the most profligate and disorganizing sentiments."[1] Something is apparently out of joint when such doctrine earns such a reading. The main Jeffersonian political principles were in no sense fighting words in the New York of the 1830's. And how should the generalities of laissez faire connote a Jacobin violence in nonfeudal, preindustrial American society?[2]

### The Outer Limits of Free Trade

There have been plenty of radical libertarians in the American past, but none, I think, surpasses William Leggett as an unconditional, almost obsessive advocate of laissez faire. Whatever the apparent subject of his discourse, the conclusion inevitably rediscovers the natural order of equal liberty, the natural laws of free trade. In a polity as close to economic liberty as we shall ever see, he took alarm at trivial or routine uses of political authority in the economic realm: denounced the public post office, state charities, emergency price con-

[1] Hone, *Diary*, I, 240; see also pp. 241, 399. For Leggett's editorial views I have drawn upon *A Collection of the Political Writings of William Leggett*, ed. Theodore Sedgwick, Jr.

[2] For a valuable discussion of Leggett as a bourgeois radical, see Richard Hofstadter, "William Leggett, Spokesman of Jacksonian Democracy," *Political Science Quarterly*, LVIII (December 1943), 581–94. Cf. Dorfman, *Economic Mind*, II, 653–54.

trols, usury laws, police regulation of butchers and bakers, public weighmasters; and even questioned state intervention against monopolistic combinations. Leggett's concern with these fringe violations of equal-rights and free-trade principles reveals important overtones of the laissez-faire argument as many radical Jacksonians understood it.

In almost every instance of Leggett's laissez-faire extremism there is an explicit primary concern with rights and power; strictly economic considerations form to the rear of the argument. Thus for him the proposal for a state asylum for insane paupers is fundamentally wrong because it would give excessive power to the governor, multiply the evils of patronage and corruption. Such an institution would lead next to a grand state poorhouse for the sane, and on to an indefinite proliferation of public charities; thus "one abuse of government would step upon the heels of another."[3] He attacks the government post office on the same grounds: such an institution inevitably serves as a political machine (even, he confesses, under Jackson's benign rule), as another instrument of patronage and corruption.[4] To regulate the weight of bread there must be more official parasites, prying inspectors, laws and more laws.[5] Every public weighmaster appointed would enlarge the band of placemen serving the combined monopoly and officeholder interest which already rules the state.[6] Altogether these criticisms develop out of Leggett's deep distrust of ambitious government, draining the people's livelihood to support a corps of pliant officeholders and employing the public power in the interest of a privileged clique. In view of the reputation of Jacksonian Democracy as creator of the spoils system—a deserved reputation but a considerably exaggerated one, as Leonard White and other recent scholars have shown—it may be difficult to recognize the force of the Jacksonian plea to cut the power, cost, and clientele of government.[7]

A related evil is the tendency to carry political controls into the details of private life. Provoked by a scheme for municipal licensing of butchers and the legal enforcement of certain apprenticeship rules, Leggett warns that local officials may well be expected to "take upon

[3] Leggett, *Political Writings,* I, 82; see generally pp. 79–83.
[4] *Ibid.,* I, 245–47.
[5] *Ibid.,* II, 120–22.
[6] *Ibid.,* I, 256–59.
[7] See Leonard D. White, *The Jacksonians; A Study in Administrative History, 1829–1861.*

themselves to regulate your private affairs, reader, or our own."[8]
Again, will government be satisfied to dictate a uniform size for bread
loaves; or will it not soon demand that everything be cut to one
measure, even—for once Leggett permits a faint show of humor—
coats and pantaloons?[9] His opposition to the public weighmaster can
be compressed into a simple dictum: "The weighing of merchandise
is a matter with which legislation has nothing to do."[10] Here is a Jeffersonian principle brought literally down to the municipal level, and
turning in the process from a promise to a grumble.

The plea for a free-trade postal service suggests another element
in Leggett's special use of the language of laissez faire. Not only
would a private, competitive postal system reduce the evils of patronage and corruption; it would almost certainly improve operating efficiency. Under the laws of supply and demand adequate mail service
would be provided without the burden of supporting a useless and
indeed harmful political machine. And—the point for emphasis—the
expansion of private service would follow the guidance of "the system
of nature and reason."[11] Public enterprise has created a "hot-bed" or
"force-pump" system of development, based on the practice of extending service prematurely to remote areas. Justified as an encouragement to rapid settlement, the policy often leads only to the special
advantage of land speculators who can steer emigrants to regions
"which perhaps God and nature meant should remain uninhabited for
ages to come." Under the governance of free trade, mail service would
be expanded gradually and prudently; it would not try blunderingly
to anticipate and lead, but would watch and wait until natural lines of
growth could be known and followed with reasonable security.[12] There
is very little of the bull in the Jacksonian economist as free trader:
big government means for him not a tendency toward bureaucratic
conservatism but the perpetual threat of reckless initiative, of wasteful
adventure. The root evils, of course, are still power concentration and
class privilege; but these related economic characteristics of reckless-
ness and wastefulness add material to moral and political costs.

[8] Leggett, *Political Writings,* II, 220.
[9] *Ibid.,* II, 120–22.
[10] *Ibid.,* I, 259. One is reminded a little of Pierre Poujade's appeals to the indignant small taxpayers of France in the mid-1950's—the curdled leftover of a long-lived
sentiment.
[11] *Ibid.,* I, 247.
[12] *Ibid.,* I, 245–47.

Leggett's editorials discussing voluntary economic combination are in many ways his most drastic assertion of confidence in laissez-faire principles. For here he makes the natural laws of trade a self-enforcing mechanism powerful enough to smash any nonpolitical attempt at defiance by economic combinations. The laws are found not only normative (as the formula for an efficiency model) and statistical (as a summation of the consequences of alternative modes of action), but literally self-enforcing and inviolable. If monopolistic combinations were discovered on the business or the labor side, Leggett "would hold them responsible only to those natural and immutable principles of trade which will infallibly teach them their error, if they do not graduate the price according to the relations of demand and supply."[13] He affirmed the right of workingmen to organize, as a legitimate application of the general liberal principle of freedom of association; this was for the time and in the practical situation an unconventional, even a courageous, stand. Yet it is clear that Leggett, a major editorial spokesman for the "radical" Loco-Foco forces in New York, saw no more positive merit in trade unions than in business combinations as agencies to control the terms of the economic bargain. On the contrary, he could tolerate their misguided monopolistic efforts only because of their manifest futility.[14]

The one editorial which speaks with full favor of "the great instrument of the rights of the poor—*associated effort*" refers neither to the ordinary functions of "business" unionism nor to any labor efforts of a proto-socialist or welfare type. The specific action Leggett approves is an effort to organize a public meeting of mechanics and laborers to protest the payment of wages in uncurrent bank notes. Thus he supports a quasi-political combination to limit the effects of a monopoly banking system, resting upon a political grant of privilege. And for this end he would prefer the direct use of political authority: public measures to prevent government from dispensing those chartered privileges which lead to the circulation of an unstable paper currency.[15]

Now most writers in the laissez-faire tradition would allow a significant role for government in maintaining the free-market framework; and if they argue that the laws of trade cannot be defied with

[13] *Ibid.*, II, 224.
[14] *Ibid.*, II, 125–26, 128–31, 221–25.
[15] *Ibid.*, II, 125–26.

impunity, they mean that the general community must pay the costs of monopolistic advantages in the form of excessive and inflexible commodity prices, productive inefficiencies, misallocated resources. Leggett's extreme faith in the immediate, automatic effectiveness as well as the objective rightness of the market mechanism, and his relative indifference toward the contrary schemes of men (so long as they do not command the instrumentalities of the state), suggest two alternative interpretations: either he conceives the market as an irresistible natural force impersonally determining the affairs of a mass economic society; or he sees the market as a personalized trading center, the meeting place of agents relatively equal in economic power and fully informed about each other's business.

Leggett's characterization of these combination cases and his manner of arguing them seem to me much closer to the latter view. The main instances relate to flour, coal, and local wage payments. The alleged monopolists—interestingly, Leggett is not inclined to credit tales of business conspiracy where no governmental act is involved— are local dealers in consumer goods. None, with the partial exception of the *labor* monopoly, is conceded strength enough to manage prices even within the municipal market. His general remedies for the evil of combination are wonderfully simple and undemanding: patient waiting until the natural causes of shortage and high price pass; rooting out all those politically based privileges and costly offices which tax and dislocate trade. A special recommendation to the consumer faced with high coal prices is revealing: if—against the probabilities —he is convinced that the dealers have put together a temporary monopolistic combination, then he may escape the burden simply by importing his own coal from Pennsylvania.[16] One is moved to give a literal interpretation to Leggett's notion of the market process as "the free exercise of confidence between man and man."[17]

---

[16] *Ibid.*, II, 128–31. It is curious that this doctrinaire free-trader, unlike some of his rival New York editors, argued against an Albany inquiry to determine whether a combination of dealers had forced coal prices up. Even if there were an improper combination, "the laws of trade are a much better defense . . . than any laws which the legislature at Albany can make." Of five reasons Leggett offered for the high coal prices, four referred directly to governmental acts: monopolistic grants to producers and carriers, tariffs, municipal fees. The fifth referred to an inflationary spurt which, in Leggett's theory, derived from government banking policy. *Ibid.*, II, 130–31. Cf. Adam Smith's comment: "People of the same trade seldom meet together, even for merriment and diversion, but the conversation ends in a conspiracy against the public, or in some contrivance to raise prices." *The Wealth of Nations*, p. 128.

[17] Leggett, *Political Writings*, II, 334.

The combined testimony of all these fringe cases does not challenge Richard Hofstadter's classification of the author as a doctrinaire economic liberal of the most extreme sort. It does perhaps suggest some further clues to the way free-trade extremism might have been construed by Leggett's readers—friendly and otherwise—as the expression of a radical appeal. The leading economic trends which were accelerating during the Jacksonian era, especially in Leggett's rising metropolis, lend almost nothing directly to his discussion. The movement toward the factory, toward a national market, toward a vast credit network—in short, toward industrial and finance capitalism—lends nothing to his free-trade faith. Leggett is not Jefferson—his world is the city and its business life—but he is even less an early prophet of the liberty which perpetually revolutionizes the economic basis of life, plunges men into bold ventures, detaches them from customary neighborhood dealings, reorients them to the great society of strangers linked by the cash nexus.

Neither can Leggett reasonably be called a herald of a new laborite welfare democracy. Rather, on the evidence of his extreme positions, he is a good Jacksonian for whom economic liberty is in the first instance a negative principle: an escape from legal privileges and controls deriving from the state for the power and profit of the few. Within the formal outlines of Leggett's free-trade order the reader finds, in local illustrations and examples, signs of a realm of simple, man-to-man exchanges. Liberty comes to represent the slow and prudent pace, correcting as it goes all kinds of error, from false weights and measures to improbable wanderings of the mail express. Authority in economic affairs portends privilege and exploit, of course; but also petty inquisition, gnawing taxes, and forced—thus false and wasteful—progress.

## The Simple Order of Nature

But one must move in from the margins toward the center of Leggett's editorial message. "This day," he wrote when Jackson retired from the presidency, "completes a period that will shine in American history with more inherent and undying lustre, than any other which the chronicler has yet recorded, or which perhaps will ever form a portion of our country's annals." The greatness of Jackson has not been in what he has created but in what he has prevented and restored. The tide of "aristocratic innovation" has been stopped, perhaps forever, and equal liberty is again the rule in the republic. Reckless, corrupting government expenditures have ceased; the poisonous Bank conspiracy has been arrested; there is a full treasury; foreign tangles have been settled by the "direct and manly character" of Jackson's diplomacy. Posterity will inherit the example of this man of "intrepid bravery, earnest patriotism, keen sagacity, nice honour, inexorable honesty, and invincible firmness." *Fidei Defensor.* Jackson's administration may well appear in retrospect the decisive moment of American history.[18]

This image of Jackson brings into focus the main theme of Leggett's argument. The great end for Democrats, he writes, is "to institute the natural system in all matters both of politics and political economy." Men need only follow this "simple order of nature" to approach true dignity, happiness, and prosperity. In politics the rules are equal rights, few laws, simple government; in the economy, "the free exercise of confidence between man and man."[19] Government must not tamper with private industry "a single hair's breadth beyond what is essential to protect the rights of person and property"; and it must leave the office of assisting distinct classes of citizens exclusively to "an overruling Providence."[20] Since the good social order is a manifest attribute of nature, it does not have to be invented; only recognized and protected against—above all—monopoly. By monopoly Leggett refers to every species of corporation "created for the purposes of gain, and gifted with privileges which others do not and cannot possess or exercise."[21] Privilege lies at the root of evil. Known by their consequences, monopolies are "the most sly and dangerous enemies to the general prosperity that ever were devised by ingenious cupidity."[22] From them arise these "extremes of wealth and poverty, so uniformly fatal to the liberties of mankind."[23] And whatever special advantages they may promise, nothing can compensate for the "corruption and abuse" they create, for the "open or secret infringements of the sanctity of Equal Rights."[24]

Leggett appeals to "the enlightened farmers and labouring classes": the country must retrace the path pursued for the past twenty or thirty

[18] *Ibid.*, II, 237–39.       [19] *Ibid.*, II, 333–34.
[20] *Ibid.*, I, 163.       [21] *Ibid.*, I, 91.
[22] *Ibid.*, I, 73.       [23] *Ibid.*, I, 78.       [24] *Ibid.*, I, 77.

years. There must be an end to the chartering of privileged corporations.[25] The simple remedy would be a general incorporation act
opening to all "the privileges proper to be bestowed upon any."[26] Then
enterprise and competition would create a proper system of credit and
exchange, manage trade, initiate sound projects, and generally conduct
the economic affairs of society with justice and efficiency.[27] We must
achieve "the complete emancipation of trade."[28]

At this general level of argument a few salient characteristics
emerge. The family origins of Leggett's principles are fairly obvious;
but his treatment of the ideas is so starkly simple and monolithic that
one is not encouraged to pursue intellectual genealogy very far. Rather
the interest seems to lie in the rhetorical clues to his intention. Here is
a radical libertarian appeal; and into what brave private ventures does
it lead? Remarkably, into none. Restoration of free trade and equal
rights—undoing the errors of the past generation—promises two great
ends: an uprooting of the tangled evils sprung from privilege; and a
stable, prudent adjustment to the order of nature. The utmost liberty,
propounded in the most doctrinaire terms, carries the hope of a just
social peace, founded upon equal rights. Freedom is not a wager on
the unknown but an investment in the familiar and reliable: freedom
*from* chartered exploitation, from "aristocratic innovation." Jacksonian readers of the *Evening Post* and the *Plaindealer* could scarcely
have taken from Leggett's editorials an incitement to dynamic progress. What they understood from the formal terms of laissez faire
will be clearer, I think, if one investigates the concrete attributes of
privilege in Leggett's arguments.[29]

### Banks and Values

Like all good Jacksonians, William Leggett substantially identifies
privilege with paper-money banking, and then derives all the ills of
man from the banking system. Whether retrospective judgment calls

[25] *Ibid.*, I, 95–96.    [26] *Ibid.*, II, 139.
[27] *Ibid.*, II, 136–40.    [28] *Ibid.*, II, 313.
[29] I do not mean to suggest here that Leggett's economic attitudes represented a
full-blooded conservatism; far from it. He does not share the Tory Democracy of
Fenimore Cooper. There would be progress enough for American society under his
simple order of natural liberty. But I do insist that the motions of nature were, for
Leggett, extraordinarily smooth, gentle, measured; that he abhorred all efforts to
quicken nature by concerted action; that this world of economic liberty, opened to
petty craftsmen and tradesmen, bore few marks of that modern economic society which
was emerging in New York while he wrote.

this a mythology or a shrewd analysis, the fact remains that banks stood for much more than banking and that the Jacksonian bank discussion supplies the best single source for a study of their general economic and social values.

Leggett is always conspicuously careful to insist that his party is the true conservator of property, and that commerce is to be prized as "the efficient instrument of civilization and promoter of all that improves and elevates mankind." He has a good word for banking itself: "We are no enemy to banking. It is a highly useful branch of trade."[30] Nevertheless his readers saw little of the uses and much of the abuses of banking in the 1830's. On principle: "Our primary ground of opposition to banks as they at present exist is that they are a species of monopoly."[31] The bank charter allows a favored group to combine greater resources than the unincorporated can command; it exonerates the chartered few from liabilities common to the rest of the community; and it arbitrarily limits entry into a branch of private business.[32] These evils the banking corporation shares with all forms of chartered monopoly. The banking system has become "an essentially aristocratic institution" which must be put down "or the days of democracy are numbered." The good fight must go on "until every vestige of monopoly has disappeared from the land, and until banking —as most other occupations are now, and as all ought to be—is left open to the free competition of all who choose to enter into that pursuit."[33] Banking, in short, is condemned as the glaring violation of the rule of laissez faire, and as a powerful threat to the very existence of democracy.

In terms of the principles of equal liberty this is the heart of Leggett's argument, a direct and simple derivation from the simple order of nature; in terms of persuasion it is only a fair start. Leggett tells a "typical" bank story: A knot of speculators get their hands on a legislative charter by the usual arts of collusion, bribery, political management. At first they lend their own limited capital. But soon, if business is active, they set their paper promises afloat. Large profits accumulate. Business in general seems to flourish. Merchants expand their operations, hiring large stores, importing heavily from abroad, and selling on easy terms to country dealers. The eager merchant will get the country dealer's note discounted and expand further. So the

---

[30] *Ibid.*, II, 306–7.  [31] *Ibid.*, I, 97.
[32] *Ibid.*, I, 97–99.  [33] *Ibid.*, I, 56–57.

appearance of prosperity whets the general appetite. Others increase their borrowing of flimsy paper from the bank to start new business enterprises; more to buy lots, build houses, initiate vast railroad and canal projects. The economy experiences a feverish boom: labor is in great demand, property prices mount, and the wide world of speculators is agog with dreams of sudden wealth. Reverse pressure begins with an unfavorable trade balance. Bank notes pour in with insistent demands for specie. The merchant pleads for increased accommodations to carry him through the period of pressure, but the bank is in distress, must call its loans, retrench its operations. Then merchants fail, banks cut back credit further, and business failures reach epidemic proportions. Finally, the bank suspends specie payments and the defenseless holders of its notes are left with worthless rags. The whole community is involved in crisis and depression.[34]

Leggett does not neglect to point the obvious morals. The paper basis of the banking system is radically wrong. Banks should have a foundation which cannot be destroyed by panic, fraud, mismanagement. There must be security for the billholder; i.e., money must be hard, certain in value. More than a fraud upon the people, this paper banking system is a kind of narcotic, arousing a feverish thirst for wealth and exciting deluded speculations. The "legitimate means of honest, patient industry, and prudent enterprise" are defeated or ignored. Fraud, failure, insolvency—once marked as evil things—are condemned no longer by our perverted commercial standards. The bank system "has changed the meaning of words, it has altered the sense of things, it has revolutionized our ethical notions." The man who ventures beyond his business depth is now judged "enterprising and ingenious"; once he would have been called no better than rash and dishonest. For the reckless speculator who comes to ruin, and buries with him the mass of industrious mechanics and laborers, there has ceased to be the least "censure and contempt," the old and the proper judgment for such conduct.[35]

When Leggett develops his argument, that banking is "building up a privileged order, who, at no distant day, unless the whole system be changed, will rise in triumph on the ruins of democracy,"[36] he is

[34] *Ibid.*, I, 99–101.
[35] *Ibid.*, I, 101–3. See also *ibid.*, I, 41, 248–49; II, 85–87, 310–13.
[36] *Ibid.*, I, 103.

again saying far more than can be deduced from the abstract doctrine of "Equal Rights." Indeed, the disruptive and divisive effects of bank privilege can be followed into the general political process, into the formation of rival parties and social classes, into the creation of opposed character types and antagonistic values.

Initially the very act of soliciting a charter has deep corrosive effects upon the democratic political process. The "political quackery of ignorant legislators, instigated by the grasping, monopolizing spirit of rapacious capitalists," is coming to dominate the life of the state: "They give the tone to our meetings; they name our candidates for the legislature; they secure their election; they control them when elected."[37] This grave menace is no sudden phenomenon; historically, the banking issue has always been the touchstone of party divisions in America. For or against the Bank has meant for aristocratic, consolidated government or for popular and limited government.[38] Whatever the "earnest and painful efforts of the Bank party to rid themselves of that appellation" and claim the honorific name of Whigs, there can be no doubt that "the Bank is the band which holds this ill-assorted party together—it is the magazine which furnishes them with weapons—it is the treasury which supplies them with means."[39] Traditionally the anti-Bank cause enlists the farmers, mechanics, laborers, "and other producers of the middling and lower classes (according to the common gradation by the scale of wealth)," while the Bank party attracts "the consumers, the rich, the proud, the privileged," all those would-be aristocrats who seek to "monopolize the advantage of the Government, to hedge themselves round with exclusive privileges, and elevate themselves at the expense of the great body of the people."[40] The very intemperance of party politics, the sharp decline from principled contests to mere public brawls, may be traced to the demoralizing influence of special legislation, and to the provocative actions of beardless boys—clerks and the like—egged on by their well-hidden, irresponsible masters of the privileged class.[41]

---

[37] *Ibid.*, I, 104.   [38] *Ibid.*, I, 64–66.
[39] *Ibid.*, I, 155–61.   [40] *Ibid.*, I, 66–67.
[41] *Ibid.*, I, 58–62. Leggett charges that "these youngsters" invade the lower-income wards "to pry into the ballots of such tradesmen, mechanics, and labourers, as may be in the employment of the lordly master they themselves serve." Fortunately, the "hard hands, sturdy limbs, and honest hearts of the democracy" are adequate to the defense of their voting rights. *Ibid.* See also *ibid.*, II, 322–27.

Deeper than the party split, and far more distressing, is the corresponding cleavage of society into rich and poor: the "scrip nobility" and the "serfs of free America."[42] The "vast disparity of condition" which has developed in American society has but one source, special privilege, mainly in the form of bank charters. If inequalities of condition bore any true relation to natural differences, "there would be no cause to complain." But plainly our "princely fortunes" originate not with patient industry or superior wisdom, not even with inheritance—scarcely a dozen wealthy New York City families can trace the bulk of their property back one generation—but only with unequal privileges coaxed from government.[43]

There are no chartered privileges for farmers, laborers, mechanics, shopkeepers—the " 'common people,' who look to their industry for their support." Government shows a shameless solicitude for "charter-mongers and money-changers," men who "choose to live in idleness by their wits rather than earn an honest livelihood by the useful employment of their faculties." As special privilege explains the wealth of our paper aristocracy, so it fixes the destiny of the poor, who groan and sweat under a weary life of unrewarded toil.[44] Can this be a reflection of differences in intelligence, vigor, industry, virtue? In his answer Leggett broadens the economic categories, omitting the restrictive adjectives, paper and privileged; and he makes the farmer stand for all decent common folk.

Take a hundred ploughmen promiscuously from their fields, and a hundred merchants from their desks, and what man, regarding the true dignity of his nature, could hesitate to give the award of superior excellence, in every main intellectual, physical, and moral respect, to the band of hardy rustics, over that of the lank and sallow accountants, worn out with the sordid anxieties of traffic and the calculations of gain? Yet the merchant shall grow rich from participation in the unequal privileges which a false system of legislation has created, while the ploughman, unprotected by the laws, and dependent wholly on himself, shall barely earn a frugal livelihood by continued toil.[45]

In effect, then, American government comes to represent a conspiracy of the rich. A "low-minded, ignorant, and rapacious order of money-changers" control the power of the state indirectly, monopo-

42 *Ibid.*, II, 122–25.   43 *Ibid.*
44 *Ibid.*, II, 162–63.   45 *Ibid.*, II, 164.

lize the main sources of profit, and "wring the very crust from the hard hand of toil." Rapidly America is coming to ape the class system of Europe. Wall Street becomes our *"Street of the Palaces."* Already three-fourths of the state legislators owe their first loyalty to the scrip nobility and devote themselves to preserving and extending privilege.[46] Thus, to come back to party politics:

The rich perceive, acknowledge, and act upon a common interest, and why not the poor? Yet the moment the latter are called upon to combine for the preservation of their rights, forsooth the community is in danger! Property is no longer secure, and life in jeopardy. This cant has descended to us from those times when the poor and labouring classes had no stake in the community, and no rights except such as they could acquire by force. But the times have changed, though the cant remains the same.[47]

If in old despotic Europe a legal and hereditary aristocracy could advance some pretense to superiority, in the United States "the claims of wealth and aristocracy are the most unfounded, absurd, and ridiculous." These overnight "creatures of the paper credit system" seem to forget that in America the people—"we mean emphatically the class which labours with its own hands"—cumulatively hold ten times more of property and intelligence than the aristocracy. Who are the rich? Most of them men who started poor, with ordinary educations and a marked gift for intrigue. Are they made wiser by their carriages, their money (commonly, their mere credit), or their splendid houses? Does patriotism grow with the acquisition of a French cook and a box at the opera? Do learning and logic improve through the study of "day-book, ledger, bills of exchange, bank promises, and notes of hand?" "What folly is this?"[48]

It would be more accurate to say of this paper lord: "His soul is wrapped up in a certificate of scrip, or a Bank note." The "labouring classes" may discover here sufficient provocation for combining "against the only enemy they have to fear as yet in this free country, monopoly and a great paper system that grinds them to the dust." Their enemy is old greed and ambition under a new name and form, the "chartered libertine": "a mighty civil gentleman, who comes mincing and bowing to the people with a quill behind his ear, at the head of countless millions of magnificent *promises.* He promises to make

---

[46] *Ibid.,* II, 123–24.     [47] *Ibid.,* I, 106.     [48] *Ibid.,* I, 107–8.

everybody rich; he promises to pave cities with gold; and he promises to pay." By trade the Great Deceiver is, more often than not, a monopoly banker. Yet he is to be found everywhere, coiled within the small deceivers, the would-be privileged of society.[49]

This argument on banking presents a severe challenge to most standard interpretations of Jacksonian Democracy, especially in its Loco-Foco form. Leggett's first premise is "the simple order of nature"; his final conclusion is: *"Let us alone."* Between the beginning and the end, however, he exposes and condemns many substantial flaws in Jacksonian society. Logically his conception of the banking system and its effects may be regarded as the consequence of a tight laissez-faire argument. And yet the characterization of ill effects becomes a large component of Leggett's message to his readers. Social valuations emerge which condition the meaning of the laissez-faire appeal, valuations which in some respects quite upset one's rational expectations. Further, Leggett's program—the free banking proposal, for instance—ought to appeal to the interests of one particular economic group, ambitious new business enterprisers; but his whole message barely acknowledges its logical beneficiaries, often abuses their traits and ways, and unmistakably favors other social types whose economic interest could be promoted only negatively and indirectly by such measures. In brief, Leggett's banking argument will not reduce to an example of free-trade logic.

The particular villain of the piece is the monopoly banker, who stands for the class of the seekers, holders, granters, and beneficiaries of privilege; politically, for the Whig-Bank party. Here is the antagonist of Jacksonian Democracy defined by essential enmity to free trade and equal rights. To characterize and judge the enemy the Leggett editorials have a vocabulary less narrow and abstract. The primary identity—monopoly-banker-Whig—is drawn out, amplified, and turned until it expresses emergent qualities which could not be deduced from the first statement, although they do not contradict it. In all these guises the essential villain may be seen: as aristocrat, consolidationist, authoritarian, corruptionist; as charter-monger, money-changer, schemer, sharper, plutocrat, consumer, idler; as the creature of avarice, ambition, pride, vanity, deceit, indolence, indulgence; as the lank and sallow merchant, the mincing and bowing confidence man. Leggett's distrust of power and ambition is evident in the evaluative

[49] *Ibid.,* I, 108–10.

terms. Privilege is of course marked for condemnation. The manipulation of intangibles is suspect, most obviously in the case of charter-mongering, still plainly for money-changing, and ambiguously for trading as such. Mere passive possession is unworthy, especially when the object is inordinately great and the possessor proud, vain, and self-indulgent. There is an indeterminate boundary between self-interest and avarice, but there is sufficient emphasis upon the demeaning aspect of avarice to cast a shadow upon self-interest proper.

It would be sheer impishness, of course, to suggest that Leggett unknowingly shaped the *enemy* of laissez faire into a caricature of economic man. A milder irony does emerge quite clearly from the evidence. An enterprising Leggett disciple of the period, seeking the main chance in a free market but still avoiding all the evils alluded to by his master, could scarcely make his way in the more promising routes to economic success; he could not readily adventure in the new industrialism, the new finance, the new commerce, or the wonder-working business of real estate. As a free-trade radical, William Leggett assigns all evil formally to privilege; specifically to the consequences of privileged banking. And yet he packs in so much of the emerging economic order under his condemnation of privilege that it becomes difficult to imagine the two elements detached: corporations without monopoly, credit without scrip, banks without charters, promotion without fraud, investment without speculation, wealth without aristocracy. In Leggett's adjectives and examples there is an ambivalent, suspicious, sometimes openly hostile greeting to the roles, ways, institutions, and values which expansive laissez-faire capitalism promised for America. This free-trade doctrinaire did something with his prose to earn the name of revolutionary—logically, an absurd designation—from nervous capitalists like Philip Hone. For political and moral support, it must be insisted, Leggett turns not to the enterprising "new men" of America but to the "producers of the middling and lower classes": farmers, laborers, mechanics, and shopkeepers. Before a Jacksonian audience in America's first city he offered the plowman in his field as the symbol of the highest excellence, physical, intellectual, and above all moral.

Liberty and moral reformation are not a perfect match. The paradox lay originally with the Jacksonians, and an interpretation of their politics must somehow embrace it. Perhaps the paradox concealed a contradiction; wisdom after the event would seem to say so.

Logically and historically the laissez-faire principle led toward the city, the factory, the complex market and credit economy; the simple agrarian republic of virtue could not stand against it. But the Jacksonians, I think, held their paradox in suspension, aided by a selective vision of the world and especially by a theory which made certain privileged institutions and practices exclusively responsible for problems which we know to have a broader provenience. The peculiar character of the Jacksonian persuasion, as William Leggett gave it expression, lies in its demand for economic liberty strictly on its own terms. If Jacksonians did not bend the world to their difficult purpose, they did enlist a vast following among the classes they appealed to: among the "producers of the middling and lower classes," who caught the traditional message of equal liberty in terms addressed to their grievances, their resentments, their fears of the newly rich and the strangely new.

# 10

# A PROGRESSIVE VERSION

## ROBERT RANTOUL, JR.

❧

Robert Rantoul, Jr., of Massachusetts belongs to a new political generation which reached maturity during the age of Jackson. His varied reform interests—in temperance, public schools, lyceums, capital punishment, the Dorr Rebellion, slavery, legal codification—place him with a large nonpartisan group of mid–nineteenth century "progressives." He was at the same time a firm Democrat who defended the basic items in the Jacksonian program and took an active part in state and local politics. Although Wendell Phillips in an obituary piece found good reason to link Rantoul's name with William Leggett's—the two men shared a number of reform enthusiasms as well as Democratic party membership—still I find the differences worth attending to. Loco-Foco radicalism in New York City was not the same as Democracy plus general progressivism in Salem, Gloucester, or Boston.

Rantoul was born and bred in Essex County—the heart of the old Federalist country—educated at Phillips Andover and Harvard, and trained in the law by a Pickering and a Saltonstall. He married a relative of a prominent New Hampshire Democrat, Supreme Court Justice Levi Woodbury. In his career as a Democratic attorney confronting first in Salem and finally in Boston the snobbish exclusiveness of the Whig upper class—this is the picture his memoirist gives—there is some resemblance to the career of Martin Van Buren, making his professional way against the cold contempt of the Columbia County Federalist luminaries. During his Gloucester residence in the mid-1830's Rantoul served four terms in the state legislature, and he later held appointments as member of the state board of education, federal customs collector for the Port of Boston, and United States district attorney. As a lawyer, Rantoul represented the defense in several *causes célèbres* of reform: the Hunt labor conspiracy case, the Rhode Island political trials, and the Sims fugitive-slave case. In a quite different direction Rantoul became during his later years agent for a group of Eastern capitalists and chief promoter of the Illinois Central Railroad project. Some of these elements of *milieu,* associations, and career will, I think, be apparent in the version of Jacksonian Democracy which Rantoul propagated in the genteel journals, in the local party press, in the legislature, and among Fourth of July celebrants around the state of Massachusetts.[1]

### The Rule of Gold: From Virtue to Interest

All Jacksonians seem to be moralizers who, in their political capacity, have much to say of proximate good and evil in a practical setting. Robert Rantoul's interest in education and his access to the lofty atmosphere of the *North American Review* supply a rare Jacksonian sketch of some higher goods, if not the highest. Here the discussion is disengaged from banks and parties, from the dated American character and situation, and takes on for a moment the problem of man and society. The result, to anticipate, is a higher synthesis of self-interest and social obligation, fused by the "divine light" of "moral science."[2]

By "moral cultivation" (the central task of education), in the light of moral science, Rantoul's man of virtue is created. "Goodness is the imprint which the sense of truth stamps indelibly upon the character." The child is given "salutary precepts" and correct habits; the man inherits "solid and substantial" character, sound maxims for his guide, an understanding of the good, and a conscience trained to rule his life.[3]

The content of Rantoul's moral science is elusive, though its marvelous powers are fulsomely intoned: "Before its purifying beams,

[1] See the memoir by Luther Hamilton in *Memoirs, Speeches, and Writings of Robert Rantoul, Jr.,* ed. Luther Hamilton, pp. 1–71; also the obituary by Wendell Phillips, *ibid.,* p. 855. There is further biographical matter in Allan Nevins, *Ordeal of the Union,* I, 113, 209, 387, 391; II, 6, 18, 23, 201. On Rantoul's business activities see Paul W. Gates, *The Illinois Central and Its Colonization Work,* pp. 53–65, 70. The sketches of the Rantouls in the *Dictionary of American Biography* are a helpful guide.

[2] "Remarks on Education" (first printed in *North American Review,* October 1838), in Rantoul, *Writings,* pp. 73–112.

[3] *Ibid.,* pp. 82–84.

all evil thoughts and low desires vanish as the noonday splendor dissipates the mists of the valley."[4] In the most pious terms, moral cultivation teaches men to find supreme happiness in "the solid satisfactions of duty well performed," to scorn ignoble objects and to aim at "a comprehensive benevolence."[5] When in another essay Rantoul comes to specify the ultimate moral code, he names the Golden Rule, Love Thy Neighbor, and, in one word, "philanthropy."[6]

At the same time, Rantoul does not rely entirely on noble intentions for the keeping of the philanthropic code: "It is the correct understanding of his own true interests that makes one man happily virtuous, and it is because he is not thus enlightened that another becomes miserably vicious."[7] Somehow, through the agency of moral enlightenment, a man may learn to serve himself, discharge his duty to the world, secure his own virtue, and give the quality of goodness to his acts. No systematic reconciliation of self-interest and social obligation is proposed, however; and the divine light of moral science can be perceived only in reflections from solid objects.

Wealth, Rantoul continues, leads to happiness, through the gratification of the senses. The main road to wealth is simply "the rule that 'honesty is the best policy.'" This is a rule confirmed by history and practice. Morality, as applied to economic conduct, has demonstrated its validity by its efficacy. Thus, of successful men who have been "artificers of their own fortunes," rarely has one risen "in defiance of the obligations of morality." And when one finds the exception, watch him closely; almost invariably some "sudden catastrophe, the consequence of his violation of the principles of rectitude," sends him tumbling down. Tens of thousands of "self-made men," Rantoul writes, "have risen, not by strength of talents, but by an unexceptional course of direct and upright dealing in all their concerns." Talents ruled by wickedness earn men "nothing but poverty, wretchedness, and just contempt."[8]

Once he has made property the immediate object of men's aspirations, Rantoul no longer invokes directly the ethic of "philanthropy," defined as neighborly love and social duty. A "correct moral educa-

[4] *Ibid.*, p. 83.
[5] *Ibid.*, p. 81.
[6] "The Education of a Free People" (address before the American Institute of Instruction, 1839), *ibid.*, pp. 125–26.
[7] "Remarks on Education," *ibid.*, p. 85.
[8] *Ibid.*, pp. 92–94.

tion" would root out the vices productive of economic failure: "idleness, habitual procrastination, and prodigality" and their yet graver consequence, intemperance, "the parent of every woe and crime"; and it would cultivate the corresponding virtues for success: industry, punctuality, frugality, and, of course, temperance. With success conditioned by character, and character by moral education, each man becomes finally responsible for his fate; and the condition of society is a resultant of the way all its individual components use their responsibility. The greatest part by far of human distress can be directly assigned to individual neglect of the simple economic virtues, to flaws in character.[9] "We are all travelling onward towards perfection," Rantoul happily reports, "and nothing can retard our progress but our own wickedness or our own folly."[10]

Yet the happy convergence of virtue and policy cannot be the last word for Rantoul. Morality is the way to wealth, but "heaven forbid that morality should ever be dissevered from religious motives, and debased to a sordid calculation of profit and loss."[11] The final justification of moral training is that it equips man with a sovereign conscience which is the true source of individual happiness. A properly cultivated youth will achieve "the feeling of independence," the result and then the safeguard of a well-developed conscience. He will not "follow the multitude to do evil against light and conviction." Virtue promotes policy; but beyond this: "We should live in an honest and straight-forward world."[12]

It would be easy, but misleading, to discount Rantoul's higher goods as a mere façade for the acquisitive virtues, and these in turn as polite disguises for naked interest. As his Monday-morning sermon descends further into the workaday world, less and less is said explicitly of noble ends, and more of calculated interest. Yet it is always self-interest with a difference, operating under limits and toward ends which cannot be understood without reference to values outside the narrow interest calculus. The cardinal value of "philanthropy"—of love and social duty—must, it is true, be cut down to modest proportions, for it never was meant as an end in itself and it demands no significant self-sacrifice. The virtuous act ought to satisfy private

[9] *Ibid.*, pp. 94–95.
[10] "Education of a Free People," *ibid.*, p. 119.
[11] "Remarks on Education," *ibid.*, p. 95.
[12] *Ibid.*, pp. 84–85.

conscience; it cannot run against true interest; and in the area of economic conduct it is peculiarly the effective instrument of material interest.

With these reservations, Rantoul's higher values provide a useful key for the interpretation of his detailed views on society, politics, and economy. If the highest reach of his code does not transcend interest, the lowest does not escape morality. If "philanthropy" does not emerge self-justified and self-sufficient, neither can calculation operate alone in terms of selfish advantage. Thus Rantoul subjects interest, the functional lever of conduct, to the final requirements of social obligation : however free the pursuit of interest, it cannot be justified entirely in its own terms. Nor is the pursuit quite so free as one might think, for the acquisitive virtues—the lowest form of the highest morality— are not indefinitely flexible, and they are finally *virtues,* with an instrumental use for acquisition. Honesty, industry, punctuality, frugality, temperance, the five attributes of good character, promote material success of a certain kind, and in a certain way; the kind and way would change if the recommended qualities were, for example, sharpness, daring, flexibility, and ambition. Finally, the judgment of men's actions is made by private conscience, not by calculation of material success. A sense of inner satisfaction is the sign that true interest has been served. By a happy arrangement of the universe, the man in this state will not want for grosser goods.

This smiling view of moral cultivation tells too little of Rantoul's judgment of his times. To learn what manner of Democrat Rantoul was, we must observe him when he lets his values play upon the surfaces of the Jacksonian world.

## Republican Society: The Utopia of the Present

Jacksonians typically view their own society in alternating perspectives: now as a great realm of social peace and unity sustaining the good life and rising toward the better; now as the battleground of hostile forces, with evil on the verge of triumph and good a valiant cause entrusted with the last and best hope. Different Jacksonians reconcile these two views differently; all, it seems to me, adapt some version of the restoration theme. In the political-battle view, an alien element in the community—often a mixture of prerepublican aristocracy and postrepublican promotional and speculative capitalism— stands opposed to the sound Revolutionary-republican tradition. In

the social-peace view, the Jacksonian is satisfied that reactionary innovation has not yet mutilated the republican social order or the republican character, and that these, restored to their original nature and
defended by a plain and simple government, constitute the worthy
substance of the good community. What gives the fierce tone to Jacksonian politics is the sense that extraneous forces within society,
powerless on their own to prosper and persuade, conspire to seize the
government and convert it to an engine of despotism, theft, and
corruption.

A survey of contemporary social classes and institutions convinces
Rantoul that the world he sees before him (or what he chooses to
perceive), secured and perfected by a proper system of moral training,
contains the promise of the good republican order. The press becomes
the people's library, politics a popular school; wealth is widely scattered, land divided; family fortunes rise and fall within three generations; most estates originate from the industry, skill, and economy of
present owners; and the landscape is reassuringly filled with small,
independent farmsteads.[13]

In this world, the merchant class will not seek special privilege if
they comprehend their true interest, for in the present condition of
society the rapid swing of fortune would make the quondam privileged,
or their posterity, potential victims of this very privilege. Even bankruptcy can be a salutary force in Rantoul's sanguine view, since it
strikes widely and often, opening new places in the business world
and dissolving old positions before they can become the permanent
bases of an aristocracy. Manufacturers similarly hold no serious
menace for republican society; they will not form an entrenched
aristocracy, for their wealth and power pass to strange hands in regular
cycles. Rantoul's argument, in short, is that inequalities are tolerable
in a free society as long as social mobility within and between generations is effective; above all, the *consciousness* of that impermanence
discourages the adoption of a system of class privilege. The capitalist
class proper is small—in New England a few hundred, in the whole
Union a few thousand—and held in check by the same grand principle
of turnabout: a half century changes almost the entire class roster.
Their aggregate wealth is but a small fraction of total community
wealth, and cannot overawe the people. Free schools and a free press

---

[13] "Education of a Free People," *ibid.*, pp. 135–36.

make an informed public which cannot be manipulated by the rich and their hired brains.[14]

Two further broad classes or interests, "talent and skill" and "labor," hold an unprecedented measure of honor, rewards, and influence under the American system of popular institutions and general education; indeed their high achievements mark the success of the republican order. The class of "talent and skill"—including skilled mechanics, business overseers, public administrators, authors, editors, professionals—is, Rantoul notes with favor, the growing interest in America: "Its power augments every day." Labor, meaning probably the wage-earner class, has always merited respect for its numbers, but for want of knowledge, laborers historically have been the tools of the few, and they have "starved in the midst of the plenty they had created." Only in American society has education changed such an "unnatural" dispensation, and taught labor both to claim its fair share of the product and to keep peace with capital by not demanding more than it deserves.[15]

In this formulation, then, the republican utopia which is on the verge of being does not draw its character from the peculiar constitution and behavior of distinct occupational classes; rather it restrains or augments their influence according to the prior requirements of republican society. The active agencies of republicanism are politics, press, and education; the defining economic conditions are wide dispersion of wealth and land, circulation of fortune and power, and the keying of success to industry, economy, and virtue. Indirectly, some occupational preference is expressed in Rantoul's cautionary approach to merchants, manufacturers, and capitalists; in his satisfaction with the rising influence of "talent and skill" and "labor"; in his specific inclusion of a small-farm landscape as a fundamental aspect of republican society.

In an "Address to the Workingmen of the United States of America," published in the "Workingmen's Library" series, Rantoul moves farther from the analysis of actual, operative social-economic groupings and states a view of classes, more a judgment, in what I have termed above the social-peace perspective. The intended special audience does not, I think, divert Rantoul from the views consistently expressed elsewhere, though it lends a distinctive emphasis to the

[14] *Ibid.*, pp. 136–37.
[15] *Ibid.*, pp. 137–38.

discussion. "Society," he begins, "as you very well know, is divided into two classes—those who do something for their living and those who do not." The "bees" do; they "have a right to all the honey which they make" and a duty to "keep the drones as nearly in a state of starvation as their compassionate feelings will allow them to."[16]

The distinction originates in a restatement of the social-obligation theme: Society protects the fruits of our labor, protects our persons, and, briefly, "enables us to enjoy peaceably all that we have." In return we have an obligation "to do something for the welfare of society." Social duty, as it soon appears, is no heavy burden. The roster of drones, or nonworkingmen, is instructive, taking names exclusively from those along the margins of ordinary respectability: the pauper, the idler, the beggar, the spendthrift, the swindler and gambler, the "vagabond demagogue."[17]

This obviously leaves about all of legitimate society in "the party of genuine workingmen," a community "of interest and feeling" dedicated to the proposition that "honest industry should be respected and rewarded." Membership is open to all "who furnish to society some equivalent for the protection and the benefits which society affords them, in whatever field of industry they exert their strength or their talents, or employ their time or their capital." And not the least among them is the man who "superintends the employment of capital acquired by diligence and prudence" and "sends its fertilizing streams through the community, while the profits of every judicious enterprise increase his power of doing good": he is "really and truly a worthy hard workingman." If his "workingmen" readers should be surprised to find nonmanual workers included in their class, Rantoul refers them to "common sense," which would surely enroll in "our party" such workingmen as Stephen Girard, Newton, Franklin, Priestley, Washington, Shakespeare, Fulton. At last all walls crumble: "All honest men belong to one party because they have all pure intentions and a common object—the greatest good of the greatest number."[18]

In the same address, Rantoul outlines a set of workingmen's rights which might serve as a parody on the modern interpretation of Jacksonian Democracy as an expression of proletarian needs and aspira-

---

[16] "Workingmen" (1833), *ibid.*, pp. 219–20.

[17] *Ibid.*, pp. 221–22. Note the similarity to Sedgwick's "idler" class. This is, of course, a common nineteenth-century view.

[18] *Ibid.*, pp. 220–23.

tions. The statement of rights embodies Rantoul's standards for evaluating economic conduct, and his estimate of the prevailing conditions of Jacksonian society. As it turns out, the rights assigned to workingmen claim little but the existing opportunities within the structure of the competitive market system; only the claimant's private efforts are required to secure his rights. What, then, can the "workingman" claim from society? (1) The right to his faculties, and the products of their use; (2) the right to choose the terms on which he will employ his time; (3) the right to steady wages at the highest going rate; (4) the right to education; (5) the right to respect; (6) the right to advancement in life.[19]

Each of the rights, with the partial exception of education, is already available, Rantoul thinks, in American republican society; it needs only to be recognized. Thus the workingman's right to his time means that he may decide what to do with it, for how long, and for how much, *so long as he recognizes that any decision not regulated by going market rates and standards will be meaningless.* Competition always fixes hours and rates at a point mutually advantageous to buyers and sellers of time; if we should want to work only ten hours, for example, in a twelve-hour market, "we must not wonder that nobody accepts our offer." There is a further right to one's *spare* time: allowing twelve hours to work and eight to sleep, one has four free hours to devote to education and self-improvement, the certain means of increasing the value of labor.[20]

What sounds at first a most sweeping claim—the right to steady wages at the highest level, remunerating time, skill, and effort spent— becomes the right to give and take the prevailing market rate. Rantoul decrees that "all combinations forcibly *to raise or to lower* the rate of the wages accruing under either of these denominations [strength, talents, fidelity, and time], are direct and inexcusable infringements of this right." If manual labor "takes more than its share of wages," then managerial skill and capital get less than their share; although of course no such "derangement" can be permanently effective, since the discipline of the market will reassert itself in the long run.

Our right then to wages steady and permanent is not like the themes of demagogues, something to be declaimed about in public, and jested about in private, but a right to be prized, defended, and improved; and all laws

[19] *Ibid.,* pp. 224–50.
[20] *Ibid.,* pp. 232–34.

intended to force capital, or talent, or labor, out of one pursuit into another, thereby producing ruinous fluctuations; and all combinations to raise violently one kind of wages, thereby producing a corresponding diminution in other kinds, are highanded violations of this our undeniable right.[21]

From these arguments it is a short step to declaring the free market in effect an expression of the general economic will, and all "artificial" contrivances (tariffs, privileges, costly governments and armies, economic combinations) agencies "to prevent the will of the working classes from being effectually promulgated." Under the prevailing conditions of the United States,

let us be grateful for the blessing, the rights of all classes of producers stand on an equal footing, and he that begins in one, may easily, if nature has fitted him for it, transfer his services to either of the others. The wages of labor are high enough among us to allow the laborer time for the acquisition of skill and information. The wages of labor and skill when he earns both, will enable him to accumulate capital with considerable rapidity; and the wages of labor, skill, and capital combined, being *all* at high rates among us, will soon, if he has a tolerable degree of economy and prudence, place him in an independent affluence, and leave him at liberty to choose his subsequent pursuits according to his fancy. Not only, therefore, have we a right to remunerating wages, but it is a right of which we enjoy at present the full and undisturbed possession.[22]

Education alone among the rights of workingmen legitimately involves public authority and the public treasury, preferably through "the little democratic corporations," the towns. But schools are only one resource: others are lyceums, social libraries, newspapers, the company one keeps, the job or residence one chooses. Rantoul does not omit the classic liberal formula: "We have a right to have the career kept fairly open to talent, and to be brought equally and together up to the starting point at the public expense; after that we must shift for ourselves."[23]

The culminating right, "to advancement in life," is developed by Rantoul from a right to an instinct. "There is," as he puts it, "a peculiarity implanted by its Maker in the human mind,—never to rest satisfied with its present condition. . . . We cannot be contented; and it is well for us that we cannot." The "desire of improving our

---

[21] *Ibid.*, pp. 234–36.
[22] *Ibid.*, p. 238.
[23] *Ibid.*, pp. 240–43.

condition" merits a loftier title: *"the instinct of perfectibility."* In general, the instinct should be encouraged to the utmost; that is to say, men should be urged not to reform society but to perfect themselves.

We are travelling onward towards perfection, and nothing can retard our progress but our own wickedness or our own folly. . . . In no time since the creation . . . have workingmen beheld that open path before them, in which we are invited to walk. . . . Let no man deceive us. Let no man control us. Let us pursue steadfastly our best interests, and hold, with an iron gripe, these our invaluable rights.[24]

What image of the world can be construed out of all these judgments and perceptions, from the higher goods down to the market rights? First, the image is intended to reflect the world at Rantoul's fingertips, already formed by republican experience and only waiting to be fully grasped. Between present institutions and perfection, character is the vital link, a style of character natural to the given social order and shaped by the lessons of experience. Our wickedness and our folly are willful interference with a process grounded in sound tradition, affirmed by reason, recorded in a set of present institutions, moved by instinct, and jointly validated by personal success and social welfare. The Jacksonian design, as Rantoul preaches it, is to attain perfection by way of the established and familiar order and character of society; man and the world need not be anything but what they have been, nearly are, and easily can become. The mood is hopeful, optimistic, because so little need be done and all the means for doing it are tested and available.

So the higher goods entail no sacrifice of self-interest which cannot be repaid with surplus. True self-interest pursues a course of hugging to the moral shore of industry, parsimony, temperance. Certification to the ranks of virtue comes to all honest men who do something for a living. Workingmen's rights are not something to be gained, but something not to be lost from the present dispensation.

The market still remains as a mechanism of risk, uncertainty, and impersonal disposition of fortune, but it is rigged by moral law. The simple, cautionary virtues must bear off the rewards, and even talent, skill, and ingenuity are made subordinate to character and morality. Although the market seems autonomously to register economic verdicts (the right to going wages, hours, and so on), its verdicts are

[24] *Ibid.*, pp. 248–50.

construed by Rantoul as a collective act of will and judgment by the "workingmen" of society, and thus a reflection more of moral preferance than of relative values linked to objective economic prospects. Rantoul projects a flexible and mobile system, but its essential process is the individual workingman's rise to independence through virtue, and not the accommodation of men and institutions to maximum productive effectiveness. In the usual Jacksonian way, he approaches only vaguely and remotely the great rising institutions of the time—the factory, for example—and shows no grasp of their impending social consequences.

Briefly, then, Rantoul bases progress on the normal processes of the established order, and reads the meaning of the status quo in its most stable and familiar features. In society as he sees it, strong movement is mainly confined to the circular path of generations and the linear path of individual workingmen up to propertied independence. The general scene is dominated by modest independent properties, not least the farmsteads of "that glorious agricultural community, which, after all, makes the backbone of the American nation."[25]

Undeniably Rantoul's system has the practical effect of endowing the free-market mechanism with breath-taking powers and capacities: to express the general will, dispense essential rights, assign status, direct mobility; to embody and enforce the principles of moral science, or true interest. It is just this superabundance of endowments which finally leads one to doubt his reliance upon the autonomous authority of the market in the narrow economic sense: the mere higgling of buyers and sellers, it seems, could not be the marvelous, almost providential power which gives bread, order, and final justice to mankind.

### Republican Society: One Nation, Divisible

The Jacksonian moods of war and peace are, as I have suggested, different but complementary elements of a common temperament and outlook. In party politics, if there is no conflict, one must be invented; more accurately, conflicts and tensions must be brought into sharp focus even when they are in fact ambiguous and diffuse. Jacksonians who are full of peace and contentment when contemplating the good

---

[25] Speech at Salem, October 6, 1848, *ibid.*, p. 688.

life in American society breathe fire when party issues come up. Some of this fury comes undoubtedly out of the old pro's bag of tricks; but I think it will be better understood as honest passion provoked by fears for the purity of the republic. An interesting mixture of the moods, illuminating both the pacific phase and the belligerent, can be found in Rantoul's Fourth of July orations and campaign speeches around the state of Massachusetts.

The "great experiment of our independence," Rantoul told the Democrats of Worcester in 1837, has proved successful beyond all expectations. There has been not only a prodigious growth in wealth and population since the Revolution, but a triumphant vindication of our great American beliefs: that men are born free and equal; that our constitutions guarantee freedom as a natural and inalienable right; that all just powers derive from "the general will" of the governed; that magistrates are the agents of a sovereign people; that the only legitimate object of government is the general welfare, and the only legitimate means to this end are the preservation of social order and the protection of each man in the enjoyment of life, liberty, and property according to standing equal laws. Such is not only the general theory of democratic government, but the specific theory of the Massachusetts constitution and, with some reservations, the Federal Constitution. So much for unity.[26]

But in human nature, Rantoul continues, lie the seeds of three *ur*-types of political party: the democratic, the aristocratic, and the anarchist. The innate aristocrats are men of talents, wealth, and energy whose lives are unrestrained by moral principle. They are given to forming systematic plans for self-aggrandizement, directed toward monopoly power and its associated benefits for their own order. They hold fast to ancient laws and usages, in so far as these promote the accumulation of property and power for the few. Though they style themselves "conservatives," they are in fact "retrogrades" seeking to reintroduce an antiquated status regime.[27]

The ideal democratic, or "popular," party includes "both rich and poor, learned and unlearned, those endowed with genius, and those unblessed by nature; but its greatest strength resides in what is often called the middling interest, and especially in the substantial yeomanry

[26] Speech at Worcester, July 4, 1837, *ibid.*, pp. 558–60.
[27] *Ibid.*, p. 561.

of the country, for they have seldom any interest adverse to the common good of all." In its purposes, the Democracy is the party of

equal rights, equal laws, equal privileges, universal protection. Its foundation rests upon the eternal principles of equity and justice. Its creed is in the ordination of Providence, the constitution of nature, and the wisdom of revelation. . . . Its policy is honesty, and its counsellors are common sense and an enlightened conscience. . . . It neither plunders the rich nor oppresses the poor. . . . It achieves and participates largely in those bold efforts for improvement which characterize our times, but it is not blown about by every wind of doctrine. . . . [It is the party of] prudent, judicious, well-considered reform.[28]

Anarchy is the cause of a "desperate and depraved" handful who would "pull down all above them to their own miserable level." These wild men of reform, Rantoul insists—in standard Jacksonian fashion—have nothing to do with wholesome, sensible Democracy. Alone they are quite harmless; but enlisted under unprincipled aristocrats—"bold, bad men," gnawed by ambition and ready to employ any kind of force to "reign in hell"—they are a grave menace to society. The "not unnatural" coalition becomes a conspiracy of the two extremes "to aggrandize and enrich themselves from the plunder of the masses."[29]

Thus Rantoul appoints the Jacksonian Democratic party sole custodian of the national and democratic tradition. On an earlier Independence Day Rantoul restated Democratic objects in terms closer to party slogans: "free trade, no bank, no debt, light taxes, and an economical government are the American doctrines." Government is confined to its proper functions: providing a sound currency, taking care of foreign relations, defending the national honor, preserving the Union. In relation to the American citizen, said Rantoul, "the whole object of government is negative. It is to remove, and keep out of his way all obstacles to his natural freedom of action."[30]

From this definition of the Jacksonian creed, Rantoul draws his conception of historical party conflicts in the United States. Whiggery, or "British liberty," was the first faith of our fathers; then in the course of the Revolutionary War, "they ceased to be British Whigs, and became American Democrats." Although there have been some later editions of the British type, Rantoul sees such "Whigs" as

[28] *Ibid.*, pp. 561–62.
[29] *Ibid.*, pp. 562–65.
[30] Speech at Scituate, 1836, *ibid.*, p. 283.

only "antiquities and curiosities,—few and far between, contrasting oddly enough with rational American democrats." The majority of the people are not and never again can be Whigs; they have cast off "that British influence" so repugnant to our institutions, condition, and character. From the base line of the Revolution, Rantoul sees the split into the party of "anarchy" (extreme antifederalism) and the "high-toned and aristocratic" Whigs (extreme federalism). The United States Constitution represented a good expedient, mediating between the parties. With the establishment of Federalist control over the new government, Whiggery again became, temporarily, the dominant persuasion; and the "disposition of power to arrogate to itself more power" was fully demonstrated by the original Federalist sin, the chartering of the first Bank of the United States, and its aftermath, the steady build-up of national power by tortured constructions of the Constitution.[31]

Opposition to this policy was "the criterion and the substance of democracy." Under "the immortal Jefferson" the people again rallied and deposed "the aristocracy," the "lovers of power and wealth." Jefferson "disallowed the binding force of British precedents, and undertook to conduct the government upon American principles," although even he could not entirely restore the "primitive purity" of the system: "the British virus" had penetrated too deep. Not until Jackson's presidency was the original Constitution of the republic restored: his "immortal" Bank veto struck down the money power through "the first, the last, the greatest and the worst of these innovations, of foreign origin and uncongenial to our institutions, which had fastened themselves with pernicious influence, upon the beautiful simplicity of our government." The Bank, Rantoul proposes, and power-bent loose construction generally, have been the great divisive issues of American politics.[32]

At an early stage of Jacksonian party warfare, Rantoul could occasionally soften the image of mortal combat with the reflection that "our party contests have not that intrinsic importance, with which the lively fancies of the heated partisans often invest them." Perhaps the

[31] *Ibid.*, pp. 252–56.
[32] *Ibid.*, pp. 254, 256–60. See also excerpts from Rantoul's speech at Lynn, 1851, *ibid.*, p. 142, and from his article for the *Gloucester Democrat*, 1834, *ibid.*, pp. 143–45. In the latter, he opposes Democratic "equal rights, equal burdens, and free trade" to the Clay-Calhoun-Webster formula of "partial privileges, partial taxes, and universal restrictions."

warming atmosphere of a Fourth of July celebration brought him to concede that even the great "moral revolutions" of Jefferson and Jackson had been substantially moderated by established routines and practical policy considerations; for, Rantoul observed, "when outs become ins, they view questions of policy under different bearings, and of course come to different conclusions."[33]

Such knowing tolerance is not, however, Rantoul's normal point of view toward partisan divisions. Wealth and politics is the theme of an address to Berkshire County Democrats; and all other lines of party opposition—aristocracy and democracy, pro- and anti-Bank, loose and strict construction, big and little government—converge upon the issue of how wealth is to be managed. Wealth is the great, perhaps the decisive, influence upon the shape of power in society.

Ought the laws, and the action of government, to favor the accumulation of wealth in masses, and its concentration in a few hands? The immediate interests of the aristocratic faction impel them to decide this question in the affirmative. The welfare of the popular masses, and the permanent interests of the whole nation are most decidedly on the other side. . . . This is the division, between these parties in the contest, everywhere.[34]

At the peak of his fury—addressing an anti-Bank meeting at Salem in the crisis year of 1834—Rantoul wholly embraced the partisan antagonisms of the time. He and his fellow Democrats, he says, have been called "ignorant, a rabble, mechanical, base, no gentlemen, incapable of governing ourselves, but created to be trampled on." The opposition will object that Rantoul speaks like a party man; then:

Sir, I confess it. I have spoken as a member of that party, blessed be God! [representing] nine tenths of this nation, whose creed is that the American government was instituted for the good of the American people,—not to serve the purposes of a joint stock company,—not to pamper this man nor that man,—but to protect equally every man's interests. . . . In the name of that party I have spoken,—that party who, rising in the might of righteous indignation, are even now about to overturn the tables of the money-changers, and purge the sacred temple of their liberties from the foul contamination of unholy mammon.[35]

Now Rantoul's harmonious hive of workingmen becomes the scene of venomous contention. Class-party alignments are sharply drawn:

[33] Speech at South Reading, July 4, 1832, *ibid.*, pp. 180–83.
[34] Speech at Lenox, July 4, 1838, *ibid.*, p. 301.
[35] Speech at Salem, March 31, 1834, *ibid.*, pp. 533, 557.

"Why, what is the democratic party in the United States? It is the mass of the laboring people of the United States. And what is the whig party? It is the mass of the capital of the United States."[36] If the class antagonisms underlying American party politics do not always show through, he argues in another speech, it is because massed wealth can purchase clever talent: the Whig politicians "seldom make a full avowal of their creed, but content themselves with steadily acting up to it, as often as they dare, giving way to the pressure from without whenever they are satisfied that it is useless to resist it longer."[37]

### An Old Roman General

The course of Rantoul's argument leads inevitably to the character and program of Andrew Jackson. Jackson had established his party's position "on the people's side"; Rantoul would fix it there:

We go against monopolies, against exclusive privileges, against unequal taxes, against all other usurpations and oppressions on the one side, against disorganization, disunion, and civil war on the other. . . . We go for equal rights, equal laws, equal taxes, equal privileges,—for liberty for the democracy, for the whole people.[38]

But Jackson was not to be understood alone by his official policy commitments. The scheming of the aristocratic party made it necessary that there be one sure resource to preserve the original purity of the Constitution: "an energetic, democratic chief magistrate" who could confront the Bank forces, the consolidationists, the whole "British party" in the United States, with "old Roman" vigor, courage, and honor, and scatter them as he had scattered the British veterans at New Orleans.[39]

Rantoul proudly recalls Jefferson's endorsement of the Old Hero: Jackson " 'has more of the Roman in him than any other man now living.' " In his own right Rantoul exalts the "brave and wise old man" who, as soldier, statesman, patriot, and philanthropist, has vindicated republican principles. Here is a great republican risen from humble poverty by honest industry and prudence to an easy affluence; from "friendless obscurity" by the exercise of "heroic virtues" to a

---

[36] Speech at Salem, October 6, 1848, *ibid.,* p. 686. The context here is an attack on Whig protectionism and Whig resistance to territorial expansion.

[37] Speech at Lenox, July 4, 1838, *ibid.,* pp. 301–2.

[38] Article for *Gloucester Democrat,* n.d., *ibid.,* p. 150.

[39] Speech at Scituate, July 4, 1836, *ibid.,* p. 287; speech at Worcester, July 4, 1837, *ibid.,* p. 566.

splendid eminence. The three great American names, for Rantoul, are Washington, Jefferson, and Jackson, and he is taken particularly with the Washington-Jackson resemblance. Both were criticized for a lack of formal education, for being military chieftains. Both were in fact "self-made" men with natural capacities for leadership. In battle, both saved the republic, and both owed military success to the school of Indian warfare. Both took presidential office at a time of crisis and prevented the victory of the "consolidating" forces. Both enjoyed unlimited popular confidence. Both were men of solid judgment rather than brilliance, who deliberated carefully and acted with implacable firmness; and both revealed their humanity in occasional towering rages.[40]

The Jefferson-Jackson parallel is more formal: they were reformers vastly abused and vastly popular, both unfairly charged with operating a spoils system. In ends and means, all must concede, "Jacksonism is but a revival of Jeffersonism." After Jackson, Van Buren is the legitimate heir: "our clear-sighted yeomanry" recognize the justice of the succession. Van Buren has weighty claims to public esteem in his "well balanced character," his knowledge of history, his wisdom and experience, his courage to dare and fortitude to suffer in the good cause, his generous philanthropy. But all Van Buren's claims are underwritten by "the guaranty of his uniform course . . . that he will follow in the footsteps of Andrew Jackson."[41]

## March and Countermarch

Rantoul's speeches and essays represent, in this discussion, a progressive version of the Jacksonian persuasion. If the heart of the Jacksonian appeal was a judgment of the new world that was coming by the values of the Old Republic, any sort of progressive would find difficulties and tensions in relating his views to those of Andrew Jackson and his followers. Rantoul exhibited such tensions, and a summary statement of his position must deal with the partial and uneasy solution that he reached. To introduce the problem, one might add just one more piece of evidence: Rantoul's attack upon common-law survivals in the American legal system. The broad animus of his speech runs against foreign influence in literature, in manners, and

[40] Speech at Scituate, July 4, 1836, *ibid.*, pp. 261–76.
[41] *Ibid.*, pp. 276, 294–95.

in legislation: America must throw off the foreign yoke and affirm the native genius. So, in manners, let "our sound, substantial yeomanry, our intelligent mechanics, our hardy tars" keep a firm check upon "the corrupt portion of the population of our great cities."[42] And in legislation there must be "a positive and unbending text" to replace that "labyrinth of apparent contradictions, reconciled by legal adroitness," which constitutes the corpus of the common law. The law must be made intelligible to all and equal in operation, and must provide cheap and prompt remedies. The task of Massachusetts is to revise its laws: to systematize, condense, simplify, modernize, and especially to substitute a uniform, written code for the many lingering remnants of common law. The common law derives from the times of "folly, barbarism, and feudality"; as judge-made law it represents a usurpation of the legislative power, and a species of special and *ex post facto* legislation. Statutes "speak the public voice," whereas judges are out of the reach of popular influence. Moreover, to judges "precedents are everything; the spirit of the age is nothing."[43]

One could start at either end and make a persuasive case about Jacksonian values: down with relics and survivals, up with the spirit of the age; or down with flexible wording, up with the positive, unbending text. As much as any Jacksonian I know of, Rantoul speaks the language of utility, progress, rational self-interest: the language of free marketing and legal codification. Yet the axe is laid to the *dark* past—feudality, barbarism, aristocracy—not to the golden past of the American republic, dated *circa* 1776. The public voice is free to speak the spirit of the age; but the record will in fact be a rigid text, legitimate only so far as it conforms to the traditional principles of the republic. (The Jacksonian executive looms above the public councils, ready with his veto-bolt for any deviations.) When judges are warned off, with their precedents and esoteric tricks, they are equally enjoined from opening up the pure original text and turning it about for present purposes. The Jacksonian's aristocrat is a strange fellow, a reactionary innovator whose essence is privileged status, whether on the oldest or the latest terms. Judges commonly fall in with the purposes of this species, and are not to be handed the weapon of the common law to turn against the interests of the republic.

In their barest meaning, Jacksonian principles as defined by Ran-

---

[42] *Ibid.*, p. 277.
[43] *Ibid.*, pp. 278–81.

toul take the determination of most value questions out of politics: the whole object of government is negative. The private citizen makes the value judgments; politics exists only to protect his "natural freedom of action."[44] If this stark commitment to individual liberty were all one had to go on, and it were placed in contrast with a properly traditionalist doctrine, then Jacksonian Democracy would appear the chosen political instrument of progress, of flexibility, of open-ended change. I have already discussed at length Rantoul's nonpolitical constraints—by education and exhortation—upon the actual use of liberty by men. So, too, his more detailed comments on politics, especially on the divided aspect of party politics, fill out the meaning of liberty in the Jacksonian persuasion.

Rantoul's ideal Democratic party thus emerges as something other than the embodiment in organized politics of the pure principle of liberty. In composition it is variegated, but still strongly dominated by "the middling interest, and especially . . . the substantial yeomanry of the country."[45] One may say that this is the inevitable ceremonial tribute to the farmer in a nineteenth-century political speech; but its very inevitability reveals the persistent need and wish to identify political forces with the major social constituency and its way of life.

The "desperate and depraved" band of anarchists would shake society to death; and the "bold, bad men" of aristocracy would lead them on in the hope of forcing America back to the dark ages. But the permanent tendency of the Democracy runs toward "prudent, judicious, well-considered reform." The great popular party, whose creed is grounded in—no less—"the ordination of Providence, the constitution of nature, and the wisdom of revelation," would adjust government to the spirit of the age.[46] That spirit, as nearly as one can tell, contains the "beautiful simplicity" of Old Republicanism, rejuvenated and somewhat clarified.[47] Rantoul cannot cease wondering, *fortissimo,* how the Bank party, the party of reactionary foreign innovation, can dare to label rational American Democrats as Jacobins, levelers, agrarians, anarchists. Whig conservatism, he notes, is a remarkably loose garment which finds a fit whenever "the peculiar

[44] *Ibid.,* p. 283.
[45] Speech at Worcester, July 4, 1837, *ibid.,* pp. 561–62.
[46] *Ibid.,* pp. 561–63.
[47] Speech at Scituate, July 4, 1836, *ibid.,* p. 260.

interests of a select coterie" are involved.[48] Fundamentally Rantoul divides the political field between the British reactionaries, ready to play any new game that serves class power and profit, and the republican purists, willing to absorb new elements that are wholesome and fully consistent with the fixed ideal of the Jeffersonian polity.

The image of Jackson as Old Roman adds one last revealing touch to Rantoul's delineation of Jacksonian values. It is always worth remembering some of the things Jackson might have been, but was not, in the rhetoric of his political advocates: an unwashed fellow out of the West, perhaps; a genius of reform; a worker's worker; a patron of men on the make. But Rantoul made him the energetic, democratic chief magistrate whose force of character, applied at the strategic center of republican politics, the presidential office, routed the "British party" as it had once routed the British army. From Jefferson he took his principles; from Washington his example.

Thus in Rantoul's politics the old inviolate ideal, the locked Constitution of the Fathers, the party of the steady middle element ringed by its yeoman guard, the resistance to reactionary innovation and reckless radicalism—all put to a severe discipline the bare principles of universal liberty and the full, free play of public will. In speaking of republican society at peace, the utopia of the present, Rantoul came as close as a Jacksonian could to eulogizing progress by way of laissez-faire capitalism. The enveloping Jeffersonian polity and the censorious moral precepts serve to moderate his enthusiasm for capitalist progress a little—not much. But these were principally his sentiments addressed to genteel readers of the *North American Review,* and to humble self-improvers who would consult the "Workingmen's Library." When the occasion was political, even in the benign atmosphere of a Fourth of July celebration, Rantoul tended to make his "bees" the plain hard-working folk of farm and shop, his "drones" the greedy money-changers, the privilege seekers, the aritsocracy in love with its own wealth and power. Even in Massachusetts, where Jacksonian Democracy made a relatively dim impression upon political life, a Democrat had to reach somehow toward the grievances, suspicions, and fears aroused by social changes in the early nineteenth century.

To the Democratic voters of Lynn and Gloucester and Scituate,

[48] Speech in Massachusetts House of Representatives, March 22, 1836, *ibid.,* pp. 352–53.

of Lenox and Worcester, Robert Rantoul said nothing of railroad promotion, little of his favorite reforms or of the market-given rights of workingmen. He spoke of the "primitive purity" of the republic, and of Jefferson's and Jackson's labors to restore it. He spoke of the conspiracies of the rich and powerful to subvert democracy, corrupt its government, exploit its ordinary citizens. Americans of the Jacksonian persuasion took their doctrines of liberty and laissez faire—within the universe of party politics—not as a stimulant to enterprise but as a purgative to bring the Old Republic, not very old of course, back to moral health.

# 11

## A DIALOGUE OF PARTIES

~

Jacksonian political encounters down to 1840 were, as Judge Jabez Hammond of New York recalled them, "incessant, fierce and at times ferocious—each party charging the other with designs fatal to the prosperity of the state and the rights of the people."[1] Contemporary reports generally suggest that party conflicts were no mere public entertainments. A large sporting element in politics did help to draw the mortal sting from party thrusts; still the game assumed the gravity of moral drama, with salvation or damnation in the balance. An Ohio witness, in lamenting that "the great Jackson era" had turned the public mind from religious to political engagements, alludes to just this earnest quality of Jacksonian party politics.[2] The unkempt peace of post-election morning—the silent streets with their pointless campaign litter—could amaze the foreign visitor who had seen the high emotion of election eve and awaited the violent climax.[3] There were no great revolutionary issues in Jacksonian America; not even contrary policy alternatives consistently maintained. And yet there was a war of words arraying hostile persuasions under rival party standards. The protagonists found a public eager to receive its own unformed sentiments toward social ways and institutions in pointed rhetoric, and to respond with votes and loyalty.

Recording this impassioned dialogue of parties over several decades in the press and in the capitols and courthouse squares of America—the sources are oppressively rich—must be reserved for another enterprise. For our purposes, two quick impressions of party discourse, one before the Jacksonian era and one at its close, can help to reveal the special mark Jacksonian Democracy made upon the language and

[1] Hammond, *History of Political Parties*, II, 533.
[2] Howells, *Recollections*, p. 120. See also Ford's *Illinois*, pp. 39–40, and the penetrating remarks of D. W. Brogan in *The American Character*, p. 18.
[3] For example, see Francis Lieber, *Stranger*, I, 25–38; II, 24–27.

purposes of a political generation. In the 1821 and 1846 constitutional conventions in New York, Jacksonians and Whigs, and their party predecessors—of sorts familiar through the Northern states at least—may be discovered in the act of fitting partisan persuasions to concrete public wants; revising the organic law of the state in full view of an audience directly concerned with the outcome.

During the Jacksonian era New York was normally a Democratic state, although the Whigs were strong enough to carry a large minority, win certain extensive regions consistently, and swing the majority under ideal conditions. The parties thus were in serious competition for support and highly sensitive to popular attitudes and interests. By contemporary standards New York was relatively mature in social and economic development; but it was also remarkably heterogeneous in ethnic composition, physical and social conditions, stages of growth. In the metropolitan area and several secondary centers one found the substantial beginnings of a modern capitalist society. But parts of New York were just emerging from frontier conditions; most of the state was occupied by stable agricultural communities; and over a wide area boom towns were springing up one after another. New Yorkers fully experienced all the great social trends of the Jacksonian era: the transportation and communications revolutions, industrialization, immigration, migration, community building, popular education, and much more. Old Yorkers, recent Yankees, and raw immigrants mingled in the population, bringing a wide range of regional and ethnic influences into politics. Finally, New York contributed important spokesmen to the Jacksonian party and served as an acknowledged Democratic tutor for the newer Western states.

My reading of party debates in New York suggests first that the basic issues of political democracy were substantially resolved before the Jacksonians took command. The Federalism of the Founders died young in the popular political arena: in the third decade of the nineteenth century its survivors could claim a hearing only on the strength of personal prestige. Moreover, these survivors spoke a language of yeoman virtues curiously reminiscent of Jefferson in the past and curiously suggestive of Jackson in the future. In effect, then, Jacksonians and Whigs learned to act and talk within a democratic universe: there they discovered their differences, pursued them fiercely, and developed rival followings. Political democracy as such was not an issue that divided men into parties.

The second reading, for 1846, reveals how elusive in practical meaning, and yet how vitally important for other purposes, had been the raging quarrels of Jacksonian politics. Here, toward the end of an era, the antagonists found themselves slipping into concord on most of the incendiary issues of two decades—banking and corporations, public debt and public works—and uniting with no perceptible friction on long-settled principles of majority rule. For the Whigs, public promotion and enterprise no longer seemed essential for accelerating economic progress. For them the "free" bank and the equal-rights corporation now seemed most excellent ways to wealth; for their Jacksonian opponents the same devices looked attractive, partly in the same way, partly as devices for keeping the economic world honest and straightforward, and in the orbit nature had prescribed.

But still they could not let their differences go. If only by the shading of a constitutional clause, a Whig must press his special concern for endless progress under democratic capitalism, stimulated by the state. A Jacksonian must insist that the changing world is full of terrors, and hint at least that once there was a better, even as he helps perfect the instruments of change.

## Genesis

By 1821 political democracy in New York was ready to register its penultimate decrees in the state constitution; the old Federalism of patroons and wilderness promoters, merchant princes and legal dignitaries, had shrunk to an elegant shadow. In the elections for the state constitutional convention of that year, such Federalist magnates as the Chancellor, James Kent, and the Patroon himself, Stephen Van Rensselaer, assumed the winning name of "Independent Republicans."[4] Dixon Ryan Fox has definitively characterized the 1821 convention as a public ceremony solemnizing the passage from republican aristocracy to prudent democracy in the politics of New York.[5]

The convention debates[6] illuminate the relation between the Jacksonian movement and the triumph of majority rule in America. Jack-

---

[4] Fox, *Decline of Aristocracy*, p. 237.

[5] *Ibid.*, chap. viii and *passim*. Judge Hammond's *History of Political Parties* provides a sane and richly informative commentary on political men, institutions, and issues in New York before and during the convention.

[6] Nathaniel H. Carter and William L. Stone (reporters), *Reports of the Proceedings and Debates of the Convention of 1821: Assembled for the Purpose of Amending the Constitution of the State of New York*.

sonian Democracy is rightly associated with "the rise of the common man"; it is wrongly identified with the fight for the acceptance of the principles of political democracy, which had been fought and won before Jackson's party came on the scene. On the contrary, political democracy was a necessary condition for the emergence of Jacksonian Democracy: it defined the political situation for Jacksonians and for their opposition as well. The Federalists' pride in a lost cause and their rusty rhetoric in its honor leave a fairly clear mark in the 1821 debates, but their majestic style should not divert attention from the modest substance of their "aristocracy." Politically defunct but personally commanding Federalists in the 1821 convention had found a chance to appropriate the opposition role, and so give the debates a somewhat archaic, unreal tone of urgency and vital conflict.[7] But the record of debates suggests unmistakably, first, that the road from Chancellor Kent's conservatism to political democracy was not so long or hard as commonly reported; second, that the main body of New Yorkers were very near the end of that road in 1821, well before the Jacksonian movement took form.

Proposals to extend the right of suffrage provoked the most intense and fundamental argument in the New York convention. The major "aristocratic" proposal directed its qualifications to the state senatorial electorate alone, and then estimated the difference between worthy citizens and the rabble at the modest value of $250 in the form of freehold property or an equitable equivalent. The practical effects of such a limitation would not have been trivial; yet the mere naming of the standard measures the "aristocratic" pretensions of New York Federalism in 1821. And the more than 5-to-1 rejection of that faint-hearted confinement of democracy argues that political democracy was largely an accomplished fact when the convention met.[8]

Chancellor Kent's dramatic plea for maintaining a selective franchise has come down as the model of American conservatism *in extremis*. The convention, Kent dolefully concluded, stood "on the very edge of the precipice."[9] And yet, without excessive forcing, the same speech can be read as a quasi-Jeffersonian performance, darkened

[7] My impression of the preconvention state of the parties was largely formed by Hammond, *History of Political Parties,* I, 422–571. Fox estimates 110 "Democrats" out of 126 delegates: *Decline of Aristocracy,* p. 239.

[8] *Debates* (1821), p. 270. Fox calculates some effects of suffrage limitation: *Decline of Aristocracy,* pp. 252 n, 262 n.

[9] *Debates* (1821), p. 222.

by antique usages. The nobility who would save the state from ruin if only they might hold the senate turn out to be: "freeholders of moderate possessions"; "free and independent lords of the soil"; "that wholesome population" in whom one always finds "moderation, frugality, order, honesty, and a due sense of independence, liberty, and justice." Defense against the democratic cataclysm is entrusted to the great body of the people of New York—the chosen many of republican ideology—to the yeoman class whose natural habits and sympathies guaranteed the safety of property and all private rights.[10]

For the Chancellor the menace of extreme democracy lay in the future, fast approaching, when America would no longer comprise so many "plain and simple republics of farmers." As cities like New York took on the European pattern and grew in numbers, commerce, manufactures, wealth, and luxury, misery and vice would fester in American society. Inevitably the alienated poor would come "to covet and to share the plunder of the rich"; the majority "to tyranize [sic] over the minority"; the "indolent and profligate, to cast the whole burthens of society upon the industrious and the virtuous." Then, too, the "master capitalist" would march his hundred hirelings to the polls and overwhelm the "farmers of small estates." Against this concrete social background Kent put the case for saving the ancient (i.e., 1777) constitutional foundations of New York; for protecting the tradition of "well balanced government" against the ultrademocratic "delusion of the day."[11]

Each of the distinguished Federalist spokesmen took a similar broad line in justifying suffrage restrictions. Elisha Williams, the young Van Buren's brilliant adversary in the courts of Columbia County and chief figure in the haughty Columbia Junto, explicitly dared the Democratic delegates to confront the reasoning of their great god Jefferson on the moral influence of cities. Would Jefferson's disciples spread "the contents of those [urban] sores through the whole political body" and so expose the yeoman interest to the will of "the ring streaked and speckled population of our large towns and cities, comprising people of every kindred and tongue"? "These cities," Williams warned, "are filled with men too rich, or too poor to fraternize with the yeomen of the country."[12] With Kent, he placed

[10] *Ibid.*, pp. 219–20.
[11] *Ibid.*, pp. 220–22.
[12] *Ibid.*, p. 253.

the democratic menace in the city and the future, deriding all attempts
to identify the Federalist suffrage plan with present aristocracy:
"Who ever before heard of a privileged order of all the freeholders
of the state—of an aristocracy of two-thirds of the whole body of the
people—of 250 dollar aristocrats?" Thus, Williams asserted:

If the time shall ever come . . . when the needy shall be excited to ask
for a *division* of your property, as they now ask for the right of governing
it, I would then have a senate composed of men, each selected from a district
where he should be known, by the yeomanry of the country—by the men
who . . . "wake their own ploughs with the dawn, and rouse their har-
rows with the lark."[13]

This lumpy Yorker mixture of bucolic poetry, squire's rights, and
well-balanced government, of class alarms and nativist snobbery, of
Jefferson, John Adams, and (in thin disguise) tax strategy, begins
to form a pattern.[14] The pattern becomes clear when debate turns to
a most important practical concern: finding a new system for selecting
some 15,000 public officials. Serious contention started with various
proposals for choosing justices of the peace and sheriffs, petty local
officers who had come to exercise, as Judge Jabez Hammond shrewdly
noted, a crucial role in maintaining state-wide party discipline.
Through them the party controlling appointments could systematically
exert its influence at the town and county level in every part of the
state.[15]

Most Federalists were quite ready to extend the electoral principle
to a vast number of local offices, even to find virtues in a direct popular
choice. (Martin Van Buren cruelly teased the orthodox Federalists,
reminding them that it was "wrong in principle to elect judicial officers.")[16] Their hostility was concentrated against the centralized
patronage system which had given the dominant Democratic party a
seemingly unbreakable political monopoly. For the Clintonians, part-

[13] *Ibid.*, p. 254. Abraham Van Vechten echoed Williams' annoyance with Democratic class-baiting: "This sound of aristocracy must by this time, I think, have lost
its force." *Ibid.*, pp. 371–72. He was quite wrong, of course.

[14] The tax-strategy component, the fear that the landless would shift the tax
burden entirely to the landlord, is suggested rather clearly in speeches by the Patroon,
Van Rensselaer, and by Elisha Williams, *ibid.*, pp. 182–83, 253.

[15] Hammond, *History of Political Parties,* II, 76–79, 479. Delegate Rufus King
insisted that control over the appointment of some 2,500 justices brought more political
power than would a monopoly over all the remaining patronage in New York. *Debates*
(1821), p. 315.

[16] *Ibid.*, pp. 321–22, 341.

ners and indeed effective masters in the New York anti-Democratic coalition, the whole point was to open local opportunities for their party. If the orthodox Federalist was not above such calculations, still he required a grander mission.

Again the Chancellor fixed the course of argument. The introduction of "downright" democracy by the proposed amendments to the old state constitution shook him to his depths: "an awful power" was emerging which might, like gunpowder or the press, "be rendered mighty in mischief as well as in blessings." The worst was certain, Kent thought, if the majority were allowed to concert its power through the agency of the party. America's great peril lay in "the disciplined force of fierce and vindictive majorities" stirred by "inflammatory appeals to the worst passions of the worst men." So New York must apply "something like quarantine laws" to isolate "this great moral pestilence," party spirit. Having unleashed "the power of the evil genius of democracy," the convention must not take the final, fatal step of leaving a great mass of appointments under the control of the Albany administration.

The great value of these local appointments is, that they weaken by dividing the force of party. They will break down the scheme of one great, uniform, organized system of party domination throughout the state, and they will give to the minor party in each county, some chance for some participation in the local affairs of the county.[17]

As always in the speeches of the Chancellor, there is a jarring incongruity between the ominous language of the warning and the modest plans for the defense. If New York were "on the very edge," a system of selecting certain petty public officers locally—some by direct election—would not be much help. The Federalist appointment scheme would be no more adequate to the defense of aristocracy than the $250 senatorial franchise.[18] One readily understands why Louis Hartz, a most rewarding analyst of American political divisions, concludes that Federalist conservatives were really confused liberals of a European cut, who believed imported nightmares and mistook ac-

[17] *Ibid.,* pp. 318–19.

[18] Hammond, from his contemporary observations, discounts the significance of a $250 qualification: this sum he considers "but a feeble evidence, in this country, of a man's prudence and sagacity . . . ; and it is still less an evidence of pecuniary independence." A suffrage qualification of $1,000, at least, would be necessary to give the senate to "the middle class." *History of Political Parties,* II, 51.

quisitiveness in their common countrymen for bloodthirsty agrarian-ism.[19] But the evidence of the convention debates indicates rather a different explanation of the paradox of seething democratic mobs and delicate restraints.

The New York Federalists found their ideal polity in an informally stratified republic, where a wholesome freeholder population chose leaders from among their well-born, well-trained, well-off neighbors —leaders who would maintain the rights and interests of the whole community, with a special regard for property rights. Their fear was for the imminent coming of anonymous democracy, detached from soil, neighborhood, custom, tradition—detached above all from the guiding influence of wise stewards. What they sensed specifically was not, I suspect, a physical threat to their lives and property titles, but a slipping of their relative income and influence. Their remedies were designed to check not revolution but the coarsening and demeaning of public life, the erosion of minority rights and interests within the legal democratic framework, the careless dispossession of a natural republican elite. If the Federalist proposals still promised little suc-cess, they were at least relevant to the end in view.

Further, the convention Federalists tended to see political virtue— and their own survival—in the locality, where weighty individuals would count for more and general party affiliation for less. Thus Kent found the last defense against the evil genius of democracy in the local choice of sheriffs and justices. In homelier language a stiff-necked Federalist judge—no "clamorous advocate for the people," as he assured the members—recommended the local election of justices as a way of clipping the power of "the constables and pettifoggers of the county," local politicians bound to the administration party who usurped the name of the people. Given the inevitable "tumult and commotion" of popular elections, he argued, one could nevertheless expect the substantial and enlightened men of the neighborhood to dominate such local contests.[20]

The New York Federalists, then, were not so blind to their situ-ation as an unwary reading of their most extravagant rhetoric might

<hr />

[19] Louis Hartz, *The Liberal Tradition: An Interpretation of American Political Thought Since the Revolution*, pp. 3–86 and *passim*. I have been much reassured in finding myself in agreement with Hartz on many points, especially on the value of Tocqueville for understanding American political thought and experience.

[20] *Debates* (1821), pp. 333–37.

suggest. New leaders were indeed rising, and the popular party organization was their vehicle. Old proprieties were threatened as social rank lost its claim to deference and thus to authority. If Federalists unreasonably despaired of the urban lower depths, they could cite Jeffersonian sources and air their fears in good Democratic company, as we shall see shortly. Certainly their gory prophecies of democratic violence to come out of the Europeanized city were false. They could imagine neither the flexible capacity of a popular regime to reconcile order with equality, nor the power of middle-class values among the unprivileged classes. They badly needed lessons from Tocqueville's "new science of politics."

The strangest Federalist error may have been to misread the future role of popular parties, in their bitterness over the rejection of their own stewardship. A sober contemporary chronicler and politician, Judge Hammond, struck brilliantly upon the character of the new party leadership, which made universal suffrage safe.

In every neighborhood . . . in this great state, there are to be found sober and thinking men, belonging to each of the two great parties, whose opinions regulate and give tone to public opinion in such neighborhood. These men, generally, have no interest other than the preservation of their right to personal liberty and property, and the general interest and prosperity of the country. There is, therefore, no danger, there can be no danger, that such men will countenance any palpably absurd or dangerous measure. It is the office and business of their less informed neighbors to decide upon the conflicting opinions of the leading men of these little circles.[21]

These were the men despised and feared as "pettifoggers" by the Federalists; they built sound party structures close to the ground and organized the political action of the masses. One thinks here of the Albany regency machine, just assuming control of Democratic operations, as an almost perfect case of the new leadership which could at once respond to popular sentiment, excite strong partisan emotions, and exercise a firm discipline over public opinion and action, generally in the direction of social order, governmental economy, and the maintenance of private rights under the rule of law.[22] One is reminded, too, of Tocqueville's persuasive suggestion that the lawyers, who dominated party affairs, were the supple, colorless and odorless po-

[21] Hammond, *History of Political Parties,* II, 50.
[22] An interesting study in this connection is John A. Garraty's *Silas Wright;* see also Shepard's *Van Buren.*

litical aristocracy of democratic America.[23] When the rich, the well-born, and the able lost touch with their community, the fluent, agile, self-taught, law-abiding party lawyer, aided by the local editor and some respectable farmers and small businessmen, took the main responsibility for ordering political life. They may not have been Jefferson's "natural aristocrats"; but within their limits they did well enough.

The Federalists arrived in 1821 a small, personally distinguished minority, already overshadowed even in their own camp by the followers of DeWitt Clinton; they departed a hopeless remnant in the politics of New York. Their contribution to the party dialogue was essentially a final reminiscence of the Fathers, unsuccessfully adapted to instruction of the errant sons. The man of the future was Martin Van Buren, in 1821 a prudent young lawyer who had risen quickly through the party ranks into the ruling circle of New York Democracy.

Astutely Van Buren confronted Kent and his allies first with the absurdity of their fears for democracy and then with the utter uselessness of their remedies if such dangers were accounted real. The Chancellor's catastrophic prophecies were patently delusory, Van Buren argued: scrapping the freehold franchise did not mean abandoning New York to the fury of the mob. The same step had been taken elsewhere with no sign of impending anarchy or confiscation. The question was simply this: Why disfranchise those many citizens who had families, households, "everything but the mere dust on which they trod to bind them to the country?" Why exclude mechanics, professionals, small farmers, men who paid taxes and gave militia service—"the bone, pith, and muscle of the population of the state?" But the suffrage question for the delegates, all considerable freeholders and most of them practical farmers, was already closed: guided by republican principles, they had come to the convention prepared to share political power with all but "the worst population of the old counties and cities," and could do so with no risk to basic private rights or social order.[24]

[23] Tocqueville, *Democracy in America*, I, 272–80.

[24] *Debates* (1821), pp. 255–59, 366–68. Van Buren opposed a suffrage scheme so broad as to admit the lower depths of the metropolitan area and so "drive from the polls all sober minded people." This was an early indication that the center of gravity for New York's Jacksonian party was to rest upstate, although Van Buren and his colleagues soon learned a higher appreciation of the urban lower classes. Some of Van Buren's "conservative" phrases in the 1821 convention came to haunt him in the 1840 campaign, when Whig orators were making him out the gaudy sybarite. *Ibid.*, pp. 366–68.

Democratic "radicals" went beyond Van Buren's views only in detail, and in their determination to identify Federalism with its most conservative rhetoric—its references to class balance, to mobs and terror—and thus deepen the social gulf between the parties. "We are all of the same estate—all commoners," Erastus Root protested. The imported dogma of "balanced government" had no relevance for "brothers of the same family, whose interests are similar."[25] All commoners; no superior aristocracy of property; but possibly, the radicals hinted, some higher virtue on the *other* side. Thus Peter R. Livingston of the powerful clan which gave New York several Democratic leaders:

But look to the higher classes of society. . . . Look to the republics of Greece. They were all destroyed by the wealth of the aristocracy bearing down the people. . . . And whom do you find in your armies in time of war? The miser? The moneyed Shylock? The speculator? No, sir; it is the poor and hardy soldier who spills his blood.[26]

Another delegate refused the gift of "thirty-two grave turf senators" to correct the follies of the common folk;[27] and General Root defiantly predicted that there would be a special merit in the voting of unpropertied young militiamen: "Not one out of ten . . . would vote for a haughty, proud, and domineering aristocrat;—they will vote for *republicans.*"[28]

Finally, however, the Democratic radicals made plain, as Van Buren had, that a broad franchise posed no threat to property rights— though such a threat was admittedly a "fatal objection" if the danger could be proved.[29] A one-class society, and that class safely committed to private property, was free of revolutionary risks. If we are brothers of the same family, we are brothers who share the burdens of the state, who in some way have an "anchorage" in the country.[30] Faced with Federalist proposals extending equal voting rights to Negroes, the radicals—in the universal American fashion—immediately discovered the concrete conditions in their abstract democratic case. Federalist fear of the political influence of rootless men, men with no social stake to guarantee independent conduct, migrated across the house. Indignantly Erastus Root portrayed the situation of New York City, where

25 *Ibid.,* pp. 223–24.  See also pp. 178–79.
26 *Ibid.,* pp. 224–25.        27 *Ibid.,* p. 238.
28 *Ibid.,* p. 360; see also p. 235.
29 *Ibid.,* pp. 179–80.        30 *Ibid.,* pp. 185–86.

"a few hundred free negroes of the city . . . , following the train
of those who ride in their coaches, and whose shoes and boots they
had so often blacked, shall go to the polls of the election, and change
the political condition of the whole state."[31]

"Property or People?" So Dixon Ryan Fox heads his chapter on
the 1821 New York convention. This is surely too severe a formulation for the dialogue on suffrage; too stark to capture the real differences between a dying Federalism which could list the vast majority
of the state in its select class of freeholders, and a prudent Democracy
which found at varying points the need for limiting the franchise
according to political capacity and community attachment. The Federalists had indeed more reservations about universal suffrage and a
much greater willingness to voice them candidly: they hoped still to
reinstate within a popular regime the political hegemony of a fairly
exclusive leading class. The Democrats were already mastering their
new style: stating emphatically—not assuming, as Federalists inclined
to do—the case for popular rule; lauding the wisdom and virtue of
the people; finding the main enemy in a vaguely conceived Tory
aristocracy of wealth; translating the democratic prudence of the
Founders into a popular idiom; creating a legitimate place for the
party organization which secured their rule. Efforts along these last
two lines were to be of great importance in Jacksonian politics, and
warrant further notice.

The New York convention agreed quickly to abolish the Council
of Revision (a mixed body of executive and judicial agents set up to
review legislation) and to vest the veto power exclusively in the governor. A majority on both sides approved the conventional American
two-thirds rule for passing over vetoes. But an amendment introduced
by Peter Livingston to weaken the veto power launched a prolix debate
on the relation of the people to legislature and executive.

Here the Federalists relied principally on the traditional doctrines
of John Adams, Madison, and Hamilton: armed with an effective
veto, Judge Jonas Platt advised, the governor would be a firm and
independent guardian against the "infirmities and vices inherent in
our form of government," peculiarly in large popular assemblies.[32]
The supporting arguments of Democratic moderates differed mainly

[31] *Ibid.*
[32] *Ibid.*, pp. 52–57. See also Kent's speech, *ibid.*, pp. 63–64.

by dropping references to endangered property rights, and by distinguishing more sharply between the virtues of the people and the vices of their representatives.[33] On a diminished scale this was the difference between Jefferson and Adams in their reasons for supporting a system of intragovernmental checks and balances.

More interesting for the future was a dispute within the radical contingent. "Sir," General Root intoned, "I deprecate that firmness which grows out of an independence of the popular voice, to oppose the popular will." Coming out of the common ranks and sharing the common interest of the community, the people's representatives needed no royal hand to control them.[34] If independent courts and frequent elections would not prevent legislative tyranny, Peter Livingston added, nothing else would: "When the tyrant of democracy arrives, it will be when the body politic is corrupted."[35]

The strongest retort came from Colonel Samuel Young, a convention "radical" who later, after some political wanderings, followed a long career as a middle-level Jacksonian leader in New York. Young denied that "by a sort of transmigration" the virtues of the people passed into their representatives. The innocent principal could not be blamed for the sins of his deputy (e.g., taking bribes for granting bank charters). Further, it was "altogether preposterous" to view the legislature as the peculiarly popular branch of government. Representatives drew their support from the counties and might easily form unprincipled combinations of local and special interests opposed to the broad majority interest of the state. The governor, on the contrary, was elected by and responsible to the whole people; his veto power could not be called aristocratic, or inconsistent in any proper sense with democratic principles.[36]

Looking beyond 1821, one finds the veto controversy significant mainly as a sign that Democrats were coming to regard this power as a weapon for the "real" majority against the pseudo-majorities formed in the legislature under lobby pressure. Twelve years of Jacksonian rule—the veto era of the American presidency, one might

---

[33] See speeches by Ogden Edwards and Van Buren, *ibid.*, pp. 59–61, 70–76.
[34] *Ibid.*, pp. 61–62, 100.
[35] *Ibid.*, pp. 92–93. See further remarks by Livingston, *ibid.*, pp. 51–52; see also the Tompkins speech, *ibid.*, pp. 79–82.
[36] *Ibid.*, pp. 101–4.

almost say—confirmed the Democratic preference and taught many Whigs the merits of the radicals' defense of the legislative power. It is surely revealing that the two leading critics of the veto power in the name of legislative authority, Livingston and Root, found their way into the Whig party, whereas Colonel Young, as noted above, supported the Jacksonians.[37] Even in Van Buren's argument for the Democratic moderates one can begin to see how a political device originally conceived as a rein upon the masses was finally to be valued by Jacksonians as a popular weapon of defense against a scheming aristocracy.

If the Democrats of 1821 were divided and unsure in their support of the executive veto power—it was not easy to forget that governors had once been royal appointees—they were still more hesitant about coming openly to the defense of parties as practical organizations with patronage needs. New Yorkers were notoriously adept in party management even at this time, but they were not quick to claim their honors; men seldom are in this matter. Nevertheless, the question of appointments brought the issue of parties and patronage forward in the convention, and here we may find a revealing final view of the party dialogue in 1821.

Most Federalists, it will be recalled, preferred local control and made a violent attack on party rule. The Democrats were badly split on the question: radicals and moderates alike were led by ideology to favor popular choice, by party interest to maintain a centralized patronage system. Doctrine prevailed, partially in the convention and completely in a later amendment. But Van Buren used the occasion to educate his Democratic colleagues in the value of party organization as a legitimate and necessary instrument of majority rule. No "distrust of the people" controlled his judgment.[38] The evils of patronage were not so obvious as men seemed to think. He would "go as far as any man, in endeavoring to curtail dangerous patronage in distinct bodies of men; but he would not go so far as to cut every cord that binds together the people to the government."[39] The supremacy of the state-wide majority, fairly won in free elections, need not be given

---

[37] Party affiliations of Root and Livingston are noted in Hammond, *History of Political Parties,* II, 323–24, 411, 517. References to Young's career are thick in the same volume.

[38] *Debates* (1821), p. 340.

[39] *Ibid.,* pp. 321–22.

away. Patronage power should be "put in the hands of the executive, not for himself, but to secure to the majority of the people that control and influence in every section of the state to which they are justly entitled."[40]

Van Buren tried to bring into the open the not yet respectable notion that democratic merit lay with general majorities, gathered and guided by party; that patronage could be something more than dirty politics. It was a lesson Democrats and Whigs came to know and practice well, although they generally preferred to learn and teach it silently, and even denounced it on appropriate occasions.

This was the sound of party dialogue in 1821. The wary republicanism of the Founders, even freshened with wholesome yeoman democracy and the spice of nativism, could no longer speak to American democrats. Henceforth the issues of political debate were to be formed entirely within a framework of democratic institutions and democratic language. No leading politician would again publish his descent from high Federalism, or treat democracy as a black box with a loud tick. This is not to say that Americans abandoned all the intricate machinery of prudence which the Founding Fathers built into the structure of democracy. Rather, they exposed the system more fully to direct popular influence—in confidence that social order and private rights were well secured by the position and habits of the American majority—and found good democratic reasons for maintaining much of their political inheritance. The old skepticism about the virtue of the people, and the accompanying restraints, went underground, so to say, and out of mind.[41]

### Exodus

The twenty-five years between constitutional conventions marked the era of Jacksonian Democracy in the politics of New York. When the 1846 convention met, political democracy was no longer a divisive issue: democratizing proposals, in a common language, came from all parts of the house, distinguishable only in their implications for practical party advantage or for social-economic policy. In the debates of 1846 one hears the falling echo of Jacksonian party quarrels beneath the surface of partial policy agreements, often most ambiguous,

---

[40] *Ibid.*, p. 341.
[41] David Riesman has guided me toward this notion of underground restraints in American democracy.

formed in the years of bold improvement projects, booming progress, and severe depression. Again in 1846 the political compass was drifting. Within two years many of the state's top Democratic leaders, behind their veteran chief, Van Buren, could desert to a Free Soil coalition and win more New York votes than the regular Democratic organization. Within a decade, the Whig party was dead.

The primitive Jacksonian persuasion, as it evolved in national politics, was always more a decalogue of moral prohibitions than an articulate set of social ends and means. Jackson roared his vetoes; his party sought to preserve the gift of popular favor, to claim a share of Jackson's potent magic, under the exacting conditions of political responsibility. Now in 1846, with the great Bank Monster slain and many little beasts dehorned by general incorporation laws, Jacksonians were left without a master symbol and a simple program to express their judgment of the times: life had met their policy demands and still defied their expectation of a moral restoration. Jacksonian ambivalence toward the rising economic order grew ever more pronounced: liberty pulled against stability, the main chance against the freehold idyll, new capitalistic ethos against old republican ethos. Most Democratic leaders were compelled to understand that corporations close to home provided jobs and means of payment, goods and services, and attractive investment opportunities for their constituents; that public enterprise and aid — "paternalistic government" in the equal-rights idiom—made market routes for isolated farmers, raised land values, opened areas to settlement. A restoration of the old republican order and its ways might still be preached and even hoped for; but this region wanted its canal or railroad, that town its bank, before the next election.

Adjusting persuasion to political circumstance was not in 1846 exclusively a Jacksonian need. The Whigs—most of them instantly, a few reluctantly—had absorbed the lessons of the democratic market place: they had acquired popular manners under the electoral whip and adapted their program and appeal to prevailing public attitudes and desires. The Democratic game, both grave and gay, of tying the can of aristocracy to Whigs' tails spurred many a Whig to outdo the Jacksonians in popular appeals; and the Whigs' broad program for social progress, requiring vigorous legislative action, gave them a fair claim to democratic and equalitarian purposes. From another side, the hard experience of depression, corporate failures, and state fiscal crisis had by 1846 turned many Whigs toward Jacksonian skepticism. Whig party voices were partially attuned to the anxious mood of the public which saw the tax bill written on the risky public loan or project and doubted mere assertions printed on a bank note. Much more easily Whigs had accepted—taken over, in some cases—the once radical Loco-Foco program of free banking and general incorporation, of laissez faire in general.

Thus the final passages of Jacksonian party dialogue are wavering, uncertain. Yet old antagonisms between the parties had been not so much resolved as patched up or evaded under the force of circumstance. Even at the end the tension between Old Republican values and nineteenth-century experience sustains, with some support from bitter memories, a muted battle of persuasions. There is far more of Monsters, debts, and ditches in the 1846 New York convention than of Mexico and slaves; and on these main concerns Jacksonians and Whigs did not go blithely, hand in hand, to meet the coming age of industrial and financial capitalism.[42]

The address which the convention delegates of both parties adopted to introduce their work to the public provides a useful index to political consensus in 1846. They had designed smaller electoral districts to give a better representation to local patches of opinion, had made most state and local offices elective (including the courts), had abolished costly surplus posts, had reduced and decentralized patronage. They had made strict provision for retiring the public debt, for cautiously concluding the discontinued improvement projects, and for drawing a substantial contribution to public revenues from the canals. They had written general incorporation articles which would restrict business monopoly, and had recommended stockholder-liability measures to make corporations sounder and more responsible. They had particularly looked to the safety and responsibility of banking corporations. In broad terms, the address proclaimed, the convention had worked to protect the private rights of person and of property against the abuse of delegated authority, the authority of the legislature in

[42] Discussions of general American social and economic conditions in Chapters 1-6, *supra,* are highly relevant to the case of Jacksonian New York. Useful works include: Robert G. Albion, *The Rise of New York Port, 1815–1860*; Blake McKelvey, *Rochester: The Water-Power City, 1812–1854*; Don C. Sowers, *The Financial History of New York State from 1789 to 1912*; O. L. Holley, *New York State Register,* 1843, 1845, 1846; Alexander C. Flick (ed.), *History of the State of New York,* Vol. VI; Fox, *Decline of Aristocracy.*

particular. And they had given the people a greater voice in initiating constitutional amendments.[43]

That an overwhelming majority (104 to 6) could finally agree to the amended constitution embodying such changes makes plain the limited character of party differences in 1846 upon the old issues of New York and national politics. Yet this vote cannot be taken quite literally: an affirmative vote, as several delegates insisted, expressed approval of some features and a willingness to tolerate the rest of the document as the best to be had by compromise. The difference in party perspectives which appeared in the debates was not less real because it fell within the limits of accommodation when broad social attitudes were translated into constitutional policy.[44]

The general values of political democracy were in 1846 so deeply rooted than even a minor departure from them could shock the convention. Everyone loved the people, bowed gladly to their sovereignty, celebrated their virtue and their judgment. No agrarian furies were planted in the wings, to sweep down with the first break in the rules of balance and decorum. Either men had come to read the pacific nature of the American masses; or they had learned the necessities of competitive politics in a democracy; or—most likely—both. When debate flowed through this channel, only a trace of party difference could be seen; a rather unexpected sort of difference. Democratic speakers, confident of their sole ownership of a legitimate democratic pedigree, seemed to feel less need to advertise their popular sympathies than many leading Whigs, who had to counteract the lingering aristocratic reputation of their party. On the whole, references to the people in the debates had a diffuse, generic, doctrinaire quality: one gets little feeling for the kind of people the People were; their character and ways, the source and type of their virtue. The people ruled by right and necessity; to say more was to court misunderstanding.

There is a well-worn tale to the effect that, all at once in 1840, the Whigs experienced a mock-conversion to democracy. Granting that the Log Cabin campaign was both novel and *ersatz,* one must still doubt the suddenness, the recency, the falsity, alleged of Whig democracy. Major party figures did not in a few years master a radically

---

[43] S. Crosswell and R. Sutton (reporters), *Debates and Proceedings in the New York State Convention for the Revision of the Constitution* (1846), p. 852. An alternative source for the 1846 convention is Bishop and Attree (reporters), *Debates and Proceedings* (1846).

[44] *Ibid.,* p. 839; for speeches qualifying affirmative votes, see pp. 837–39.

democratic rhetoric; did not, for example, learn to say with Alvah Worden that "Every attempt to throw obstructions in the way of the free and full exercise of the popular will, served only to make an artificial machine that would not and could not work beneficially for the public interest."[45] The Federalist legacy which some writers have awarded to the Whigs was, for the leading party spokesmen, an alien, unclean thing. "It was," charged Worden, "the last expiring effort of dying old Federalism that we saw here laboring to incorporate into this constitution this exploded idea, as to the exercise of popular power."[46] The source of his alarm, be it noted, was a proposal requiring routine age and residence qualifications of the governor; the source of that proposal was a committee dominated and chaired by Democrats. Not even the democracy of Jeffersonian times—the standard for *conservative* Whig delegates—was pure enough for Worden, as he denied the obligation of piety to ancient usages:

He was of opinion that the people had sent them here to sweep away as many absurdities as there were in it [the state constitution], and to conform it to the spirit of the age, and the advancement of the public mind. . . . His colleague [Whig Robert Cary Nicholas] had found the principle of this restriction in the democratic creed of 1798. . . . He really hoped his friend had come down to the democratic creed of 1846, and was not going to rest himself on the old doctrine of 1798. Why at that period it was sound democratic doctrine as then understood, that a property qualification was necessary to enable a man to vote for the office of Governor. But since 1798, we have made advances in the science of civil government; the public mind has progressed on that subject, and has become more intelligent, and the people are now better able than they were then to discharge the duties of administering and arresting and controlling their government.[47]

As debate touched an obviously tender spot—the growing presence of Irish and German immigrants, concentrated in the cities and especially in the great national port of entry—a latent antagonism could be felt, if seldom seen. The groanings of a Kent—even of Van Buren —which told the 1821 convention of the perils of great cities in the making, with their hordes of unwashed strangers, sores upon the body politic, were barely whispered now: cities and strangers had come,

45 *Ibid.,* p. 138.
46 *Ibid.,* p. 203.
47 *Ibid.,* p. 161. For an example of a Jacksonian trying to steal back the thunder of democracy, see the speech of Levi Chatfield, *ibid.,* pp. 216–19.

and the worst one could say to a general political audience was that ethnic politics would distract the state from its proper business. Delegates Murphy and O'Conor apart, most Democrats seemed again content to record their proprietary claim upon the immigrant vote, with little rhetorical reinforcement; while enterprising Whigs now urged their friendship for the alien as their Governor William H. Seward had earlier when he recommended aid to parochial foreign-language schools and showed his distaste for discriminatory voter-registration laws.[48] Admittedly, whatever open or cryptic nativist appeal there was in the convention came from a few Whigs who publicized the resentments of "large and respectable bodies" of native Protestants,[49] and no doubt the existence of this minority got through, with broadened party connotations, to the publics most sensitive on this question. Still, the most impressive characteristic of these debates was a cautious adaptation to cross-pressures: one prominent Democrat could hedge his opposition to all qualifications for the governor with an assurance that his own votes would almost always go to native candidates.[50]

The Democratic chorus came alive only when debate approached the social uses of democracy implied by the executive veto provision. Some Whigs labored to restore the image of the veto as a royal British ghost, and to invest the legislature with all the glories of the sovereign people.[51] But most of that party now saw too many political traps in that direction, not least the mortal risk of raising Andrew Jackson from his fresh grave. The initiative was seized by the Jacksonians, all the wrathful radical lieutenants, who denied that the people lent their virtues to highly corruptible legislative delegates. The people divided into hungry little bands of interest seekers were not the same as the whole people with a common interest: the legislature tended to tap the spurious layer of group interest; the governor a broader, deeper level of community values. For ordinary business the legislature would of course make policy; but when the agents grew too hot with spend-

[48] See especially the speeches of George Patterson, Elijah Rhodes, and Worden, *ibid.*, pp. 130–31, 131–32, 162–63.

[49] Speech of John T. Harrison, *ibid.*, pp. 269–70. A similar attitude appears in speeches by William Penniman, George Simmons, and William Angel (all relatively minor figures), *ibid.*, pp. 137, 139, 269.

[50] *Ibid.*, p. 271.

[51] Examples are William B. Wright, Penniman, and Ira Harris; for their speeches see *ibid.*, pp. 261–64, 265–66, 283–84.

thrift visions, the people needed to rely upon a single figure, utterly
exposed, generally responsible, probably Democratic, to say: No,
unless you have two-thirds. So had died the Monster Bank, the Mays-
ville policy, the latest threat to New York's trembling fiscal virtue:
all by the moral power of the veto.[52]

With the veto discussion it became clear that the Barnburner
Democrats, orthodox Jacksonians with a free-soil tinge who controlled
the important committees, would seek to load the new constitution
with detailed policy prescriptions, and thus to "tie up the power of
the legislature," as one of their leaders put it, "and limit the large
discretion now exercised by them."[53] Certainly this purpose was felt
most urgently with reference to public debt and public works; but it
extended also to the subject of corporations and banking, classic Jacksonian matter. Symbolic tilting with bank villains was never quite
convincing in the local situation. Previously, at the general and remote
level of national issues, the diverse tendencies in the Jacksonian appeal
—toward competitive "private" enterprise, toward social equality, toward rustic simplicity and Old Republican virtue—could be caught up
in a single flow of rhetoric aimed *against* representative forces of evil
like the Bank, which was made to stand for monopoly, class privilege,
consolidated federal power, capitalistic organization, political corruption, economic instability, financial chicane. But now the scene was
set for a confused, attenuated argument on the old Jacksonian economic issues, leading toward a policy of hesitant accommodation to
the inevitable: the further spread and growing influence of corporate
organization and paper-money banking.

New York in 1846 had long since passed the stage at which corporations could be identified primarily with little local bridge and
turnpike enterprises, academies and benevolent institutions: for all
the delegates the term suggested banks and insurance companies, railroads and factories—large-scale profit enterprises playing powerful
roles in a market and credit economy. Further, corporations were
peculiarly associated with large tasks of innovation and development,
in transportation, industry, finance. If the concept of the corporation

[52] The keynoter on the veto question was Michael Hoffman; see *ibid.*, pp. 285–87.
He was joined by nearly every consequential Democrat of the orthodox Jacksonian
persuasion, e.g., William Taylor, Arphaxed Loomis, John Brown, Lemuel Stetson,
and C. C. Cambreleng: *ibid.*, pp. 259–60, 260, 260–61, 264–65.

[53] Speech of Robert Morris, *ibid.*, p. 225.

as a quasi-public instrument had not wholly disappeared, yet such measures as the early acts permitting general incorporation in manufacturing and then the crucial Free Banking law of 1838 had gone far toward dissociating state and corporation. Indeed, C. C. Cambreleng —perpetual Jacksonian congressman with a background in railroading and a taste for the country which led him to report his occupation simply as Suffolk County farmer—deliberately phrased his bank-reform proposals "as much as possible to avoid the word 'corporation.'" Cambreleng objected to the use of the word "because he desired to get rid of it—as applied to every thing but municipal establishments." For him "the word associations was sufficiently descriptive of the character of all other bodies."[54]

The chief Democratic spokesman on the corporation question, a prominent Barnburner named Arphaxed Loomis, carefully affirmed that his party's purpose was not a ritual slaughter of legal monsters.

The committee have not deemed these incorporations an injury to the public, but on the contrary, an essential benefit. They viewed them as very useful institutions for the employment of capital, the development of enterprise, and to carry on the business which requires greater capital than individuals or limited partnerships can conveniently furnish. They had therefore made provision so as to render them safe, and put restraints on their abuse, corresponding with the restraints which nature has imposed on natural persons. It made no difference, in the estimation of the committee, whether business was to be carried on by corporators or others, so long as the business was legitimate. . . . But this system would allow men of small means to come in and unite in carrying on business. The principle was democratic; but when these privileges were limited to the few . . . it was opposed to every principle of democracy.[55]

A simple cure for monopolistic privilege, Loomis argued, was the prohibition of special acts of incorporation, opening this business form to all who would meet a few general requirements. But the lack of personal liability in corporations posed a most difficult problem: how could they purify the institution without killing it?

An incorporation is a person—a legal person. . . . It is impelled on to action by the same motives of gain which impel private citizens, but it is not restrained by the same motive of benevolence and of humanity, and of fellow feeling, which exists in the mind of every individual person, and which restrain[s] his selfish propensities in the acquisition of gain. Nor

[54] *Ibid.*, p. 761.
[55] *Ibid.*, p. 174.

were they restrained by those prudential considerations which prevent individuals from embarking their capital rashly, in the desperate hope of
gain, reckless of loss.

Thus Loomis, for his committee, offered an elaborate set of correc-
tives: corporations should be obliged to give full publicity to their
business records and to confine their debts within fixed limits; stockholders should be liable for corporate losses in proportion to their
claims on corporate profits. But he would offer large exemptions to
two major classes of corporations—insurance companies and railroads
—which could not survive under a personal liability rule.[56]

A few inflexible Jacksonian voices rose to a generic damnation
of the corporation as the instrument of an alien way of business.
Ex-Mayor Robert Morris of New York City—whose flourishing
political career was soon to carry him to the state supreme court bench
—declared himself "in the broadest sense of the term an anti-corpo-
rationist." A proper constitutional rule would prohibit passage of
"any act of incorporation to do that business which is done by individuals or any voluntary association of individuals."[57] His essential
object, Morris said,

was to prevent the establishment of the same kind of society here which
had been described as existing in other countries. He did not wish to see
women and children carrying baskets for the emolument of those who did
not labor, or children from an early age trudging off to factories to toil from
early day to night-fall for the good of others. . . . He proceeded to show
that what primogeniture did on the other side of the Atlantic, corporations
would do here.[58]

The feeble attempts at corporate regulation proposed in the convention
struck him "as a mere 'tub to the whale,' to amuse the people with the
idea that they were safe from these corporations."[59]

Another sort of radical appeal—grown almost obsolete in New
York politics within a brief decade—was the Old Jacksonian harangue
on corporate privilege as the root of all social evil, delivered in the
convention by a young mechanic-politician of Kings County, Conrad
Swackhamer.[60] It is difficult to say how far this was a special message

[56] Ibid., pp. 172–73.
[57] Ibid., p. 744.
[58] Ibid., p. 762.
[59] Ibid., p. 779.
[60] Bishop and Attree (reporters), Report of the Debate and Proceedings (1846),
pp. 971–72. Interestingly, one has to turn to the reports sponsored by the Barnburner
newspaper, the Albany Atlas, for an adequate record of this speech.

for the metropolitan worker constituency, how far the anachronism of an obscure young man who missed a change of party signals. In any case the speech was politically out of touch, in trying to revive the issue of monopolistic charters when the parties had almost reached common ground. And yet the old-time rhetoric of class antagonism allowed him to touch a reality which eluded the speeches of his fellow delegates: the facts of poverty and social immobility, not as the special curse of immigrants and Negroes, not as the sad material for charitable rescue operations, but as the continuing condition of a large class of urban laborers and mechanics. The career from journeyman to respectable, independent mechanic-businessman was indeed breaking down before the spreading influence of market-oriented production, organized by merchant capitalists and factory owners.[61] It was not Swackhamer's fault, perhaps, that protest had to be formed in the only convenient language, Loco-Foco, even as the terms grew obsolete.

The Whig response to proposed corporate regulations was generally mild and accommodating: they granted some need for reform, rejected detailed constitutional prescriptions as awkward and crippling, discouraged punitive measures, and broadly referred as much as possible to legislative discretion.[62] Attorney Richard P. Marvin of southwestern Chautauqua County led the major Whig attack upon strong stockholder-liability rules, presenting his party's case for the wholesome democratic corporation. The whole notion of individual liability for stockholders was false: it was of the essence of the corporation that only its collective property could be reached by creditors. Imposing personal responsibility for corporate debts would, in effect, place the poor man seeking capital for worthy enterprises and his advancement wholly at the mercy of "the wealthy capitalists," since men of moderate means would not dare invest under such conditions. Then, Marvin warned, "none but your John J. Astors would have any control of this matter." "If that was democracy," he announced, "to enrich the rich against the poor, then he wished to have nothing to do with it."[63] A colleague from Whig country east of the Hudson

---

[61] For a brief indication of the mechanic's changing position, see Taylor, *Transportation Revolution*, pp. 215–20, 223–24, 250–52, 294–300.

[62] A fair example of this Whig moderation may be found in the speech of Charles Kirkland: Crosswell and Sutton (reporters), *Debates and Proceedings in the New York State Convention* (1846), p. 741.

[63] *Ibid.*, pp. 746–47.

joined in denouncing unlimited liability "as the essence of aristocracy, and as calculated to drive out the middling classes from corporations, and let in the rich only."[64]

The decisions of the 1846 convention on the general subject of corporations reflect the mixture of sentiments evident in the debates.[65] Quite plainly a majority of both parties had determined to accept the corporate era with the mixed emotions a respectable farm or burgher couple might feel on receiving into the household a flashily successful son-in-law of uncertain character. They would try to treat the corporation as if it were like any other kind of enterprise, by making the device broadly accessible; yet the special utility of the corporation seemed to depend on the concession of certain unique privileges and immunities, and the resulting public perils demanded some degree of public regulation and control. Strict constitutional provisions were necessary to combat the potential dangers of the corporation; but lest such provisions prove too clumsy and discouraging, the legislature must be left a significant range of discretion.

The final compromise on corporations enlisted broad consent, and there was rarely a frontal collision of radically opposed views in the debates. Yet the parties did divide, if only in spirit and emphasis. Deep hostility found expression only at the Democratic fringe; enthusiastic acceptance (in the context of New York politics, 1846) appeared only among the Whigs. Even toward the middle ground of opinion important distinctions persisted. The dominant Barnburner Democrats were more concerned about the hazards, more inclined to strict constitutional prescription, and, with some lack of essential consistency, more determined to obliterate all traces of privilege preserved in special charter terms; although this doctrinaire application of the equal-rights principle might prevent the legislature from imposing more careful controls on public-service corporations. (Jacksonians assumed, of course, that legislative discretion could only lead to laxity and indulgence where special interests were involved.) Whig spokesmen cared more for the benefits in view, the positive stimulus to business enterprise; made more of the corporation as everyman's

[64] Speech of George Simmons, *ibid.*, p. 779. George Patterson and Horatio Stow, both upstaters, made similar Whig speeches for the corporation as the poor man's friend: *ibid.*, pp. 748, 762.

[65] They adopted a milder version of the Loomis reform proposals. See the amended constitution, Article viii, Sections 1–3, *ibid.*, p. 848.

way to wealth; worried more about the frustrating effects of severe
government regulations; looked to a flexible legislative policy rather
than a fixed constitutional rule. Within the range of attitudes de-
limited by economic and political experience down to 1846, New
Yorkers still separated by parties according to their Whig hopes or
Democratic fears, stirred by that supple instrument of economic
growth and change, the business corporation.

For the future it was more significant, perhaps, that the range of
differences had shrunk, that the question had been reduced to the
terms, the spirit, of acceptance. Here, however, where we are con-
sidering the convention as an epilogue to Jacksonian Democracy, felt
differences, no matter how vestigial, count for more than a new, reluctant, uneasy consensus. The Jacksonians of New York had been
trapped by history: the symbols of their discontent had been reformed
to meet their political standards; and the discontent which still remained, intensified in some respects, would have to await the new
conventional language of a later stage, when the simple, natural order
of equal rights and free trade seemed less perfect, when monopoly and
privilege and conspiracy assumed new shapes.

In the heat of mid-July the convention reached at last the battleground which Democratic strategists had instinctively chosen for a
mortal struggle: the field of public works and public finance. Viewed
in retrospect this angry dialogue of debts and ditches may seem an
*opéra bouffe* affair of wooden swords and ketchup wounds: a passionate dispute among men closely agreed on fundamentals—and knowing
it. None thought of repudiating the public debt without a shudder of
horror; only a matter of timing divided parties—ten years' difference,
more or less, in the projected data of deliverance from debt. None
thought of a large new career for state enterprise, although there was
some question of how tightly the legislature would be bound in its
discretionary use of credit. None considered liquidating the state's
interest in the major public works, despite some irritating disagree-
ments over the value and fate of two half-completed lateral canals.
In brief, the issues of public policy at stake in 1846 were, in this
domain, quite limited and specific. The dispute over debts and ditches
was not in fact a mortal battle; it went as deep as party differences
could be made to go in 1846 over state economic policy, that is to say,
just deep enough to stir the hostile persuasions of the Jacksonian era.

Michael Hoffman—a senior Democrat and an old comrade of

Van Buren, of Governor Silas Wright, of all the major New York figures in the pure Jacksonian line—advanced a highly detailed program for inclusion in the constitution. One set of proposals laid out exact priorities for distributing surplus canal revenues, with overwhelming emphasis on quick retirement of the public debt. Provisions were made for strict enforcement of state claims against corporate debtors. The legislature was required to levy taxes—there had been a prolonged tax holiday during the period of canal construction and debt accumulation—whenever the sinking funds failed to meet due claims. A second set of proposals was directed generally at "the power to create future state debts and liabilities, and in restraint thereof."[66]

Here is a chart of the Jacksonian conscience, indignant at what it has seen, half-ashamed at what it has condoned, and fiercely resolved to extirpate forever one whole order of public evil. In Hoffman's appeal for this program he seems almost to take pleasure in painfully probing the state's financial wounds. (Whig wits hinted that he had gone a little mad brooding so long over the mysteries of Jacksonian comptrollers' reports.) His demand for a return to direct state taxation appears as much a matter of expiating guilt as of solving fiscal problems. New York's drunken era of deficit financing and tax dodging had produced, he said, the cancer of "a British debt" in a republican society; a foundation for "perpetual, endless debt and taxation —to wither, blight and blast every branch of human industry." All dreams of painless salvation from rising revenues produced by salt or auction duties, or especially by surplus canal tolls, could lead only to repudiation, a monstrous crime, or to perpetual debt bondage. The "debtor system" of Governor Seward's Whig regime had exhausted and depressed state credit, brought on bank failures, amassed a $28,000,000 debt, and bequeathed to New York only the debris of worthless uncompleted works.[67]

Charged with enmity toward internal improvements, Michael Hoffman insisted that he opposed only that "debtor system" which "made pauperism, produced crime, misery, and distress in all countries."[68] He would let "all men who had means . . . engage in any project they might judge for their own interest"; but never should the people of the state be "sold into bondage" in order to force such

[66] *Ibid.*, pp. 355–56.
[67] *Ibid.*, Appendix, pp. 917–38.
[68] Bishop and Attree, *Report of the Debates and Proceedings* (1846), p. 873.

schemes into premature existence. The equally noxious system of lending the credit of the state to corporations had encouraged unscrupulous promoters to forage on the public treasury while plundering their own stockholders.[69] Other Democratic speakers echoed the same themes: denounced the British-Federalist-Whig system of finance; shuddered at the prospect of going again to "the sign of the three balls" to mortgage posterity; praised those "correct and liberal principles of political economy"—equal rights and laissez faire—which Jacksonians had established in Albany and Washington. No other convention subject, save possibly the veto, drew from the old-style Democrats such concerted, passionate appeals; no other debate so clearly engaged all that remained of Jacksonian vitality.[70]

The Whigs in the convention, quietly aided by some Hunker Democrats (minimalists on economic reform, with closer Southern ties), conceded the main field to the Hoffman-Barnburner policy and carefully deployed their strength to save a few secondary positions. DeWitt Clinton or the William Seward of 1838 would have been ashamed of such spineless heirs. Obviously the Whigs shared the horror of the radical Democrats at the thought of debt repudiation. And there can be no doubt that the very real troubles New York had encountered with its recent promotional spree demanded a long retreat from Clintonian enthusiasm, Clintonian grandiloquence, of the party which had taken no political hedges against the program's failure.

But the most important element, I think, in the Whig shift toward a Jacksonian position was represented in a low-ranking delegate's statement that "the time had gone by, when in view of the great resources and wealth of this state, it would be necessary to create new debts."[71] New York's economy had matured remarkably in the past generation: the canal system had been built close to its useful limits; and private enterprise and capital now seemed capable of taking in hand the new central phase of the state's economic development, railroad building. Even Michael Hoffman had dropped broad hints that the Barnburner critique of the public works program had clearly in view the declining economic importance of the canals as railroad com-

[69] *Ibid.*, p. 856.
[70] See the speech of Lemuel Stetson, *ibid.*, p. 865; also speeches of John H. Hunt and Conrad Swackhamer in Crosswell and Sutton, *Debates and Proceedings in the New York State Convention* (1846), pp. 706–7, 716–17.
[71] Speech of Ansel Bascom, *ibid.*, p. 723. See also George Patterson's speech, *ibid.*, p. 724.

petition grew: within two decades, he predicted, the railroads would be making a major bid for the interstate and local freight business.[72]

But just as the Democratic attack meant, politically, something more than a flexible accommodation to shifting channels of economic development, so the shuffling Whig retreat was not reducible to economic realism plus political embarrassment. Fighting for the life of the last two canals, or pleading for five years' delay in paying off the debt, Whig speakers revealed some of the attitudes and values which had given New York voters a choice of persuasions during the political era now coming to an end.

Thus William Angel—merchant, farmer, and local politician of Allegany County, on the line of an unfinished canal—resisted the appeal to "cold-hearted, frozen avarice" in Hoffman's theme of "tax and terror." In sober fact New York was in the position of a man on a fine $10,000 farm, enjoying excellent health, and $200 in debt. One should cheer, not weep; it was time to speak again to the "more liberal" feelings of the people. A penny-pinching policy would mean a stupid miscalculation of the tremendous potential of the western trade, a selfish denial to the neglected areas of facilities available to the rest of New York. Would the convention "look coldly on and see the people of Allegany and Cattaraugus pine in suffering and poverty, when they can be relieved without a call upon your pockets?" And why should these radical Democrats display such extreme solicitude for the rich creditor who held state bonds? The state, he argued, was just as fully committed to the thousands of farmers, mechanics, tradesmen, and laborers who had bought property or changed residence on the public promise to complete the works.[73] This Democratic "stop and tax" policy, a young Whig farmer added, reflected the pressure of Wall Street brokers, anxious for their public bond investments; and it matched a little too well the interests of railroad stockholders.[74]

When the convention had at great length gone through the original committee proposals, adopting the essential restraints on deficit financing as well as the basic plan for debt retirement, Michael Hoffman voiced his satisfaction at the results:

Taken together, they would preserve your faith—they would pay your debt. . . . He predicted that our labors had overcome the greatest dis-

72 *Ibid.*, pp. 922–24.
73 *Ibid.*, pp. 661–66, 702–3.
74 Benjamin Bruce's remarks, *ibid.*, pp. 703–5.

grace ever attempted to be cast on free institutions. And if you would go on, and fix the individual liability of the banker, compel corporations to be formed under general laws, and guard the power of municipal corporations to make debts, you would have achieved . . . that which you had not had for a quarter of a century—a legislature in these halls.[75]

Alvah Worden responded for the Whigs:

The difference between us had not been one of principle . . . Mr. W. concurred with the gentleman from Herkimer as far as he went. He thought it would be a proud monument to the integrity of the state, and that our action would go forth to the world evincing that we had met here and kept steadily in view the great object for which we convened—which was to make some provision for placing our credit beyond contingency or doubt. He congratulated the state and the convention on having secured a still further object—the completion of those great works of internal improvement, which more than any thing else had enabled us to assume that high attitude and to present ourselves in the position we occupied in this Union, and which would serve more than anything else to secure to this State for all time and forever, the appellation of the "Empire State."[76]

The Hoffmans and Wordens of New York could very nearly come to terms in 1846 over a policy toward debts and improvements, state enterprise and promotion. The Jacksonian closed the record with a curse upon an era of reckless adventure in government and business, and a prayer that a future nailed down to rigid constitutional specifications might be safe; the Whig with praise for the settlement of an obligation which had served wonderfully to launch eternal progress for the Empire State. It is difficult to categorize a difference so narrow, yet so essential to an understanding of New York parties in the Jacksonian era: a difference not of principle, as Worden fairly claimed, but of persuasion on the wane.

The men of 1846 had nearly concluded a chapter of Erie: an epoch of economic development partly symbolized by the Erie state canal, which revolutionized New York and brought a costly network of unprosperous ditches in its wake, and by the sick Erie railroad, which stuck the public treasury for two million dollars. Neither Jacksonians nor Whigs imagined the wild sequel to their Erie episode which a grandson of John Quincy Adams was to record. They had no policy to touch, not even rhetoric to image, those fierce, improbable beasts, the bulls and bears, the Drews and Vanderbilts and Fisks and Goulds who were tearing at each other and at the very substance of the first

[75] *Ibid.,* p. 733.
[76] *Ibid.*

agrarian republic. Michael Hoffman and Alvah Worden closed the Jacksonian era on a hopeful note, each with his distinct expectations for the future. A quarter-century later, Charles Francis Adams, Jr., was left wondering if the incredible struggle of the Wall Street titans recorded in his *Chapter of Erie* did not point to the end of the republican experiment:

As the Erie ring represents the combination of the corporation and the hired proletariat of a great city; as Vanderbilt embodies the autocratic power of Caesarism introduced into corporate life, and as neither alone can obtain complete control of the government of the State, it, perhaps, only remains for the coming man to carry the combination of elements one step in advance, and put Caesarism at once in control of the corporation and of the proletariat, to bring our vaunted institutions within the rule of all historic precedent.[77]

But the democracy which Jacksonians had helped to shape was not at the end of its resources; and the image of the good republican life which they had brought back into focus had further services to perform in American politics. In one form or another, the Jacksonian persuasion has been a perennially powerful strain in American life. It has much to answer for, but also much to claim. In its moments of dominance, it has often obscured political choices\for the American people: it has fixed thought on oversimplified dichotomies, moralized where it should have judged, encouraged an ungenerous fundamentalism. And yet the very faults of the persuasion as a guide to prudent statesmanship may have been its strength as a call to justice. For a society inevitably committed to maximizing economic gains, this persuasion in its various forms has been the great effective force provoking men to ask what their nation ought to be. Answers must be short and blunt and vivid in democratic politics; the Jacksonian persuasion answers with an image of the Old Republic. One can imagine nobler models. Yet this one affirms substantial goods and it has commanded assent. To men of the Jacksonian generation the Old Republic was just out of reach; was seen in something like the full design that Jefferson had drawn; was still directly relevant to their condition. As the image grows remote and small, the Jacksonian persuasion tends to lose either its power or its worth: its power when the appeal to the past turns merely cranky and archaic; its worth when nothing remains but the righteous wrath.

[77] Charles Francis Adams, Jr., *A Chapter of Erie*, pp. 150–51.

# APPENDIX A

## NOTE ON TOCQUEVILLE AS HISTORICAL WITNESS

The general neglect of Tocqueville for limited historical uses is not mysterious; indeed the author invited it in his introductory confession that "in America I saw more than America; I sought there the image of democracy itself, with its inclinations, its character, its prejudices, and its passions, in order to learn what we have to fear or to hope from its progress."[1] The approach is alternately hortatory, speculative, analytic, descriptive; the contents present a seeming chaos of latent and manifest, essential and accidental traits, of French and American experiences, of glacial movements of democracy over seven centuries and the events of a decade.

Admittedly, then, there are difficulties in handling the *Democracy* as a historical source, and yet it is impossible to believe that these difficulties are as overwhelming as the common avoidance of the task would suggest. For one thing, Tocqueville has a clear mind and a lucid style. For another, consider his manifest intention: he maintains in the opening sentences of the Introduction that "the study of American society" shaped his conception of the great democratic revolution, and repeatedly he specifies the link between America and democracy not as something casual but exactly as the relationship between the case and the class.[2] America could reveal "the image of democracy" because there the social revolution "seems to have nearly reached its natural limits," and this "without having had the revolution itself."[3] "I have selected the nation . . . in which its [democracy's] development has been the most peaceful and the most complete in order to discern its natural consequences."[4] Tocqueville's modest apology is entirely consistent, at least in principle, with the design of his work: "I do not know whether I have succeeded in making known what I

---

[1] *Democracy in America*, I, 14.    [2] *Ibid.*, I, 3.
[3] *Ibid.*, I, 13.    [4] *Ibid.*, I, 14.

saw in America, but I am certain that such has been my sincere desire, and that I have never, knowingly, molded facts to ideas, instead of ideas to facts."[5]

Tocqueville's generality and abstractness unquestionably raise serious problems of method. He is by no means an empirical reporter of the American scene; a conceptual scheme of democracy informs every part of his work. Indeed Tocqueville accuses himself of attempting, on rhetorical considerations, "to carry all his ideas to their utmost theoretical conclusions, and often to the verge of what is false or impracticable"—a comment on political reasoning which has some bearing on the method of social inquiry.[6] This is not, however, to be taken as a crude confusion of logic and experience. The large conception of democracy is drawn from historical evidence, given theoretical elaboration and tried out upon the materials of observation. The question, in short, is not one of "abstraction" versus "reality" but of the value of Tocqueville's thesis in organizing and explaining American phenomena. The careful reader can nearly always tell when the text is developing the logic of the type, when it is characterizing the American (or French) situation, when it is bringing the two things into single focus.

Tocqueville's conception of the "fatal circle" of human possibilities in democratic times—i.e., his idea of democracy as a type of social system with necessary tendencies and limits—does not exclude the significance of accident and art in the determination of actual consequences. On the contrary, he insists upon the "wide verge" of the circle, within which history, place, and rational invention exercise decisive influence. Thus in his discussion of America, contingent circumstance and reasoned choice are seen to exercise substantial influence within the democratic social system.[7] Indeed, one may propose a novel criticism of the *Democracy*: that, beginning with a general conception of democracy, and then allowing for the unique varieties of American experience, Tocqueville does not attempt an integration of both elements. At most one finds a series of American themes, variously juxtaposed according to the subject of observation, all rather loosely related to a common point of departure in the framework theory.

[5] *Ibid.,* I, 15.
[6] *Ibid.,* I, 16; II, v–vi.
[7] *Ibid.,* II, 334; I, 319–22.

Other familiar criticisms of Tocqueville as a guide to Jacksonian society are, I think, less serious. His manifest concern with French prospects in the midst of American life tends to sharpen, not confuse, the discussion, for he must distinguish American, French, and universal democratic elements in order to discover a prudent policy for France.[8] The further question of aristocratic bias has generally—and rightly—been resolved in Tocqueville's favor. Beyond a rare capacity to enter sympathetically into another realm of values, he had the gift of a great curiosity about the ways of men; he typically responded to his shocks and surprises by inquiring into the actual and the possible.[9]

Finally, the rebuke to Tocqueville's gullibility—that he was taken in by tendentious conservative informants—has some truth and little consequence. The catalogue of Tocqueville's "errors," some of which are far from obviously wrong, refers primarily to chapters in the first volume constituting a kind of manual of American government for foreigners; refers, that is, to sections of the work which now hold least interest and value for the historian. The discussion of the "customs of the people"—"a central point in the range of observation, and the common termination of all my inquiries"—has errors and omissions, of course; but no critic, to my knowledge, has successfully traced these to a systematic American Whig bias.[10] It would be marvelous indeed to trace Tocqueville's strikingly original views of American democracy directly to informants who had given no sign of a like understanding.

Thorough Jacksonians like Colonel Samuel Young of New York and Robert Rantoul, Jr., of Massachusetts found Tocqueville a more than acceptable interpreter of their nation. Rantoul called him, in 1848, "the greatest political philosopher of this age."[11] Thomas Hart Benton—perhaps the severest Jacksonian critic of Tocqueville's *Democracy*—complained mainly of the unflattering treatment of Jackson himself, and ascribed *that* misunderstanding to Whig misinformants.[12] Professor George Pierson mentions a young American in Paris who must have fed Tocqueville Federalist ideas and sources. This may be;

[8] E.g., *ibid.,* I, 323–30.

[9] E.g., *ibid.,* I, 252–53; II, 331–34.

[10] *Ibid.,* I, 322; see also p. 319 n., where he defines customs broadly as "the moral and intellectual characteristics of men in society."

[11] Rantoul, *Writings,* p. 679. On Young's approval, see Dorfman, *Economic Mind,* II, 660.

[12] *Thirty Years' View,* I, 112–14.

but one should add that the young informant, Theodore Sedgwick III, was the son of a Jacksonian convert (discussed in Chapter 8) and himself became an active Loco-Foco Democrat.[18]

These brief remarks are not designed to absolve the *Democracy* of all faults, but simply to clear a way through certain general objections to the critical use of an immensely valuable historical source.

[18] See *Tocqueville and Beaumont,* pp. 731–32.

# APPENDIX B

## NOTE ON VAN BUREN'S VIEW OF PARTIES

During his political retirement Van Buren attempted an *Inquiry into the Origin and Course of Political Parties in the United States.* Although largely a stock Democratic interpretation of historical party positions, the book offers a few insights into democratic politics that are worth noting. Both the persistence and the passion which Van Buren finds in American party affiliations suggest that party meant much more than a specific interest association. Thus he observes:

Sons have generally followed in the footsteps of their fathers. . . . Neither the influences of marriage connections, nor of sectarian prejudices, nor any of the strong motives which often determine the ordinary actions of men, have, with limited exceptions, been sufficient to override the bias of party organization and sympathy, devotion to which has, on both sides, as a rule, been a master-passion of their members.[1]

There would seem to be something accidental in this hereditary transmission of loyalties; but Van Buren insists that there is strong reason in it.

At another point the venerable ex-Magician reflects upon the social sources of support for the two central political traditions, Jeffersonian and Hamiltonian, which had given direction and meaning to party struggles through the mid-nineteenth century. One is at first inclined to discount his judgments: they are too pat, too neatly fitted to the requirements of his own political principles. He takes in as Democratic supporters exactly those whom Democratic theory honors; and throws to the opposition (whether Federalist, Whig, or 1850's Republican) social groups which on Democratic principle *should* be rejected. On sober second thought—an exercise much recommended by Van Buren—one finds less reason for such skepticism: the Democrats had an ideal constituency, postulated its interests, appealed for

[1] *Political Parties,* p. 7.

its support, and in large measure got the votes of actual groups most closely matched to the ideal.

Van Buren maintains that parties in the Hamiltonian tradition (including the Whigs) were "constructed principally of a network of special interests,—almost all of them looking to Government for encouragement of some sort." Their supporters were typically—in standard Jacksonian language—men associated with banks, insurance companies, manufacturing and transportation corporations: enterprises marked by their "possession of special and, in some of these cases, of exclusive privileges." With privilege came wealth and social distinction, and power over an army of dependents: journalists, lawyers, and others attracted to "the fountains of patronage." Joined by obvious mutual interests, such men moved spontaneously toward a single goal. Among other things they had no need of caucuses and conventions; hence their righteous indignation in attacking "all usages or plans designed to secure party unity."

But the Hamiltonian parties have been doomed to failure in America: "Although Hamilton's policy was successful with many, it failed signally . . . with the most numerous and consequently the most powerful class of our citizens—those engaged in agriculture." The commercial and manufacturing interests were on the whole responsive to a political appeal which promised governmental favors; when a rare few Democrats appeared among these classes—especially in the groups most dependent upon special privilege—their party allegiance tended to dissolve: three-fourths of such Democrats soon became Hamiltonian converts. The "main-stay of the Democratic party" must always be "the farmers and planters," the classes furthest removed from "the seductive influence of the money power"; in the second rank were "the mechanics not manufacturers, and the working classes." The farmers and mechanics neither had nor wanted special favors; the only effect of the Hamiltonian appeal upon them was to increase "that antagonism to some extent between those who live by the sweat of their brow and those who live by their wits." Indeed, Van Buren prophesies: "It can only be when agriculturalists abandon the implements and the field of their labor and become, with those who now assist them, shopkeepers, manufacturers, carriers, and traders, that the Republic will be brought in danger of the influences of the money power. But this can never happen."

Literally applied to New York politics in the Jacksonian era, Van

Buren's view of class constituencies is patently untenable. (His references are all to national politics, and the applications to New York are my own extension of his remarks.) In the simplest terms the "commercial, manufacturing, and trading classes" dependent upon privilege and favor could not supply the 45 to 50 per cent of the popular vote which the Whigs regularly gathered; moreover, the farmers of the state often showed a very healthy appetite for public favors. Nevertheless Van Buren does suggest—with the authority of a participant-leader—where the Democrats looked for support, in what terms they cultivated party attachment. The "wits" and the "sweats" were, I think, real groupings in New York, to be found not only at the obvious extremes—say, speculative bankers and ditchdiggers— but also within the great occupational classes, farmers and mechanics. Van Buren at least hints at this more subtle classification of party supporters when he specifies "the mechanics not manufacturers," and when he specifies the point at which farmers would lose their political virtue, and their Democratic voting habit—i.e., the point at which they acquired the primary characteristics of speculators, traders, and the like. Again, although Van Buren's notion of privilege and favor seeking as the key to party preference cannot account for the political behavior of gross occupational classes like farmers or mechanics, it may be more persuasive when those classes are subdivided by region and special situation into groups that had least and needed most from government—canals, railroads, banks—and those that had most or asked least of such support.[2]

[2] *Ibid.*, pp. 177–231.

# BIBLIOGRAPHY

Abernethy, Thomas P. From Frontier to Plantation in Tennessee. Chapel Hill, N.C., 1932.

Adams, Charles F., Jr. A Chapter of Erie. Boston, 1869.

Adams, Henry. John Randolph. American Statesmen series. Boston, 1896.

Adams, John Quincy. Memoirs of John Quincy Adams, Comprising Parts of His Diary from 1795 to 1848. Edited by Charles Francis Adams. 12 vols. Philadelphia, 1875–77.

Albion, Robert G. The Rise of New York Port, 1815–1860. New York, 1939.

Atherton, Louis. The Pioneer Merchant in Mid-America. University of Missouri Studies, Vol. XIV, No. 2. Columbia, Mo., 1939.

Baldwin, Joseph G. Party Leaders; Sketches of Thomas Jefferson, Alexander Hamilton, Andrew Jackson, Henry Clay, John Randolph of Roanoke. . . . New York, 1855.

Bancroft, George. Literary and Historical Miscellanies. New York, 1855.

———. Martin Van Buren to the End of His Public Career. New York, 1889.

Bassett, John Spencer. Life of Andrew Jackson. 2 vols. in 1. New York, 1916.

Beard, Charles A. Economic Origins of Jeffersonian Democracy. New York, 1915.

Benton, Thomas Hart (ed.). Abridgment of the Debates of Congress from 1789 to 1856. 16 vols. New York, 1857–61.

———. Thirty Years' View. 2 vols. New York, 1854–56.

Bishop, J. Leander. A History of American Manufactures from 1608 to 1860. 3 vols. Philadelphia, 1861–68. Vol. II.

Blau, Joseph L. (ed.). Social Theories of Jacksonian Democracy: Representative Writings of the Period 1825–1850. New York, 1947.

Boardman, James. America and the Americans. London, 1833.

Boas, George (ed.). Romanticism in America. Baltimore, 1940.

Bower, Robert T. "Note on 'Did Labor Support Jackson?: the Boston Story,'" Political Science Quarterly, LXV (September 1950), 441–44.

Bowers, Claude G. The Party Battles of the Jackson Period. New York, 1922.

Branch, E. Douglas. The Sentimental Years, 1836–1860. New York, 1934.

Breck, Samuel. Recollections of Samuel Breck with Passages from His Note-Books, 1771–1862. Edited by H. E. Scudder. Philadelphia, 1877.

Bremer, Frederika. The Homes of the New World; Impressions of America. Translated by Mary Howitt. 2 vols. New York, 1853.

Brogan, D. W. The American Character. Vintage Books. New York, 1956.

Brown, Herbert Ross. The Sentimental Novel in America, 1789–1860. Durham, N.C., 1940.

Buckingham, James Silk. The Eastern and Western States of America. 3 vols. London, 1842.

Burnham, W. Dean. Presidential Ballots, 1836–1892. Baltimore, 1955.

Catterall, Ralph C. H. Second Bank of the United States. Chicago, 1903.

Chambers, William Nisbet. Old Bullion Benton, Senator from the New West: Thomas Hart Benton, 1782–1858. Boston, 1956.

Channing, Edward. A History of the United States. 6 vols. New York, 1905–25. Vol. V.

Church, Jeremiah. Journal of Travels, Adventures, and Remarks of Jerry Church. Harrisburg, Pa., 1933.

Claxton, Timothy. Memoir of a Mechanic; Being a Sketch of the Life of Timothy Claxton, Written by Himself; Together with Miscellaneous Papers. Boston, 1839.

Cobbett, William. The Emigrant's Guide. London, 1830.

―――. Life of Andrew Jackson, President of the United States of America. New York, 1834.

―――. Rural Rides. 2 vols. Everyman's Library. London, n.d.

―――. A Year's Residence in the United States. London, 1820.

Cobden, Richard. The American Diaries of Richard Cobden. Edited by Elizabeth H. Cawley. Princeton, N.J., 1952.

Cole, G. D. H. Persons and Periods. Pelican Books. Harmondsworth, Middlesex, England, 1945.

Colton, Calvin. The Rights of Labor. 3d ed. New York, 1847.

Cooper, James Fenimore. The American Democrat. New York, 1931.

―――. Autobiography of a Pocket-Handkerchief. Evanston, Ill., 1897.

―――. Correspondence of James Fenimore Cooper. Edited by James Fenimore Cooper, grandson. 2 vols. New Haven, 1922.

―――. The Crater. Vol. XV of The Works of James Fenimore Cooper. Mohawk edition. New York, 1896.

―――. Home as Found. Vol. XIV of Mohawk edition. New York, 1896.

―――. Homeward Bound. Vol. XII of Mohawk edition. New York, 1896.

―――. The Monikins. Vol. XXXI of Mohawk edition. New York, 1896.

―――. New York. Edited by Dixon Ryan Fox. New York, 1930.

————. Notions of the Americans. Vol. I, London, 1828; Vol. II, Philadelphia, 1836.

————. The Prairie. Introduction by Henry Nash Smith. Rinehart editions. New York, 1953.

————. The Redskins. Vol. XXV of Mohawk edition. New York, 1896.

————. The Ways of the Hour. Vol. XXIV of Mohawk edition. New York, 1896.

Crockett, David. A Narrative of the Life of David Crockett. Philadelphia, 1837.

Cunningham, Mary E. (ed.). James Fenimore Cooper: A Re-appraisal. Cooperstown, N.Y., 1954.

Current, Richard N. Daniel Webster and the Rise of National Conservatism. The Library of American Biography. Boston, 1955.

Curti, Merle. The Social Ideas of American Educators. New York, 1935.

Darling, Arthur B. Political Changes in Massachusetts, 1824–1848: A Study of Liberal Movements in Politics. New Haven, 1925.

Davis, Emerson. The Half Century; or, A History of Changes . . . and Events . . . Chiefly in the United States, Between 1800 and 1850. Boston, 1851.

Diamond, Sigmund. The Reputation of the American Businessman. Cambridge, Mass., 1955.

Dickens, Charles. American Notes for General Circulation. Vol. XVII of The Works of Charles Dickens. Library edition. Boston, 1867.

————. Life and Adventures of Martin Chuzzlewit. London, 1844.

Dodd, William E. Expansion and Conflict. Vol. III of The Riverside History of the United States. Boston, 1919.

Dorfman, Joseph. The Economic Mind in American Civilization. 3 vols. New York, 1946–49. Vol. II.

————. "The Jackson Wage-Earner Thesis," *American Historical Review,* LIV (January 1949), 296–306.

Doty, Sile. The Life of Sile Doty, 1800–1876. Foreword by Randolph G. Adams. Detroit, 1948.

Downing, Major Jack [Seba Smith]. Jack Downing's Letters. Philadelphia, 1845.

————. My Thirty Years Out of the Senate. New York, 1859.

Eaton, Clement. Henry Clay and the Art of American Politics. The Library of American Biography. Boston, 1957.

Ekirch, Arthur A., Jr. The Idea of Progress in America, 1815–1860. New York, 1944.

Emerson, Ralph Waldo. Journals. Edited by Edward W. Emerson and Waldo E. Forbes. 10 vols. Boston, 1909–14.

Evans, George H. Business Incorporations in the United States, 1800–1943. Publications of the National Bureau of Economic Research, No. 49. New York, 1948.

Farwell, John V. Some Recollections of John V. Farwell. Chicago, 1911.

Fish, Carl Russell. The Rise of the Common Man, 1830–1850. Vol. VI of A History of American Life. New York, 1927.

Flick, Alexander C. (ed.). History of the State of New York. 10 vols. New York, 1933–37. Vol. VI.

Ford, Thomas. A History of Illinois. Chicago, 1854.

Ford, Worthington C. (ed.). "Van Buren–Bancroft Correspondence, 1830–1845," in Proceedings of the Massachusetts Historical Society. Third Series, Vol. II (June 1909). Boston, 1909.

Fox, Dixon Ryan. The Decline of Aristocracy in the Politics of New York. Columbia Studies in History, Economics and Public Law, Vol. LXXXVI, No. 198. New York, 1919.

——— (ed.). Sources of Culture in the Middle West. New York, 1934.

Freedley, Edwin T. A Practical Treatise on Business. Philadelphia, 1853.

Gallatin, Albert. Suggestions on the Banks and Currency of the Several United States. New York, 1842.

Garraty, John A. Silas Wright. New York, 1949.

Gates, Paul W. The Illinois Central and Its Colonization Work. Harvard Economic Studies, Vol. XLII. Cambridge, 1934.

Goodman, Nathan (ed.). A Benjamin Franklin Reader. New York, 1945.

Goodrich, Carter. "The Revulsion Against Internal Improvements," Journal of Economic History, X (November 1950), 145–69.

Goodrich, Samuel G. Recollections of a Lifetime. Vol. II. New York, 1856.

Gouge, William M. A Short History of Paper Money and Banking in the United States. Philadelphia, 1833.

Grattan, Thomas Colley. Civilized America. 2 vols. London, 1859.

Greeley, Horace. Recollections of a Busy Life. New York, 1868.

Griscom, John H. The Sanitary Condition of the Laboring Population of New York. New York, 1845.

Grossman, James. James Fenimore Cooper. American Men of Letters series. New York, 1949.

Grund, Francis J. The Americans in Their Moral, Social and Political Relations. Boston, 1837.

Gurowski, Adam G. de. America and Europe. New York, 1857.

Hacker, Louis M. The Triumph of American Capitalism. New York, 1940.

Hamilton, Alexander, John Jay, and James Madison. The Federalist: A Commentary on the Constitution of the United States. Modern Library. New York, n.d.

Hamilton, James A. Reminiscences of James A. Hamilton. New York, 1869.

Hammond, Bray. "Banking in the Early West: Monopoly, Prohibition, and Laissez Faire," *Journal of Economic History,* VIII (May 1948), 1–25.

————. "Free Banks and Corporations: the New York Free Banking Act of 1838," *Journal of Political Economy,* XLIV (April 1936), 184–209.

————. "Jackson, Biddle, and the Bank of the United States," *Journal of Economic History,* VII (May 1947), 1–23.

Hammond, Jabez D. *The History of Political Parties in the State of New York.* 2 vols. Albany, 1842.

————. Political History of the State of New York from January 1, 1841 to January 1, 1847. Vol. III; including The Life of Silas Wright. Syracuse, 1852.

Hammond, J. L., and Barbara Hammond. The Bleak Age. Pelican Books. West Drayton, Middlesex, England, 1947.

Handlin, Oscar. Boston's Immigrants, 1790–1865. Cambridge, Mass., 1941.

————, and Mary Handlin. Commonwealth: A Study of the Role of Government in the American Economy; Massachusetts, 1774–1861. New York, 1947.

Hansen, Marcus Lee. The Atlantic Migration, 1607–1860. Edited by Arthur H. Schlesinger. Cambridge, Mass., 1940.

Hartz, Louis. Economic Policy and Democratic Thought: Pennsylvania, 1776–1860. Cambridge, Mass., 1948.

————. The Liberal Tradition: An Interpretation of American Political Thought Since the Revolution. New York, 1955.

Hawthorne, Nathaniel. The American Notebooks. Edited by Randall S. Stewart. New Haven, 1932.

Hoffman, Charles Fenno. A Winter in the Far West. 2 vols. London, 1835.

Hofstadter, Richard. The Age of Reform: From Bryan to F.D.R. New York, 1956.

————. The American Political Tradition. New York, 1948.

————. "William Leggett, Spokesman of Jacksonian Democracy," *Political Science Quarterly,* LVIII (December 1943), 581–94.

Holley, O. L. New York State Register for 1843. Albany, 1843.

————. The New York State Register for 1845. New York, 1845.

————. The New York State Register for 1846. New York, 1846.

Hone, Philip. The Diary of Philip Hone, 1828–1851. Edited by Allan Nevins. 2 vols. New York, 1927.

Howells, William C. Recollections of Life in Ohio from 1813–1840. Cincinnati, 1895.

Hugins, Walter E. "Ely Moore: the Case History of a Jacksonian Labor Leader," *Political Science Quarterly,* LXV (March 1950), 105–25.

Hunt, Freeman. Worth and Wealth. New York, 1856.

Hunt, Gaillard, and James Brown Scott (eds.). The Debates in the Federal Convention of 1787 which Framed the Constitution of the United

States of America, Reported by James Madison . . . International edition. New York, 1920.

Illinois Constitutional Convention, 1847. The Constitutional Debates of 1847. Edited by Arthur C. Cole. Collections of the Illinois State Historical Library, Vol. XIV. Springfield, Ill., 1919.

Jackson, Andrew. Correspondence of Andrew Jackson. Edited by John Spencer Bassett and J. Franklin Jameson. 7 vols. Washington, D.C., 1926–35.

Jefferson, Thomas. The Works of Thomas Jefferson. Edited by Paul Leicester Ford. 12 vols. New York, 1904.

————. The Writings of Thomas Jefferson. Edited by H. A. Washington. 9 vols. New York, 1835–54. Vol. VI.

Johnson, Clifton. Old-Time Schools and School-Books. New York, 1935.

Kendall, Amos. Autobiography of Amos Kendall. Edited by William Stickney. Boston, 1872.

Koerner, Gustave. The Memoirs of Gustave Koerner, 1809–1896. Edited by Thomas J. McCormack. 2 vols. Cedar Rapids, Iowa, 1909.

Kouwenhoven, John. Made in America. New York, 1948.

Krout, John Allen, and Dixon Ryan Fox. The Completion of Independence, 1790–1830. Vol. V of A History of American Life. New York, 1944.

Larcom, Lucy. A New England Girlhood. Boston, 1889.

Larkin, Oliver W. Art and Life in America. New York, 1949.

Lawrence, Amos. Extracts from the Diary and Correspondence of the Late Amos Lawrence. Edited by William R. Lawrence. Boston, 1855.

Lawrence, D. H. Studies in Classic American Literature. Anchor Books. New York, 1953.

Leggett, William. A Collection of the Political Writings of William Leggett. Edited by Theodore Sedgwick, Jr. 2 vols. New York, 1840.

Lewis, R. W. B. The American Adam. Chicago, 1955.

Lieber, Francis. The Stranger in America. 2 vols. London, 1835.

Lincoln, Charles Z. Constitutional History of New York. 5 vols. Rochester, 1906. Vol. II.

———— (ed.). State of New York: Messages from the Governors. Vols. III, IV. Albany, 1909.

McGrane, Reginald C. (ed.). The Correspondence of Nicholas Biddle Dealing with National Affairs, 1807–1844. Boston, 1919.

————. The Panic of 1837. Chicago, 1924.

McKelvey, Blake. Rochester: The Water-Power City, 1812–1854. Cambridge, Mass., 1945.

McMaster, John B. A History of the People of the United States from the Revolution to the Civil War. 8 vols. New York, 1883–1913. Vols. V, VI.

Martineau, Harriet. Society in America. 2 vols. New York, 1837.

Massachusetts Constitutional Convention, 1820. Journal of Debates and Proceedings in the Convention . . . to Revise the Constitution of

Massachusetts . . . 1820. Reported for the Boston Daily Advertiser. Rev. ed. Boston, 1853.

Massachusetts Constitutional Convention, 1853. Official Report of the Debates and Proceedings in the State Convention . . . to Revise and Amend the Constitution. 3 vols. Boston, 1853.

Mathews, Cornelius. The Career of Puffer Hopkins. New York, 1842.

———. The Motley Book. New York, 1840.

Matthiessen, F. O. American Renaissance. New York, 1941.

Meyer, Leland W. The Life and Times of Colonel Richard Mentor Johnson of Kentucky. New York, 1932.

Meyers, Marvin. "The Great Descent: A Version of Fenimore Cooper," The Pacific Spectator, X (Autumn 1956), 367–81.

———. "The Jacksonian Persuasion," American Quarterly, V (Spring 1953), 3–15.

Miller, Perry (ed.). The Transcendentalists: An Anthology. Cambridge, Mass., 1950.

Mills, C. Wright. "The American Business Elite: A Collective Portrait," in The Tasks of Economic History [Supplement to Journal of Economic History, V (December 1945)], pp. 20–44.

Nevins, Allan. Ordeal of the Union. 2 vols. New York, 1947.

New York Constitutional Convention, 1821. Reports of the Proceedings and Debates of the Convention of 1821. Reported by Nathaniel H. Carter and William L. Stone. Albany, 1821.

New York Constitutional Convention, 1846. Report of the Debates and Proceedings of the Convention for the Revision of the Constitution. Reported by W. G. Bishop and W. H. Attree. Albany, 1846.

———. Debates and Proceedings in the New York State Convention for the Revision of the Constitution. Reported by S. Croswell and R. Sutton. Albany, 1846.

Nichols, Roy Franklin. The Democratic Machine, 1850–1854. Columbia Studies in History, Economics and Public Law, Vol. CXI, No. 1. New York, 1923.

Nichols, Thomas Low. Forty Years of American Life. New York, 1937.

Norton, A. B. Tippecanoe Songs of the Log Cabin Boys and Girls of 1840. Bound with A. B. Norton, The Great Revolution of 1840. Mount Vernon, Ohio, 1888.

Ohio Constitutional Convention, 1850–51. Report of the Debates and Proceedings of the Convention for the Revision of the Constitution of the State of Ohio, 1850–1851. 2 vols. Reported by J. V. Smith. Columbus, 1851.

Ostrogorski, M. Democracy and the Party System in the United States. New York, 1926

Parrington, Vernon Louis. Main Currents in American Thought. 3 vols. in 1. New York [c. 1930].

Parton, James. Life of Andrew Jackson. 3 vols. Boston [1887–88].

Pease, Theodore C. The Frontier State, 1818–1848. Vol. II of The Centennial History of Illinois. Springfield, Ill., 1918.

Pessen, Edward. "Did Labor Support Jackson?: The Boston Story," *Political Science Quarterly*, LXIV (June 1949), 262–74.

Phillips, Willard. A Manual of Political Economy. Boston, 1828.

Pierson, George. Tocqueville and Beaumont in America. New York, 1938.

Potter, David M. People of Plenty; Economic Abundance and the American Character. Chicago, 1954.

Quill, Charles [James Wadell Alexander]. The Working Man. Philadelphia, 1839.

Raeder, Ole Munch. America in the Forties. Translated and edited by Gunnar J. Malmin. Norwegian-American Historical Association: Travel and Description Series, Vol. III. Minneapolis, 1929.

Rantoul, Robert, Jr. Memoirs, Speeches, and Writings of Robert Rantoul, Jr. Edited by Luther Hamilton. Boston, 1854.

Redlich, Fritz. The Molding of American Banking: Men and Ideas. Vol. II, Part 1, of History of American Business Leaders. New York, 1947.

Richardson, James D. (ed.). Messages and Papers of the Presidents, 1789–1897. Vols. II, III. Washington, D.C., 1896.

Riegel, Robert E. Young America, 1830–1840. Norman, Okla., 1949.

Riesman, David, with Reuel Denney and Nathan Glazer. The Lonely Crowd; A Study of the Changing American Character. New Haven, 1950.

Roosevelt, Theodore. Thomas Hart Benton. American Statesmen series. Boston, 1899.

Rossiter, Clinton. Conservatism in America. New York, 1955.

Rourke, Constance. American Humor: A Study of National Character. Anchor Books. New York, 1953.

Santayana, George. Character and Opinion in the United States. Anchor Books. New York, 1956.

Schafer, Joseph. Four Wisconsin Counties: Prairie and Forest. Wisconsin Domesday Book: General Studies, Vol. II. Madison, 1927.

Schlesinger, Arthur M. Paths to the Present. New York, 1949.

Schlesinger, Arthur M., Jr. The Age of Jackson. Boston, 1945.

Schumpeter, Joseph A. Business Cycles. 2 vols. New York, 1939. Vol. I.

Sedgwick, Theodore, II. Public and Private Economy. Part I. New York, 1836.

———. Public and Private Economy, Illustrated by Observations Made in England in the Year 1836. Part II. New York, 1838.

Sellers, Charles G., Jr. "Banking and Politics in Jackson's Tennessee, 1817–1827," *Mississippi Valley Historical Review*, XLI (June 1954), 61–84.

———. "Jackson Men with Feet of Clay," *American Historical Review*, LXII (April 1957), 537–51.

Shepard, Edward M. Martin Van Buren. American Statesmen series. Boston, 1899.

Shireff, Patrick. A Tour Through North America. Edinburgh, 1835.

Smith, Adam. The Wealth of Nations. Modern Library. New York, 1937.

Smith, Henry Nash. Virgin Land; the American West as Symbol and Myth. Cambridge, Mass., 1950.

Smith, Walter B. Economic Aspects of the Second Bank of the United States. Cambridge, Mass., 1953.

———, and Arthur H. Cole. Fluctuations in American Business, 1790–1860. Cambridge, Mass., 1935.

Smith, William E. The Francis Preston Blair Family in Politics. Vol. I. New York, 1933.

Sowers, Don C. The Financial History of New York State from 1789 to 1912. Columbia Studies in History, Economics and Public Law, Vol. LVII, No. 2. New York, 1914.

Spiller, Robert E. Fenimore Cooper. New York, 1931.

Sullivan, William A. "Did Labor Support Andrew Jackson?" *Political Science Quarterly*, LXII (December 1947), 569–80.

Sumner, William Graham. Andrew Jackson. American Statesmen series. Boston, 1899.

———. A History of Banking in the United States. Vol. I of A History of Banking in All the Leading Nations. New York, 1896.

Syrett, Harold C. Andrew Jackson. Makers of the American Tradition series. Indianapolis, 1953.

Taylor, George Rogers. The Transportation Revolution, 1815–1860. Vol. IV of The Economic History of the United States. New York, 1951.

Taylor, John. An Inquiry into the Principles and Policy of the Government of the United States. Fredericksburg, Va., 1814.

Tocqueville, Alexis de. Democracy in America. Edited by Phillips Bradley. 2 vols. New York, 1948.

Trollope, Frances. Domestic Manners of the Americans. New York, 1949.

Tryon, Warren S. (ed.). A Mirror for Americans. 3 vols. Chicago, 1952.

Turner, Frederick Jackson. The Frontier in American History. New York, 1928.

———. Rise of the New West, 1819–1829. Vol. XIV of The American Nation: A History. New York, 1906.

———. The Significance of Sections in American History. New York, 1950.

———. The United States, 1830–1850. New York, 1935.

United States Bureau of the Census. Historical Statistics of the United States, 1789–1945. Washington, D.C., 1949.

Van Buren, Martin. "The Autobiography of Martin Van Buren." Edited by John C. Fitzpatrick. Vol. II of the *Annual Report of the American Historical Association for the Year 1918*. Washington, D.C., 1920.

———. An Inquiry into the Origin and Course of Political Parties in the United States. New York, 1867.

Van Deusen, Glyndon G. The Life of Henry Clay. Boston, 1937.

————. Thurlow Weed, Wizard of the Lobby. Boston, 1947.

Waples, Dorothy. The Whig Myth of James Fenimore Cooper. New Haven, 1938.

Ward, John W. Andrew Jackson, Symbol for an Age. New York, 1955.

Webster, Noah. An American Dictionary of the English Language. 2 vols. New York, 1828. Also the same revised by Chauncey A. Goodrich. Springfield, Mass., 1849.

Weed, Thurlow. Autobiography. Edited by Harriet A. Weed. Boston, 1883.

Weisenburger, Francis P. The Passing of the Frontier, 1825–1850. Vol. III of The History of the State of Ohio. Columbus, 1941.

White, Leonard D. The Jacksonian; A Study in Administrative History, 1829–1861. New York, 1954.

Williamson, Harold F. (ed.). The Growth of the American Economy. New York, 1951.

Wilson, Woodrow. Division and Reunion, 1829–1889. Epochs of American History series. New York, 1926.

# INDEX

Greenough, Horatio, 94
Grossman, James, 70
Grund, Francis, 93, 96, 103
Gurowski, Adam G. de, 93 f., 97

Hacker, Louis, 87
Hall, James, 95
Hammond, Bray, 79–82 *passim*, 87
Hammond, Jabez D., 179, 184; quoted, 187
Hartz, Louis, 185–86
Hoffman, Michael, 204–6; quoted, 207–8
Hofstadter, Richard, 146
*Home as Found* (Cooper), 44, 55–72 *passim*
*Homeward Bound* (Cooper), 44, 55–72 *passim*
Hunt, Freeman, 95–99 *passim*

Immigrants, discussed in New York State Constitutional Convention of 1846, 197–98
*Inquiry into the Origins and Course of Political Parties in the United States* (Van Buren), 215–17
Internal improvements: successes and failures of, 85–86; party views of, in 1846, 204–8

Jackson, Andrew: as seen by contemporaries, 1–2, 10, 54, 62, 71 f., 111–13, 146–47, 173–74; relation to Jacksonian movement, 2, 8, 11–12; contrasts "the real people" with the aristocracy, 12 ff., 14–17; argument for direct presidential elections, 14; attitude toward West, 17; arguments against Bank of the United States, 17–19, paper money, 19, surplus distribution, 20; endorses Jeffersonian view of governmental functions, 20–21; his formal doctrines and rhetoric compared, 21–23
Jacksonian Democracy, conflicting interpretations of, 2–4
Jefferson, Thomas: and yeoman ideal, 7, 209; compared with Jackson, 174

Kent, James, 182–83, 185

Laissez faire, Jacksonian views on, 7–8, 21–23, 137–40, 154–56, 167–68
Land: speculation in, 60–62, 83–84; attitudes toward, 67, 102 ff.; and government policy, 117
Lawyers, political role of, 187–88
Leggett, William: radical reputation of,

141, 146, 155–56; arguments against public charities, 142, public regulation, 142–43, public post office, 143, economic combinations, 144–45; hails Jackson's achievements, 146–47; demands return to "natural system," 147–48; and banking, 148–56; identifies Whigs with Bank, 151; contrasts social classes, 152–55; paradox of his position, 154–56
Legislative power, party views of, in 1821, 190–92, in 1846, 198–99
Lieber, Francis, 92–93, 96
Livingston, Peter R., 189, 191
Loomis, Arphaxed, quoted, 200–201

Martineau, Harriet, 93, 96; quoted, 102
Marvin, Richard P., 202
Morris, Robert, quoted, 201

Negro voting, party attitudes toward, 189–90
New York *Evening Post,* 141, 148
New York State: character of Jacksonian leadership in, 43 n.; social and political conditions in, 46–47, 180; party politics in, 179–209 *passim*;—CONSTITUTIONAL CONVENTION OF 1821, 181–93; role of Federalists in, 181–82, 188; Federalist arguments against suffrage extension, 182–84, party patronage, 184–86; general goals of Federalists in, 186–87, 190; Democratic arguments on suffrage extension, 188–90; veto power discussed by Federalists, 190, by Democrats, 191–92; Democratic views on party patronage, 192–93; political consequences of, 193;—CONSTITUTIONAL CONVENTION OF 1846, 193–209; background of, 194–95; areas of party consensus, 195–97; debates on immigrants, 197–98; Democratic defense of executive veto, 198–99; corporations discussed by Democrats, 199–202, by Whigs, 202–3; compromise on corporations analyzed, 203–44; public works and debt discussed by Democrats, 204–6, by Whigs, 206–7; party compromise appraised, 207–8
Nichols, Thomas Low, 94 ff.
*North American Review,* 158
*Notions of the Americans* (Cooper), 44–55 *passim*

Parton, James, 1
Persuasion, concept of, v, 6
Peyton, John L., quoted, 104

*Plaindealer,* 141, 148
Political parties: emotional response to, 1–6 *passim,* 179–217; traditional conflicts between, 169–73, 217–19; and political democracy, 4–5, 187–88; and patronage, 142, 184–85; attitudes toward, 172–73, 185–87, 192–93; *see also* Democratic party; New York State; Social classes; Whig party
*Public and Private Economy* (Sedgwick), 125–40 *passim*
Public debt: growth of, in states, 85; party attitudes toward in 1846, 204–8

Randolph, John, 111
Rantoul, Robert, Jr.: career of, 157–58; his "moral science," 158–61; views on education, 158, 160; appraises social classes, 161–67; "Address to the Workingmen of the United States of America," 163–67; and laissez faire, 167–68, 176–78; analyzes party differences, 169–73; portrays Jackson as Old Roman, 173–74; attacks common-law survivals, 174–75
Redlich, Fritz, 79, 87
Reemelin, Charles, 98
Root, Erastus, 189 ff.

Schumpeter, Joseph, 83, 86
Sedgwick, Theodore, II: career of, 124–25; sources of his ideas, 125; links property and virtue, 126–32 *passim;* surveys American poverty, 127–29; advocates self-improvement, 129–30; condemns consumer extravagance, 130–31; contrasts producers and idlers, 132–34; justifies class hierarchy, 134; compared with Jackson and Van Buren, 135–36; ambivalence toward modern capitalism, 137–40; and the West, 139
Social classes: and party preference, 5, 105, 106 n., 169–74 *passim,* 215–17; Jackson on, 14–17; outward marks of, 51, 51 n.; Cooper on, 51–59 *passim,* 65–72 *passim;* and emulation, 96 f., 99–101; discussed by Sedgwick, 132–34, by Leggett, 152–55, by Rantoul, 161–67, by New York convention of 1821, 184, 188–89
Social mobility: characterizes Jacksonian era, 33, 92–93; dangers of, according to Cooper, 55–59; *see also* Social classes
Suffrage: early party views on, 182–84, 188–90
Swackhamer, Conrad, 201–2

Taylor, George Rogers, 88–89
Temperance reform, 131
Tocqueville, Alexis de: *Democracy in America,* 24–41 *passim;* as historical guide, 24–26, 40–41, 211–14; analyzes "individualism," 27–28; on effects of unique national experience, 29–30; portrays American as venturous conservative, 31–40; on American enterprise, 32–34, middle-class caution, 34–38, conformity, 38–40
Trollope, Frances, 94 ff.

Van Buren, Martin: early career of, 108–9; reputation as "little magician," 109–11, 113–14; shows Jackson as political model, 111–13; contrasts commerce and agriculture, 116 f.; land policy of, 117; money and banking views of, 118–22; on crisis of 1837, 116–20 *passim;* argues dangers of credit system, 120 ff.; denounces financial aristocracy, 120, 122 f.; on suffrage, 188, party patronage, 192–93; analyzes traditional party conflicts, 215–17
Veto power: party views on, in 1821, 190–92, in 1846, 198–99

Washington, George, as model of character, 1, 52–53, 72, 174
West: as viewed by Jackson, 17, by Van Buren, 117, by Sedgwick, 139; effects of, on democratic society, 30; process of settlement in, 32, 46–47; social character of, 36, 99–100; growth of, 84
Whig party: adapts to political democracy, 4, 180 f., 196–97; speaks for economic progress, 9–10; as anti-Jackson coalition, 10; retreats on Bank issue, 17–18; *see also* New York State, CONSTITUTIONAL CONVENTION OF 1846; Political parties
Williams, Elisha, 183–84
Worden, Alvah, 197, 208

Yoemen, *see* Farmers
Young, Samuel, 191

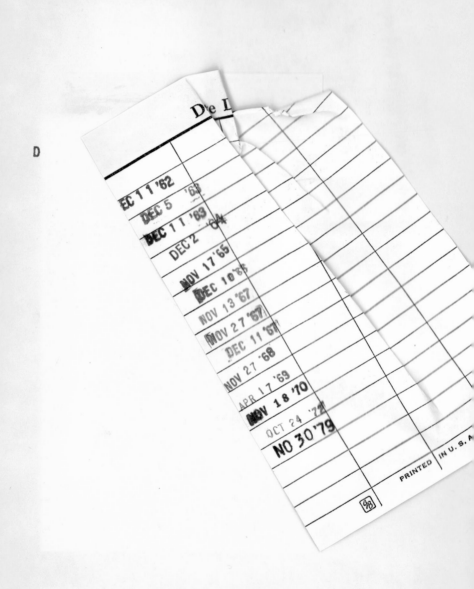